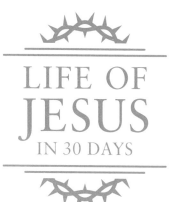

LIFE OF
JESUS
IN 30 DAYS

Compiled and with an Introduction by
TREVIN WAX

CHRISTIAN STANDARD BIBLE® | HOLMAN® BIBLES

Introduction

by Trevin Wax

Jesus—he is the central figure of the New Testament, and his life, death, resurrection, and exaltation is the heart of the gospel. His story is foretold by the Old Testament prophets, anticipated in the Psalms, and then explained by the apostles who witnessed his work. But nowhere do we see him more clearly than in the Gospels, the four biographies that reveal his ministry on earth.

"Regardless of what anyone may personally think or believe about him, Jesus of Nazareth has been the dominant figure in the history of western culture for almost twenty centuries," wrote Jaroslav Pelikan in *Jesus Through the Centuries.*

The influence of Jesus Christ is incalculable on our society, yes. But as Christians, we approach the inspired scriptural testimony not primarily as historians excavating ancient accounts, but as worshipers seeking an encounter with the living Savior. We want to see him in his glory—to be dazzled by the brightness of his revelation on the Mount of Transfiguration, to sit at his feet like Mary and drink deeply from the wisdom of his infallible words.

Journeying with Jesus

A few years ago, I adapted a centuries-old approach to reading through all 150 psalms in a month, relying on a Morning, Midday, and Evening prayer schedule. The result was a little book called *Psalms in 30 Days.*

In this volume, I follow the same structure of prayer, but with selections from the Gospels. The goal is to embark on a thirty-day prayer journey with Jesus through the major moments and teachings of his life, his death on the cross for our sins, and his resurrection and ascension.

There is precedent in the Scriptures for praying three times a day, and there is spiritual blessing in deliberately punctuating your day with moments of prayer and Bible reading. The three-times-a-day approach takes you back to the life of Jesus, so that you lift your eyes above your current circumstances and remember that the glory of our Savior is the blazing center of all things.

Prayers of Faithful Christians

Over the years, I've also found the written prayers of faithful Christians who have gone before me to be a help in my prayer life. Our praying the written prayers of saints from years gone by is a lot like children trying on the shoes of their parents. We wonder if our feet will ever fit into the spiritual shoes of the giants who have gone before us. We wonder if our devotion will match the intensity and clarity we find in their words. We want hearts that are oriented in such a way that we would ask for and desire the right things. Praying through these Gospel selections alongside other Scriptures and other faithful expressions of faith over the years is one way of forming our hearts and minds daily.

The Life of Jesus in 30 Days

This book features Gospel stories and teachings of Jesus, as translated in the Christian Standard Bible, arranged in three-times-a-day readings for thirty days. I have not sought to include every single story, parable, miracle, or moment recorded in the Gospels, but I have intentionally pulled from all four Gospel writers so that you are acquainted with each of their voices. The journey is predominantly, but not precisely chronological.

Every prayer time begins with a call to prayer, includes the Gloria and the Lord's Prayer, and closes with a biblical blessing.

The morning prayer guide includes a "confession of faith" taken from Scripture, the ancient creeds, or the "Reforming Catholic Confession," which was released in celebration of the five hundredth anniversary of the Reformation. The evening prayer guide includes a "confession of sin" and a biblical promise of absolution to all who repent.

The morning and evening prayers also include psalms, prophecies, or songs from Scripture as well as written prayers from Christians through the ages—all of them aligning with the specific themes of the day's Gospel readings. There is also time set aside for you to intercede on behalf of others and bring your personal requests to the Lord.

The midday prayer guide is abbreviated and focused on the reading from the Gospels, since this is the time of day when it may be more challenging to carve out ten or fifteen minutes for prayer.

Suggestions for Praying through the Life of Jesus in 30 Days

Praying through these Gospel selections for thirty days is a spiritual workout, much like doing daily exercises. Don't feel the pressure to make it through all the readings your first time through. If you miss a reading, you can catch up later, or you can skip it and come back to it the next month. If you get behind a day or two, you can pick up on the day that corresponds to the day of the month, or you can proceed in order, even if it takes you more than thirty days to complete the readings.

Set this book on a desk, nightstand, or table close to your bed, where you will see it. Let it be a visual reminder whenever you enter the room that nudges you to spend time with the Lord.

Pray the morning selection as soon as you wake up and the evening selection just before going to bed.

The abbreviated midday routine is ideal for a brief pause during work, but if you miss a midday prayer time, simply add that Gospel selection to the evening prayer guide in order to catch up.

If you only wish to pray through the Gospel readings and not the other selected prayers, simply jump to that portion of the prayer guide and read the Gospel selection three times daily.

My prayer is that this guide will help you make this journey with Jesus a regular spiritual discipline that strengthens your love for God and neighbor. "May the God of hope fill you with all joy and peace as you believe so that you may overflow with hope by the power of the Holy Spirit" (Rm 15:13).

Introduction to the Christian Standard Bible®

The Bible is God's revelation to humanity. It is our only source for completely reliable information about God, what happens when we die, and where history is headed. The Bible does these things because it is God's inspired Word, inerrant in the original manuscripts. Bible translation brings God's Word from the ancient languages (Hebrew, Greek, and Aramaic) into today's world. In dependence on God's Spirit to accomplish this sacred task, the CSB Translation Oversight Committee and Holman Bible Publishers present the Christian Standard Bible.

Textual Base of the CSB

The textual base for the New Testament (NT) is the Nestle-Aland *Novum Testamentum Graece*, 28th edition, and the United Bible Societies' *Greek New Testament*, 5th corrected edition. The text for the Old Testament (OT) is the *Biblia Hebraica Stuttgartensia,* 4th edition.

Goals of This Translation

- Provide English-speaking people worldwide with an accurate translation in contemporary English.
- Provide an accurate translation for personal study, sermon preparation, private devotions, and memorization.
- Provide a text that is clear and understandable, suitable for public reading, and shareable so that all may access its life-giving message.
- Affirm the authority of Scripture and champion its absolute truth against skeptical viewpoints.

Translation Philosophy of the Christian Standard Bible

Most discussions of Bible translations speak of two opposite approaches: formal equivalence and dynamic equivalence. However, Bible translations cannot be neatly sorted into these categories. Optimal equivalence capitalizes on the strengths of both approaches.

Optimal equivalence balances contemporary English readability with linguistic precision to the original languages. In the many places throughout the Bible where a word-for-word rendering is understandable, a literal translation is used. When a word-for-word rendering might obscure the meaning for a modern audience, a more dynamic translation is used. This process assures that both the words and the thoughts contained in the original text are conveyed accurately for today's readers. The Christian Standard Bible places equal value on fidelity to the original and readability for a modern audience, resulting in a translation that achieves both goals.

History of the CSB

Holman Bible Publishers assembled an interdenominational team of one hundred scholars, editors, stylists, and proofreaders, all of whom were committed to biblical inerrancy. Working from the original languages, the translation team edited and polished the manuscript, which was first published as the Holman Christian Standard Bible in 2004.

A standing committee maintained the translation, while also seeking ways to improve both readability and accuracy. As with the original translation, the committee that prepared this revision, renamed the Christian Standard Bible, is international and interdenominational, comprising evangelical scholars who honor the inspiration and authority of God's written Word.

LIFE OF
JESUS
IN 30 DAYS

DAY 1 MORNING PRAYER

Call to Prayer

Our King and Savior now draws near: O come, let us adore him.

Confession of Faith

I believe in God, the Father almighty,
creator of heaven and earth;
I believe in Jesus Christ, his only Son, our Lord.
He was conceived by the power of the Holy Spirit
and born of the Virgin Mary.
He suffered under Pontius Pilate,
was crucified, died, and was buried.
He descended to the dead.
On the third day he rose again.
He ascended into heaven,
and is seated at the right hand of the Father.
He will come again to judge the living and the dead.
I believe in the Holy Spirit,
the holy catholic Church,
the communion of saints,
the forgiveness of sins
the resurrection of the body,
and the life everlasting. Amen.
The Apostles' Creed

Canticle

My soul magnifies the Lord,
and my spirit rejoices in God my Savior,
because he has looked with favor
on the humble condition of his servant.
Surely, from now on all generations
will call me blessed,
because the Mighty One
has done great things for me,

and his name is holy.
His mercy is from generation to generation
on those who fear him.
He has done a mighty deed with his arm;
he has scattered the proud
because of the thoughts of their hearts;
he has toppled the mighty from their thrones
and exalted the lowly.
He has satisfied the hungry with good things
and sent the rich away empty.
He has helped his servant Israel,
remembering his mercy
to Abraham and his descendants forever,
just as he spoke to our ancestors.
Luke 1:46–55

Morning Readings

John 1:1–18
In the beginning was the Word, and the Word was with God,
and the Word was God. He was with God in the beginning. All
things were created through him, and apart from him not one
thing was created that has been created. In him was life, and
that life was the light of men. That light shines in the darkness,
and yet the darkness did not overcome it.

There was a man sent from God whose name was John. He
came as a witness to testify about the light, so that all might
believe through him. He was not the light, but he came to testify
about the light. The true light that gives light to everyone was
coming into the world.

He was in the world, and the world was created through him,
and yet the world did not recognize him. He came to his own,
and his own people did not receive him. But to all who did
receive him, he gave them the right to be children of God, to
those who believe in his name, who were born, not of natural
descent, or of the will of the flesh, or of the will of man, but of
God.

The Word became flesh and dwelt among us. We observed his
glory, the glory as the one and only Son from the Father, full of

grace and truth. (John testified concerning him and exclaimed, "This was the one of whom I said, 'The one coming after me ranks ahead of me, because he existed before me.'") Indeed, we have all received grace upon grace from his fullness, for the law was given through Moses; grace and truth came through Jesus Christ. No one has ever seen God. The one and only Son, who is himself God and is at the Father's side—he has revealed him.

Luke 1:26–38
In the sixth month, the angel Gabriel was sent by God to a town in Galilee called Nazareth, to a virgin engaged to a man named Joseph, of the house of David. The virgin's name was Mary. And the angel came to her and said, "Greetings, favored woman! The Lord is with you." But she was deeply troubled by this statement, wondering what kind of greeting this could be. Then the angel told her, "Do not be afraid, Mary, for you have found favor with God. Now listen: You will conceive and give birth to a son, and you will name him Jesus. He will be great and will be called the Son of the Most High, and the Lord God will give him the throne of his father David. He will reign over the house of Jacob forever, and his kingdom will have no end."

Mary asked the angel, "How can this be, since I have not had sexual relations with a man?"

The angel replied to her, "The Holy Spirit will come upon you, and the power of the Most High will overshadow you. Therefore, the holy one to be born will be called the Son of God. And consider your relative Elizabeth—even she has conceived a son in her old age, and this is the sixth month for her who was called childless. For nothing will be impossible with God."

"See, I am the Lord's servant," said Mary. "May it happen to me as you have said." Then the angel left her.

This is the Word of the Lord. Thanks be to God.

Gloria

Glory be to God the Father, God the Son, and God the Holy
Spirit. As it was in the beginning, is now, and will be forever,
world without end.

The Lord's Prayer

Our Father in heaven,
Hallowed be your name.
Your kingdom come,
Your will be done
on earth as it is in heaven.
Give us this day our daily bread.
And forgive us our debts,
as we also have forgiven our debtors.
And lead us not into temptation
But deliver us from the evil one.
For yours is the kingdom and the power and the glory forever.
Amen.

Intercessions and Personal Requests

Prayer of the Church

Almighty God, give us grace to cast away the works of darkness,
and put on the armor of light, now in the time of this mortal
life in which your Son Jesus Christ came to visit us in great
humility; that in the last day, when he shall come again in his
glorious majesty to judge both the living and the dead, we may
rise to the life immortal; through him who lives and reigns with
you and the Holy Spirit, one God, now and forever. Amen.
The Book of Common Prayer

Blessing

The grace of the Lord Jesus Christ, and the love of God, and the
fellowship of the Holy Spirit be with us all.
2 Corinthians 13:14

DAY 1 MIDDAY PRAYER

CALL TO PRAYER

God's dwelling is with humanity, and he will live with them.
They will be his people, and God himself will be with them and
will be their God.
Revelation 21:3

MIDDAY READINGS

Matthew 1:18–24

The birth of Jesus Christ came about this way: After his mother
Mary had been engaged to Joseph, it was discovered before they
came together that she was pregnant from the Holy Spirit. So
her husband, Joseph, being a righteous man, and not wanting to
disgrace her publicly, decided to divorce her secretly.

But after he had considered these things, an angel of the Lord
appeared to him in a dream, saying, "Joseph, son of David,
don't be afraid to take Mary as your wife, because what has been
conceived in her is from the Holy Spirit. She will give birth to
a son, and you are to name him Jesus, because he will save his
people from their sins."

Now all this took place to fulfill what was spoken by the Lord
through the prophet:

See, the virgin will become pregnant
and give birth to a son,
and they will name him Immanuel,

which is translated "God is with us."

When Joseph woke up, he did as the Lord's angel had
commanded him.

Luke 2:1–7

In those days a decree went out from Caesar Augustus that the
whole empire should be registered. This first registration took
place while Quirinius was governing Syria. So everyone went to
be registered, each to his own town.

Joseph also went up from the town of Nazareth in Galilee, to Judea, to the city of David, which is called Bethlehem, because he was of the house and family line of David, to be registered along with Mary, who was engaged to him and was pregnant. While they were there, the time came for her to give birth. Then she gave birth to her firstborn son, and she wrapped him tightly in cloth and laid him in a manger, because there was no guest room available for them.

This is the Word of the Lord. Thanks be to God.

GLORIA

Glory be to God the Father, God the Son, and God the Holy Spirit. As it was in the beginning, is now, and will be forever, world without end.

THE LORD'S PRAYER

Our Father in heaven,
Hallowed be your name.
Your kingdom come,
Your will be done
on earth as it is in heaven.
Give us this day our daily bread.
And forgive us our debts,
as we also have forgiven our debtors.
And lead us not into temptation
But deliver us from the evil one.
For yours is the kingdom and the power and the glory forever.
Amen.

BLESSING

May the LORD bless you and protect you; may the LORD make his face shine on you and be gracious to you; may the LORD look with favor on you and give you peace.
Numbers 6:24–26

DAY 1 EVENING PRAYER

The Word was made flesh and dwelt among us: O come, let us
adore him.

CONFESSION OF SIN

Most merciful God,
we confess that we have sinned against you
in thought, word, and deed,
by what we have done,
and by what we have left undone.
We have not loved you with our whole heart;
we have not loved our neighbors as ourselves.
We are truly sorry and we humbly repent.
For the sake of your Son Jesus Christ,
have mercy on us and forgive us;
that we may delight in your will,
and walk in your ways,
to the glory of your Name. Amen.
The Book of Common Prayer

If we confess our sins, he is faithful and righteous to forgive us
our sins and to cleanse us from all unrighteousness.
1 John 1:9

CANTICLE

For a child will be born for us,
a son will be given to us,
and the government will be on his shoulders.
He will be named
Wonderful Counselor, Mighty God,
Eternal Father, Prince of Peace.
The dominion will be vast,
and its prosperity will never end.

He will reign on the throne of David
and over his kingdom,
to establish and sustain it
with justice and righteousness from now on and forever.
The zeal of the LORD of Armies will accomplish this.
Isaiah 9:6–7

EVENING READING
Luke 2:8–38
In the same region, shepherds were staying out in the fields and keeping watch at night over their flock. Then an angel of the Lord stood before them, and the glory of the Lord shone around them, and they were terrified. But the angel said to them, "Don't be afraid, for look, I proclaim to you good news of great joy that will be for all the people: Today in the city of David a Savior was born for you, who is the Messiah, the Lord. This will be the sign for you: You will find a baby wrapped tightly in cloth and lying in a manger."

Suddenly there was a multitude of the heavenly host with the angel, praising God and saying:
Glory to God in the highest heaven,
and peace on earth to people he favors!

When the angels had left them and returned to heaven, the shepherds said to one another, "Let's go straight to Bethlehem and see what has happened, which the Lord has made known to us."

They hurried off and found both Mary and Joseph, and the baby who was lying in the manger. After seeing them, they reported the message they were told about this child, and all who heard it were amazed at what the shepherds said to them. But Mary was treasuring up all these things in her heart and meditating on them. The shepherds returned, glorifying and praising God for all the things they had seen and heard, which were just as they had been told.

When the eight days were completed for his circumcision, he was named Jesus—the name given by the angel before he was conceived. And when the days of their purification according to the law of Moses were finished, they brought him up to Jerusalem to present him to the Lord (just as it is written in the law of the Lord, **Every firstborn male will be dedicated to the Lord**) and to offer a sacrifice (according to what is stated in the law of the Lord, **a pair of turtledoves or two young pigeons**).

There was a man in Jerusalem whose name was Simeon. This man was righteous and devout, looking forward to Israel's consolation, and the Holy Spirit was on him. It had been revealed to him by the Holy Spirit that he would not see death before he saw the Lord's Messiah. Guided by the Spirit, he entered the temple. When the parents brought in the child Jesus to perform for him what was customary under the law, Simeon took him up in his arms, praised God, and said,

> Now, Master,
> you can dismiss your servant in peace,
> as you promised.
> For my eyes have seen your salvation.
> You have prepared it
> in the presence of all peoples—
> a light for revelation to the Gentiles
> and glory to your people Israel.

His father and mother were amazed at what was being said about him. Then Simeon blessed them and told his mother Mary, "Indeed, this child is destined to cause the fall and rise of many in Israel and to be a sign that will be opposed—and a sword will pierce your own soul—that the thoughts of many hearts may be revealed."

There was also a prophetess, Anna, a daughter of Phanuel, of the tribe of Asher. She was well along in years, having lived with her husband seven years after her marriage, and was a widow for eighty-four years. She did not leave the temple, serving God night and day with fasting and prayers. At that very moment, she came up and began to thank God and to speak about him to all who were looking forward to the redemption of Jerusalem.

This is the Word of the Lord. Thanks be to God.

GLORIA

Glory be to God the Father, God the Son, and God the Holy Spirit. As it was in the beginning, is now, and will be forever, world without end.

THE LORD'S PRAYER

Our Father in heaven,
Hallowed be your name.
Your kingdom come,
Your will be done
on earth as it is in heaven.
Give us this day our daily bread.
And forgive us our debts,
as we also have forgiven our debtors.
And lead us not into temptation
But deliver us from the evil one.
For yours is the kingdom and the power and the glory forever.
Amen.

INTERCESSIONS AND PERSONAL REQUESTS

PRAYER OF THE CHURCH

Almighty God, you have poured upon us the new light of your incarnate Word: Grant that this light, enkindled in our hearts, may shine forth in our lives; through Jesus Christ our Lord, who lives and reigns with you, in the unity of the Holy Spirit, one God, now and forever. Amen.
The Book of Common Prayer

BLESSING

The Lord Almighty grant us a peaceful night and a perfect end. Amen.

DAY 2 MORNING PRAYER

CALL TO PRAYER

My name will be great among the nations, from the rising of the
sun to its setting. Incense and pure offerings will be presented
in my name in every place because my name will be great
among the nations, says the LORD of Armies.
Malachi 1:11

CONFESSION OF FAITH

I believe in Jesus Christ, who, existing in the form of God,
did not consider equality with God
as something to be exploited.
Instead he emptied himself
by assuming the form of a servant,
taking on the likeness of humanity.
And when he had come as a man,
he humbled himself by becoming obedient
to the point of death—even to death on a cross.
For this reason God highly exalted him
and gave him the name
that is above every name,
so that at the name of Jesus
every knee will bow—in heaven and on earth
and under the earth—and every tongue will confess
that Jesus Christ is Lord,
to the glory of God the Father.
Philippians 2:6–11

CANTICLE

Arise, shine, for your light has come,
and the glory of the LORD shines over you.
For look, darkness will cover the earth,
and total darkness the peoples;
but the LORD will shine over you,

and his glory will appear over you.
Nations will come to your light,
and kings to your shining brightness.
Your city gates will always be open;
they will never be shut day or night
so that the wealth of the nations
may be brought into you,
with their kings being led in procession.
The sons of your oppressors
will come and bow down to you;
all who reviled you
will fall facedown at your feet.
They will call you the City of the LORD,
Zion of the Holy One of Israel.
Violence will never again be heard of in your land;
devastation and destruction
will be gone from your borders.
You will call your walls Salvation
and your city gates Praise.
The sun will no longer be your light by day,
and the brightness of the moon will not shine on you.
The LORD will be your everlasting light,
and your God will be your splendor.
Isaiah 60:1–3,11,14,18–19

MORNING READING
Matthew 2:1–23
After Jesus was born in Bethlehem of Judea in the days of King
Herod, wise men from the east arrived in Jerusalem, saying,
"Where is he who has been born king of the Jews? For we saw
his star at its rising and have come to worship him."

When King Herod heard this, he was deeply disturbed, and
all Jerusalem with him. So he assembled all the chief priests and
scribes of the people and asked them where the Messiah would
be born.

"In Bethlehem of Judea," they told him, "because this is what
was written by the prophet:

And you, Bethlehem, in the land of Judah,

are by no means least **among the rulers of Judah:**
Because out of you will come a ruler
who will shepherd my people Israel."

Then Herod secretly summoned the wise men and asked them the exact time the star appeared. He sent them to Bethlehem and said, "Go and search carefully for the child. When you find him, report back to me so that I too can go and worship him."

After hearing the king, they went on their way. And there it was—the star they had seen at its rising. It led them until it came and stopped above the place where the child was. When they saw the star, they were overwhelmed with joy. Entering the house, they saw the child with Mary his mother, and falling to their knees, they worshiped him. Then they opened their treasures and presented him with gifts: gold, frankincense, and myrrh. And being warned in a dream not to go back to Herod, they returned to their own country by another route.

After they were gone, an angel of the Lord appeared to Joseph in a dream, saying, "Get up! Take the child and his mother, flee to Egypt, and stay there until I tell you. For Herod is about to search for the child to kill him." So he got up, took the child and his mother during the night, and escaped to Egypt. He stayed there until Herod's death, so that what was spoken by the Lord through the prophet might be fulfilled: **Out of Egypt I called my Son.**

Then Herod, when he realized that he had been outwitted by the wise men, flew into a rage. He gave orders to massacre all the boys in and around Bethlehem who were two years old and under, in keeping with the time he had learned from the wise men. Then what was spoken through Jeremiah the prophet was fulfilled:

A voice was heard in Ramah,
weeping, and great mourning,
Rachel weeping for her children;
and she refused to be consoled,
because they are no more.

After Herod died, an angel of the Lord appeared in a dream to Joseph in Egypt, saying, "Get up, take the child and his mother, and go to the land of Israel, because those who intended to kill the child are dead." So he got up, took the child and his mother, and entered the land of Israel. But when he heard that Archelaus was ruling over Judea in place of his father Herod, he was afraid to go there. And being warned in a dream, he withdrew to the region of Galilee. Then he went and settled in a town called Nazareth to fulfill what was spoken through the prophets, that he would be called a Nazarene.

This is the Word of the Lord. Thanks be to God.

Gloria

Glory be to God the Father, God the Son, and God the Holy Spirit. As it was in the beginning, is now, and will be forever, world without end.

The Lord's Prayer

Our Father in heaven,
Hallowed be your name.
Your kingdom come,
Your will be done
on earth as it is in heaven.
Give us this day our daily bread.
And forgive us our debts,
as we also have forgiven our debtors.
And lead us not into temptation
But deliver us from the evil one.
For yours is the kingdom and the power and the glory forever.
Amen.

PRAYER OF THE CHURCH

O God, by the leading of a star you manifested your only Son to
the peoples of the earth: Lead us, who know you now by faith,
to your presence, where we may see your glory face to face;
through Jesus Christ our Lord, who lives and reigns with you
and the Holy Spirit, one God, now and forever. Amen.
The Book of Common Prayer

BLESSING

Now to him who is able to do above and beyond all that we
ask or think according to the power that works in us—to him
be glory in the church and in Christ Jesus to all generations,
forever and ever. Amen.
Ephesians 3:20–21

DAY 2 MIDDAY PRAYER

CALL TO PRAYER

Seek the LORD and his strength; seek his face always.
Psalm 105:4

MIDDAY READING

Luke 2:40–52
The boy grew up and became strong, filled with wisdom, and
God's grace was on him.

Every year his parents traveled to Jerusalem for the Passover
Festival. When he was twelve years old, they went up according
to the custom of the festival. After those days were over, as they
were returning, the boy Jesus stayed behind in Jerusalem, but
his parents did not know it. Assuming he was in the traveling
party, they went a day's journey. Then they began looking for
him among their relatives and friends. When they did not find

him, they returned to Jerusalem to search for him. After three days, they found him in the temple sitting among the teachers, listening to them and asking them questions. And all those who heard him were astounded at his understanding and his answers. When his parents saw him, they were astonished, and his mother said to him, "Son, why have you treated us like this? Your father and I have been anxiously searching for you."

"Why were you searching for me?" he asked them. "Didn't you know that it was necessary for me to be in my Father's house?" But they did not understand what he said to them.

Then he went down with them and came to Nazareth and was obedient to them. His mother kept all these things in her heart. And Jesus increased in wisdom and stature, and in favor with God and with people.

This is the Word of the Lord. Thanks be to God.

Gloria

Glory be to God the Father, God the Son, and God the Holy Spirit. As it was in the beginning, is now, and will be forever, world without end.

The Lord's Prayer

Our Father in heaven,
Hallowed be your name.
Your kingdom come,
Your will be done
on earth as it is in heaven.
Give us this day our daily bread.
And forgive us our debts,
as we also have forgiven our debtors.
And lead us not into temptation
But deliver us from the evil one.
For yours is the kingdom and the power and the glory forever.
Amen.

The grace of the Lord Jesus Christ, and the love of God, and the
fellowship of the Holy Spirit be with us all.
2 Corinthians 13:14

DAY 2 EVENING PRAYER

CALL TO PRAYER

Behold the lamb of God who takes away the sin of the world.
John 1:29

CONFESSION OF SIN

O Lord, the house of my soul is narrow; enlarge it that you
may enter in. It is ruined, O repair it! It displeases your sight;
I confess it, I know. But who shall cleanse it, or to whom shall
I cry but unto you? Cleanse me from my secret faults, O Lord,
and spare your servant from sin.
Augustine

The sacrifice pleasing to God is a broken spirit. You will not
despise a broken and humbled heart, God.
Psalm 51:17

CANTICLE

Blessed is the Lord, the God of Israel,
because he has visited
and provided redemption for his people.
He has raised up a horn of salvation for us
in the house of his servant David,
just as he spoke by the mouth
of his holy prophets in ancient times;
salvation from our enemies
and from the hand of those who hate us.
He has dealt mercifully with our ancestors
and remembered his holy covenant—

the oath that he swore to our father Abraham,
to grant that we,
having been rescued
from the hand of our enemies,
would serve him without fear
in holiness and righteousness
in his presence all our days.
And you, child, will be called
a prophet of the Most High,
for you will go before the Lord
to prepare his ways,
to give his people knowledge of salvation
through the forgiveness of their sins.
Because of our God's merciful compassion,
the dawn from on high will visit us
to shine on those who live in darkness
and the shadow of death,
to guide our feet into the way of peace.
Luke 1:68–79

Evening Reading
Matthew 3:1–17

In those days John the Baptist came, preaching in the wilderness of Judea and saying, "Repent, because the kingdom of heaven has come near!" For he is the one spoken of through the prophet Isaiah, who said:

> **A voice of one crying out in the wilderness:**
> **Prepare the way for the Lord;**
> **make his paths straight!**

Now John had a camel-hair garment with a leather belt around his waist, and his food was locusts and wild honey. Then people from Jerusalem, all Judea, and all the vicinity of the Jordan were going out to him, and they were baptized by him in the Jordan River, confessing their sins.

When he saw many of the Pharisees and Sadducees coming to his baptism, he said to them, "Brood of vipers! Who warned you to flee from the coming wrath? Therefore produce fruit consistent with repentance. And don't presume to say to yourselves, 'We have Abraham as our father.' For I tell you that God is able to raise up children for Abraham from these stones. The ax is already at the root of the trees. Therefore, every tree that doesn't produce good fruit will be cut down and thrown into the fire.

"I baptize you with water for repentance, but the one who is coming after me is more powerful than I. I am not worthy to remove his sandals. He himself will baptize you with the Holy Spirit and fire. His winnowing shovel is in his hand, and he will clear his threshing floor and gather his wheat into the barn. But the chaff he will burn with fire that never goes out."

Then Jesus came from Galilee to John at the Jordan, to be baptized by him. But John tried to stop him, saying, "I need to be baptized by you, and yet you come to me?"

Jesus answered him, "Allow it for now, because this is the way for us to fulfill all righteousness." Then John allowed him to be baptized.

When Jesus was baptized, he went up immediately from the water. The heavens suddenly opened for him, and he saw the Spirit of God descending like a dove and coming down on him. And a voice from heaven said, "This is my beloved Son, with whom I am well-pleased."

This is the Word of the Lord. Thanks be to God.

Gloria

Glory be to God the Father, God the Son, and God the Holy Spirit. As it was in the beginning, is now, and will be forever, world without end.

The Lord's Prayer

Our Father in heaven,
Hallowed be your name.
Your kingdom come,
Your will be done
on earth as it is in heaven.
Give us this day our daily bread.

And forgive us our debts,
as we also have forgiven our debtors.
And lead us not into temptation
But deliver us from the evil one.
For yours is the kingdom and the power and the glory forever.
Amen.

INTERCESSIONS AND PERSONAL REQUESTS

PRAYER OF THE CHURCH

Eternal Father, at the baptism of Jesus you revealed him to be
your Son, and your Holy Spirit descended upon him like a dove:
Grant that we, who are born again by water and the Spirit, may
be faithful as your adopted children; through Jesus Christ our
Lord, who lives and reigns with you and the Holy Spirit, one
God, now and for ever. Amen.
The Book of Common Prayer

BLESSING

The Almighty and merciful Lord, Father, Son, and Holy Spirit,
bless us and keep us, this night and evermore. Amen.

DAY 3 MORNING PRAYER

CALL TO PRAYER

The Lord has shown forth his glory: O come, let us adore him.

CONFESSION OF FAITH

I believe that Jesus Christ is the eternal Son of God become
human for us and our salvation, the only Mediator between
God and humanity, born of the virgin Mary, the Son of David
and servant of the house of Israel, one person with two natures,
truly God and truly man. He lived a fully human life, having
entered into the disorder and brokenness of fallen existence,
yet without sin, and in his words, deeds, attitude, and suffering
embodied the free and loving communication of God's own
light and life.
Adapted from the Reforming Catholic Confession

CANTICLE

Glory to God in the highest,
and peace to his people on earth.
Lord God, heavenly King,
almighty God and Father,
we worship you, we give you thanks,
we praise you for your glory.
Lord Jesus Christ, only Son of the Father,
Lord God, Lamb of God,
you take away the sin of the world:
have mercy on us;
you are seated at the right hand of the Father:
receive our prayer.
For you alone are the Holy One,
you alone are the Lord,
you alone are the Most High,
Jesus Christ,

with the Holy Spirit,
in the glory of the Father. Amen.
Gloria

Morning Readings

Matthew 4:1–11

Then Jesus was led up by the Spirit into the wilderness to be tempted by the devil. After he had fasted forty days and forty nights, he was hungry. Then the tempter approached him and said, "If you are the Son of God, tell these stones to become bread."

He answered, "It is written: **Man must not live on bread alone but on every word that comes from the mouth of God.**"

Then the devil took him to the holy city, had him stand on the pinnacle of the temple, and said to him, "If you are the Son of God, throw yourself down. For it is written:

> **He will give his angels orders concerning you**,
> and **they will support you with their hands**
> **so that you will not strike**
> **your foot against a stone.**"

Jesus told him, "It is also written: **Do not test the Lord your God.**"

Again, the devil took him to a very high mountain and showed him all the kingdoms of the world and their splendor. And he said to him, "I will give you all these things if you will fall down and worship me."

Then Jesus told him, "Go away, Satan! For it is written: **Worship the Lord your God, and serve only him.**"

Then the devil left him, and angels came and began to serve him.

John 1:35–51

The next day, John was standing with two of his disciples. When he saw Jesus passing by, he said, "Look, the Lamb of God!"

The two disciples heard him say this and followed Jesus. When Jesus turned and noticed them following him, he asked them, "What are you looking for?"

They said to him, "Rabbi" (which means "Teacher"), "where are you staying?"

"Come and you'll see," he replied. So they went and saw where he was staying, and they stayed with him that day. It was about four in the afternoon.

Andrew, Simon Peter's brother, was one of the two who heard John and followed him. He first found his own brother Simon and told him, "We have found the Messiah" (which is translated "the Christ"), and he brought Simon to Jesus.

When Jesus saw him, he said, "You are Simon, son of John. You will be called Cephas" (which is translated "Peter").

The next day Jesus decided to leave for Galilee. He found Philip and told him, "Follow me."

Now Philip was from Bethsaida, the hometown of Andrew and Peter. Philip found Nathanael and told him, "We have found the one Moses wrote about in the law (and so did the prophets): Jesus the son of Joseph, from Nazareth."

"Can anything good come out of Nazareth?" Nathanael asked him.

"Come and see," Philip answered.

Then Jesus saw Nathanael coming toward him and said about him, "Here truly is an Israelite in whom there is no deceit."

"How do you know me?" Nathanael asked.

"Before Philip called you, when you were under the fig tree, I saw you," Jesus answered.

"Rabbi," Nathanael replied, "You are the Son of God; you are the King of Israel!"

Jesus responded to him, "Do you believe because I told you I saw you under the fig tree? You will see greater things than this." Then he said, "Truly I tell you, you will see heaven opened and the angels of God ascending and descending on the Son of Man."

This is the Word of the Lord. Thanks be to God.

GLORIA

Glory be to God the Father, God the Son, and God the Holy Spirit. As it was in the beginning, is now, and will be forever, world without end.

THE LORD'S PRAYER

Our Father in heaven,
Hallowed be your name.
Your kingdom come,
Your will be done
on earth as it is in heaven.
Give us this day our daily bread.
And forgive us our debts,
as we also have forgiven our debtors.
And lead us not into temptation
But deliver us from the evil one.
For yours is the kingdom and the power and the glory forever.
Amen.

INTERCESSIONS AND PERSONAL REQUESTS

PRAYER OF THE CHURCH

Almighty God, whose blessed Son was led by the Spirit to be tempted by Satan: Come quickly to help us who are assaulted by many temptations, and, as you know the weaknesses of each of us, let each one find you mighty to save; through Jesus Christ your Son our Lord, who lives and reigns with you and the Holy Spirit, one God, now and for ever. Amen.
The Book of Common Prayer

BLESSING

May God be gracious to us and bless us; may he make his face shine upon us so that your way may be known on earth, your salvation among all nations.
Psalm 67:1–2

DAY 3 MIDDAY PRAYER

CALL TO PRAYER

Lord, open my lips, and my mouth will declare your praise.
Psalm 51:15

MIDDAY READINGS

John 2:1–11

On the third day a wedding took place in Cana of Galilee. Jesus's mother was there, and Jesus and his disciples were invited to the wedding as well. When the wine ran out, Jesus's mother told him, "They don't have any wine."

"What has this concern of yours to do with me, woman?" Jesus asked. "My hour has not yet come."

"Do whatever he tells you," his mother told the servants.

Now six stone water jars had been set there for Jewish purification. Each contained twenty or thirty gallons.

"Fill the jars with water," Jesus told them. So they filled them to the brim. Then he said to them, "Now draw some out and take it to the headwaiter." And they did.

When the headwaiter tasted the water (after it had become wine), he did not know where it came from—though the servants who had drawn the water knew. He called the groom and told him, "Everyone sets out the fine wine first, then, after people are drunk, the inferior. But you have kept the fine wine until now."

Jesus did this, the first of his signs, in Cana of Galilee. He revealed his glory, and his disciples believed in him.

Mark 1:14–15

After John was arrested, Jesus went to Galilee, proclaiming the good news of God: "The time is fulfilled, and the kingdom of God has come near. Repent and believe the good news!"

Luke 5:1–11

As the crowd was pressing in on Jesus to hear God's word, he was standing by Lake Gennesaret. He saw two boats at the edge of the lake; the fishermen had left them and were washing their nets. He got into one of the boats, which belonged to Simon, and asked him to put out a little from the land. Then he sat down and was teaching the crowds from the boat.

When he had finished speaking, he said to Simon, "Put out into deep water and let down your nets for a catch."

"Master," Simon replied, "we've worked hard all night long and caught nothing. But if you say so, I'll let down the nets."

When they did this, they caught a great number of fish, and their nets began to tear. So they signaled to their partners in the other boat to come and help them; they came and filled both boats so full that they began to sink.

When Simon Peter saw this, he fell at Jesus's knees and said, "Go away from me, because I'm a sinful man, Lord!" For he and all those with him were amazed at the catch of fish they had taken, and so were James and John, Zebedee's sons, who were Simon's partners.

"Don't be afraid," Jesus told Simon. "From now on you will be catching people." Then they brought the boats to land, left everything, and followed him.

This is the Word of the Lord. Thanks be to God.

GLORIA

Glory be to God the Father, God the Son, and God the Holy Spirit. As it was in the beginning, is now, and will be forever, world without end.

THE LORD'S PRAYER

Our Father in heaven,
Hallowed be your name.
Your kingdom come,

Your will be done
on earth as it is in heaven.
Give us this day our daily bread.
And forgive us our debts,
as we also have forgiven our debtors.
And lead us not into temptation
But deliver us from the evil one.
For yours is the kingdom and the power and the glory forever.
Amen.

BLESSING

May your faithful love rest on us, LORD, for we put our hope
in you.
Psalm 33:22

DAY 3 EVENING PRAYER

CALL TO PRAYER

Seek the one who made the Pleiades and Orion, who turns
darkness into dawn and darkens day into night, who summons
the water of the sea and pours it out over the surface of the
earth—the LORD is his name.
Amos 5:8

CONFESSION OF SIN

O Almighty and merciful Father, you pour your benefits upon
us—forgive the unthankfulness with which we have responded
to your goodness. We have remained before you with dead
and senseless hearts, unkindled with love of your gentle and
enduring goodness. Turn us, O merciful Father, and so shall we
be turned. Make us with our whole heart to hunger and thirst
after you, and with all our longing to desire you. Amen.
Anselm

As far as the east is from the west, so far has he removed our transgressions from us.
Psalm 103:12

Canticle

Seek the Lord while he may be found;
call to him while he is near.
Let the wicked one abandon his way
and the sinful one his thoughts;
let him return to the Lord,
so he may have compassion on him,
and to our God, for he will freely forgive.
"For my thoughts are not your thoughts,
and your ways are not my ways."
This is the Lord's declaration.
"For as heaven is higher than earth,
so my ways are higher than your ways,
and my thoughts than your thoughts.
For just as rain and snow fall from heaven
and do not return there
without saturating the earth
and making it germinate and sprout,
and providing seed to sow
and food to eat,
so my word that comes from my mouth
will not return to me empty,
but it will accomplish what I please
and will prosper in what I send it to do."
Isaiah 55:6–11

Evening Reading

John 3:1–21
There was a man from the Pharisees named Nicodemus, a ruler of the Jews. This man came to him at night and said, "Rabbi,

we know that you are a teacher who has come from God, for no one could perform these signs you do unless God were with him."

Jesus replied, "Truly I tell you, unless someone is born again, he cannot see the kingdom of God."

"How can anyone be born when he is old?" Nicodemus asked him. "Can he enter his mother's womb a second time and be born?"

Jesus answered, "Truly I tell you, unless someone is born of water and the Spirit, he cannot enter the kingdom of God. Whatever is born of the flesh is flesh, and whatever is born of the Spirit is spirit. Do not be amazed that I told you that you must be born again. The wind blows where it pleases, and you hear its sound, but you don't know where it comes from or where it is going. So it is with everyone born of the Spirit."

"How can these things be?" asked Nicodemus.

"Are you a teacher of Israel and don't know these things?" Jesus replied. "Truly I tell you, we speak what we know and we testify to what we have seen, but you do not accept our testimony. If I have told you about earthly things and you don't believe, how will you believe if I tell you about heavenly things? No one has ascended into heaven except the one who descended from heaven—the Son of Man.

"Just as Moses lifted up the snake in the wilderness, so the Son of Man must be lifted up, so that everyone who believes in him may have eternal life. For God loved the world in this way: He gave his one and only Son, so that everyone who believes in him will not perish but have eternal life. For God did not send his Son into the world to condemn the world, but to save the world through him. Anyone who believes in him is not condemned, but anyone who does not believe is already condemned, because he has not believed in the name of the one and only Son of God. This is the judgment: The light has come into the world, and people loved darkness rather than the light because their deeds were evil. For everyone who does evil hates the light and avoids it, so that his deeds may not be exposed.

But anyone who lives by the truth comes to the light, so that his works may be shown to be accomplished by God."

This is the Word of the Lord. Thanks be to God.

Gloria
Glory be to God the Father, God the Son, and God the Holy Spirit. As it was in the beginning, is now, and will be forever, world without end.

The Lord's Prayer
Our Father in heaven,
Hallowed be your name.
Your kingdom come,
Your will be done
on earth as it is in heaven.
Give us this day our daily bread.
And forgive us our debts,
as we also have forgiven our debtors.
And lead us not into temptation
But deliver us from the evil one.
For yours is the kingdom and the power and the glory forever.
Amen.

Intercessions and Personal Requests

Prayer of the Church
Gracious and holy Father, give me wisdom to perceive you, intelligence to fathom you, patience to wait for you, eyes to behold you, a heart to meditate upon you, and a life to proclaim you, through the power of the Spirit of Jesus Christ our Lord.
Benedict

BLESSING

The Lord Almighty grant us a peaceful night and a perfect end.
Amen.

DAY 4 MORNING PRAYER

Call to Prayer

Sing a new song to the LORD, for he has performed wonders; his right hand and holy arm have won him victory.
Psalm 98:1

Confession of Faith

I believe the Son of God was manifested in the flesh,
vindicated in the Spirit,
seen by angels,
preached among the nations,
believed on in the world,
taken up in glory.
1 Timothy 3:16

Canticle

A shoot will grow from the stump of Jesse,
and a branch from his roots will bear fruit.
The Spirit of the LORD will rest on him—
a Spirit of wisdom and understanding,
a Spirit of counsel and strength,
a Spirit of knowledge and of the fear of the LORD.
His delight will be in the fear of the LORD.
Isaiah 11:1–2

Morning Reading

Mark 1:21–45

They went into Capernaum, and right away he entered the synagogue on the Sabbath and began to teach. They were astonished at his teaching because he was teaching them as one who had authority, and not like the scribes.

Just then a man with an unclean spirit was in their synagogue. He cried out, "What do you have to do with us, Jesus of

Nazareth? Have you come to destroy us? I know who you are—the Holy One of God!"

Jesus rebuked him saying, "Be silent, and come out of him!" And the unclean spirit threw him into convulsions, shouted with a loud voice, and came out of him.

They were all amazed, and so they began to ask each other, "What is this? A new teaching with authority! He commands even the unclean spirits, and they obey him." At once the news about him spread throughout the entire vicinity of Galilee.

As soon as they left the synagogue, they went into Simon and Andrew's house with James and John. Simon's mother-in-law was lying in bed with a fever, and they told him about her at once. So he went to her, took her by the hand, and raised her up. The fever left her, and she began to serve them.

When evening came, after the sun had set, they brought to him all those who were sick and demon-possessed. The whole town was assembled at the door, and he healed many who were sick with various diseases and drove out many demons. And he would not permit the demons to speak, because they knew him.

Very early in the morning, while it was still dark, he got up, went out, and made his way to a deserted place; and there he was praying. Simon and his companions searched for him, and when they found him they said, "Everyone is looking for you."

And he said to them, "Let's go on to the neighboring villages so that I may preach there too. This is why I have come."

He went into all of Galilee, preaching in their synagogues and driving out demons. Then a man with leprosy came to him and, on his knees, begged him, "If you are willing, you can make me clean." Moved with compassion, Jesus reached out his hand and touched him. "I am willing," he told him. "Be made clean." Immediately the leprosy left him, and he was made clean. Then he sternly warned him and sent him away at once, telling him, "See that you say nothing to anyone; but go and show yourself to the priest, and offer what Moses commanded for your cleansing, as a testimony to them." Yet he went out and began to proclaim it widely and to spread the news, with the result that Jesus could no longer enter a town openly. But he was out in deserted places, and they came to him from everywhere.

This is the Word of the Lord. Thanks be to God.

Gloria

Glory be to God the Father, God the Son, and God the Holy Spirit. As it was in the beginning, is now, and will be forever, world without end.

The Lord's Prayer

Our Father in heaven,
Hallowed be your name.
Your kingdom come,
Your will be done
on earth as it is in heaven.
Give us this day our daily bread.
And forgive us our debts,
as we also have forgiven our debtors.
And lead us not into temptation
But deliver us from the evil one.
For yours is the kingdom and the power and the glory forever.
Amen.

Intercessions and Personal Requests

Prayer of the Church

May the strength of God pilot me, the power of God uphold me, the wisdom of God guide me. May the eye of God look before me, the ear of God hear me, the Word of God speak for me. May the hand of God protect me, the way of God lie before me, the shield of God defend me, the host of God save me. May Christ shield me today. Christ with me, Christ before me, Christ behind me, Christ in me, Christ beneath me, Christ above me, Christ on my right, Christ on my left, Christ when I lie down, Christ when I sit, Christ when I stand, Christ in the heart of everyone who thinks of me, Christ in the mouth of everyone

who speaks of me, Christ in every eye that sees me, Christ in
every ear that hears me.
Patrick of Ireland

Blessing

The peace of God, which passes all understanding, keep your
hearts and minds in the knowledge and love of God, and of his
Son Jesus Christ our Lord; and the blessing of God Almighty,
the Father, the Son, and the Holy Spirit, be among you, and
remain with you always. Amen.

DAY 4 MIDDAY PRAYER

Call to Prayer

The mercy of the Lord is everlasting: O come, let us adore him.

Midday Reading

Mark 2:1–22
When he entered Capernaum again after some days, it was
reported that he was at home. So many people gathered
together that there was no more room, not even in the doorway,
and he was speaking the word to them. They came to him
bringing a paralytic, carried by four of them. Since they were
not able to bring him to Jesus because of the crowd, they
removed the roof above him, and after digging through it, they
lowered the mat on which the paralytic was lying. Seeing their
faith, Jesus told the paralytic, "Son, your sins are forgiven."

But some of the scribes were sitting there, questioning in
their hearts: "Why does he speak like this? He's blaspheming!
Who can forgive sins but God alone?"

Right away Jesus perceived in his spirit that they were
thinking like this within themselves and said to them, "Why
are you thinking these things in your hearts? Which is easier:
to say to the paralytic, 'Your sins are forgiven,' or to say, 'Get up,
take your mat, and walk'? But so that you may know that the

Son of Man has authority on earth to forgive sins"—he told the paralytic—"I tell you: get up, take your mat, and go home."

Immediately he got up, took the mat, and went out in front of everyone. As a result, they were all astounded and gave glory to God, saying, "We have never seen anything like this!"

Jesus went out again beside the sea. The whole crowd was coming to him, and he was teaching them. Then, passing by, he saw Levi the son of Alphaeus sitting at the tax office, and he said to him, "Follow me," and he got up and followed him.

While he was reclining at the table in Levi's house, many tax collectors and sinners were eating with Jesus and his disciples, for there were many who were following him. When the scribes who were Pharisees saw that he was eating with sinners and tax collectors, they asked his disciples, "Why does he eat with tax collectors and sinners?"

When Jesus heard this, he told them, "It is not those who are well who need a doctor, but those who are sick. I didn't come to call the righteous, but sinners."

Now John's disciples and the Pharisees were fasting. People came and asked him, "Why do John's disciples and the Pharisees' disciples fast, but your disciples do not fast?"

Jesus said to them, "The wedding guests cannot fast while the groom is with them, can they? As long as they have the groom with them, they cannot fast. But the time will come when the groom will be taken away from them, and then they will fast on that day. No one sews a patch of unshrunk cloth on an old garment. Otherwise, the new patch pulls away from the old cloth, and a worse tear is made. And no one puts new wine into old wineskins. Otherwise, the wine will burst the skins, and the wine is lost as well as the skins. No, new wine is put into fresh wineskins."

This is the Word of the Lord. Thanks be to God.

GLORIA

Glory be to God the Father, God the Son, and God the Holy Spirit. As it was in the beginning, is now, and will be forever, world without end.

The Lord's Prayer

Our Father in heaven,
Hallowed be your name.
Your kingdom come,
Your will be done
on earth as it is in heaven.
Give us this day our daily bread.
And forgive us our debts,
as we also have forgiven our debtors.
And lead us not into temptation
But deliver us from the evil one.
For yours is the kingdom and the power and the glory forever.
Amen.

Blessing

The grace of the Lord Jesus Christ, and the love of God, and the
fellowship of the Holy Spirit be with us all.
2 Corinthians 13:14

DAY 4 EVENING PRAYER

Call to Prayer

May my prayer be set before you as incense, the raising of my
hands as the evening offering.
Psalm 141:2

Confession of Sin

Merciful Lord, pardon all the sins of my life, of omission and
commission, of lips, life and walk, of hard-heartedness, unbelief,
pride, of bringing dishonor on your great name, of impurity
in thought, word and deed, of covetousness, which is idolatry.
Pardon all my sins, known and unknown, felt and unfelt,
confessed and unconfessed, remembered or forgotten. Good
Lord, hear; and hearing, forgive!
The Valley of Vision

If we confess our sins, he is faithful and righteous to forgive us our sins and to cleanse us from all unrighteousness.
1 John 1:9

Canticle

When I think of you as I lie on my bed,
I meditate on you during the night watches
because you are my helper;
I will rejoice in the shadow of your wings.
I follow close to you;
your right hand holds on to me.
Psalm 63:6–8

Evening Readings

Matthew 12:1–14

At that time Jesus passed through the grainfields on the Sabbath. His disciples were hungry and began to pick and eat some heads of grain. When the Pharisees saw this, they said to him, "See, your disciples are doing what is not lawful to do on the Sabbath."

He said to them, "Haven't you read what David did when he and those who were with him were hungry: how he entered the house of God, and they ate the bread of the Presence—which is not lawful for him or for those with him to eat, but only for the priests? Or haven't you read in the law that on Sabbath days the priests in the temple violate the Sabbath and are innocent? I tell you that something greater than the temple is here. If you had known what this means, **I desire mercy and not sacrifice**, you would not have condemned the innocent. For the Son of Man is Lord of the Sabbath."

Moving on from there, he entered their synagogue. There he saw a man who had a shriveled hand, and in order to accuse him they asked him, "Is it lawful to heal on the Sabbath?"

He replied to them, "Who among you, if he had a sheep that fell into a pit on the Sabbath, wouldn't take hold of it and lift it out? A person is worth far more than a sheep; so it is lawful to do what is good on the Sabbath."

Then he told the man, "Stretch out your hand." So he stretched it out, and it was restored, as good as the other. But the Pharisees went out and plotted against him, how they might kill him.

Mark 3:13–19
Jesus went up the mountain and summoned those he wanted, and they came to him. He appointed twelve, whom he also named apostles, to be with him, to send them out to preach, and to have authority to drive out demons. He appointed the Twelve: To Simon, he gave the name Peter; and to James the son of Zebedee, and to his brother John, he gave the name "Boanerges" (that is, "Sons of Thunder"); Andrew; Philip and Bartholomew; Matthew and Thomas; James the son of Alphaeus, and Thaddaeus; Simon the Zealot, and Judas Iscariot, who also betrayed him.

This is the Word of the Lord. Thanks be to God.

GLORIA
Glory be to God the Father, God the Son, and God the Holy Spirit. As it was in the beginning, is now, and will be forever, world without end.

THE LORD'S PRAYER
Our Father in heaven,
Hallowed be your name.
Your kingdom come,
Your will be done
on earth as it is in heaven.
Give us this day our daily bread.
And forgive us our debts,
as we also have forgiven our debtors.
And lead us not into temptation
But deliver us from the evil one.
For yours is the kingdom and the power and the glory forever.
Amen.

PRAYER OF THE CHURCH

I am no longer my own, but yours. Put me in any place of service, rank me with any type of people; put me to work, put me to suffering. Let me be useful for you or laid aside for you, exalted for you or brought low by you. Let me be full, let me be empty. Let me have all things, let me have nothing. I freely and heartily yield all things to your pleasure and for your use.
John Wesley

BLESSING

The Almighty and merciful Lord, Father, Son, and Holy Spirit, bless us and keep us, this night and evermore. Amen.

DAY 5 MORNING PRAYER

Call to Prayer

An hour is coming, and is now here, when the true worshipers
will worship the Father in Spirit and in truth. Yes, the Father
wants such people to worship him.
John 4:23

Confession of Faith

I believe the Holy Spirit is the third person of the Trinity,
the unseen yet active personal presence of God in the world,
who unites believers to Christ, regenerating and making us
new creatures with hearts oriented to the light and life of the
kingdom of God and to peace and justice on earth. The Spirit
indwells those whom he makes alive with Christ, through
faith incorporates us into the body of Christ, and conforms us
to the image of Christ so that we may glorify him as we grow
in knowledge, wisdom, and love into mature sainthood, the
measure of the stature of the fullness of Christ. The Spirit is
the light of truth and fire of love who continues to sanctify
the people of God, prompting us to repentance and faith,
diversifying our gifts, directing our witness, and empowering
our discipleship.
Adapted from the Reforming Catholic Confession

Canticle

Indeed, God is my salvation;
I will trust him and not be afraid,
for the Lord, the Lord himself,
is my strength and my song.
He has become my salvation.
You will joyfully draw water
from the springs of salvation,
and on that day you will say,
"Give thanks to the Lord; proclaim his name!

Make his works known among the peoples.
Declare that his name is exalted.
Sing to the LORD, for he has done glorious things.
Let this be known throughout the earth.
Cry out and sing, citizen of Zion,
for the Holy One of Israel is among you
in his greatness."
Isaiah 12:2–6

MORNING READING

John 4:4–42

He had to travel through Samaria; so he came to a town of
Samaria called Sychar near the property that Jacob had given his
son Joseph. Jacob's well was there, and Jesus, worn out from his
journey, sat down at the well. It was about noon.

A woman of Samaria came to draw water.

"Give me a drink," Jesus said to her, because his disciples had
gone into town to buy food.

"How is it that you, a Jew, ask for a drink from me, a
Samaritan woman?" she asked him. For Jews do not associate
with Samaritans.

Jesus answered, "If you knew the gift of God, and who is
saying to you, 'Give me a drink,' you would ask him, and he
would give you living water."

"Sir," said the woman, "you don't even have a bucket, and the
well is deep. So where do you get this 'living water'? You aren't
greater than our father Jacob, are you? He gave us the well and
drank from it himself, as did his sons and livestock."

Jesus said, "Everyone who drinks from this water will get
thirsty again. But whoever drinks from the water that I will give
him will never get thirsty again. In fact, the water I will give him
will become a well of water springing up in him for eternal life."

"Sir," the woman said to him, "give me this water so that I
won't get thirsty and come here to draw water."

"Go call your husband," he told her, "and come back here."

"I don't have a husband," she answered.

"You have correctly said, 'I don't have a husband,'" Jesus said. "For you've had five husbands, and the man you now have is not your husband. What you have said is true."

"Sir," the woman replied, "I see that you are a prophet. Our ancestors worshiped on this mountain, but you Jews say that the place to worship is in Jerusalem."

Jesus told her, "Believe me, woman, an hour is coming when you will worship the Father neither on this mountain nor in Jerusalem. You Samaritans worship what you do not know. We worship what we do know, because salvation is from the Jews. But an hour is coming, and is now here, when the true worshipers will worship the Father in Spirit and in truth. Yes, the Father wants such people to worship him. God is spirit, and those who worship him must worship in Spirit and in truth."

The woman said to him, "I know that the Messiah is coming" (who is called Christ). "When he comes, he will explain everything to us."

Jesus told her, "I, the one speaking to you, am he."

Just then his disciples arrived, and they were amazed that he was talking with a woman. Yet no one said, "What do you want?" or "Why are you talking with her?"

Then the woman left her water jar, went into town, and told the people, "Come, see a man who told me everything I ever did. Could this be the Messiah?" They left the town and made their way to him.

In the meantime the disciples kept urging him, "Rabbi, eat something."

But he said, "I have food to eat that you don't know about."

The disciples said to one another, "Could someone have brought him something to eat?"

"My food is to do the will of him who sent me and to finish his work," Jesus told them. "Don't you say, 'There are still four more months, and then comes the harvest'? Listen to what I'm telling you: Open your eyes and look at the fields, because they are ready for harvest. The reaper is already receiving pay and gathering fruit for eternal life, so that the sower and reaper can rejoice together. For in this case the saying is true: 'One sows and another reaps.' I sent you to reap what you didn't labor for; others have labored, and you have benefited from their labor."

Now many Samaritans from that town believed in him because of what the woman said when she testified, "He told me everything I ever did." So when the Samaritans came to him, they asked him to stay with them, and he stayed there two days. Many more believed because of what he said. And they told the woman, "We no longer believe because of what you said, since we have heard for ourselves and know that this really is the Savior of the world."

This is the Word of the Lord. Thanks be to God.

GLORIA

Glory be to God the Father, God the Son, and God the Holy Spirit. As it was in the beginning, is now, and will be forever, world without end.

THE LORD'S PRAYER

Our Father in heaven,
Hallowed be your name.
Your kingdom come,
Your will be done
on earth as it is in heaven.
Give us this day our daily bread.
And forgive us our debts,
as we also have forgiven our debtors.
And lead us not into temptation
But deliver us from the evil one.
For yours is the kingdom and the power and the glory forever.
Amen.

INTERCESSIONS AND PERSONAL REQUESTS

PRAYER OF THE CHURCH

O God of all nations of the earth, we thank you, that you are no respecter of persons, and that you have made of one blood all people. Rend the heavens, O Lord, and come down upon the earth. Hasten that glorious time, when the knowledge of the gospel of Jesus Christ shall cover the earth, as the waters cover the sea.

Absalom Jones

BLESSING

Now to him who is able to do above and beyond all that we ask or think according to the power that works in us—to him be glory in the church and in Christ Jesus to all generations, forever and ever. Amen.

Ephesians 3:20–21

DAY 5 MIDDAY PRAYER

CALL TO PRAYER

Come and listen, all who fear God, and I will tell what he has done for me.

Psalm 66:16

MIDDAY READING

John 4:46–53

He went again to Cana of Galilee, where he had turned the water into wine. There was a certain royal official whose son was ill at Capernaum. When this man heard that Jesus had come from Judea into Galilee, he went to him and pleaded with him to come down and heal his son, since he was about to die.

Jesus told him, "Unless you people see signs and wonders, you will not believe."

"Sir," the official said to him, "come down before my boy dies."

"Go," Jesus told him, "your son will live." The man believed what Jesus said to him and departed.

While he was still going down, his servants met him saying that his boy was alive. He asked them at what time he got better.

"Yesterday at one in the afternoon the fever left him," they answered. The father realized this was the very hour at which Jesus had told him, "Your son will live." So he himself believed, along with his whole household.

This is the Word of the Lord. Thanks be to God.

GLORIA

Glory be to God the Father, God the Son, and God the Holy Spirit. As it was in the beginning, is now, and will be forever, world without end.

THE LORD'S PRAYER

Our Father in heaven,
Hallowed be your name.
Your kingdom come,
Your will be done
on earth as it is in heaven.
Give us this day our daily bread.
And forgive us our debts,
as we also have forgiven our debtors.
And lead us not into temptation
But deliver us from the evil one.
For yours is the kingdom and the power and the glory forever.
Amen.

BLESSING

May the LORD bless you and protect you; may the LORD make his face shine on you and be gracious to you; may the LORD look with favor on you and give you peace.
Numbers 6:24–26

DAY 5 EVENING PRAYER

CALL TO PRAYER

From the rising of the sun to its setting, let the name of the
LORD be praised.
Psalm 113:3

CONFESSION OF SIN

Be gracious to me, God,
according to your faithful love;
according to your abundant compassion,
blot out my rebellion.
Completely wash away my guilt
and cleanse me from my sin.
Psalm 51:1–2

The sacrifice pleasing to God is a broken spirit. You will not
despise a broken and humbled heart, God.
Psalm 51:17

CANTICLE

LORD God of Israel,
there is no God like you
in heaven or on earth,
who keeps his gracious covenant
with your servants who walk before you
with all their heart.
Now, LORD God of Israel, please confirm
what you promised to your servant David.
2 Chronicles 6:14,17

Luke 4:16–30

He came to Nazareth, where he had been brought up. As usual, he entered the synagogue on the Sabbath day and stood up to read. The scroll of the prophet Isaiah was given to him, and unrolling the scroll, he found the place where it was written:

The Spirit of the Lord is on me,
because he has anointed me
to preach good news to the poor.
He has sent me
to proclaim release to the captives
and recovery of sight to the blind,
to set free the oppressed,
to proclaim the year of the Lord's favor.

He then rolled up the scroll, gave it back to the attendant, and sat down. And the eyes of everyone in the synagogue were fixed on him. He began by saying to them, "Today as you listen, this Scripture has been fulfilled."

They were all speaking well of him and were amazed by the gracious words that came from his mouth; yet they said, "Isn't this Joseph's son?"

Then he said to them, "No doubt you will quote this proverb to me: 'Doctor, heal yourself. What we've heard that took place in Capernaum, do here in your hometown also.'"

He also said, "Truly I tell you, no prophet is accepted in his hometown. But I say to you, there were certainly many widows in Israel in Elijah's days, when the sky was shut up for three years and six months while a great famine came over all the land. Yet Elijah was not sent to any of them except a widow at Zarephath in Sidon. And in the prophet Elisha's time, there were many in Israel who had leprosy, and yet not one of them was cleansed except Naaman the Syrian."

When they heard this, everyone in the synagogue was enraged. They got up, drove him out of town, and brought him to the edge of the hill that their town was built on, intending to hurl him over the cliff. But he passed right through the crowd and went on his way.

Matthew 9:35–38
Jesus continued going around to all the towns and villages, teaching in their synagogues, preaching the good news of the kingdom, and healing every disease and every sickness. When he saw the crowds, he felt compassion for them, because they were distressed and dejected, like sheep without a shepherd. Then he said to his disciples, "The harvest is abundant, but the workers are few. Therefore, pray to the Lord of the harvest to send out workers into his harvest."

This is the Word of the Lord. Thanks be to God.

Gloria
Glory be to God the Father, God the Son, and God the Holy Spirit. As it was in the beginning, is now, and will be forever, world without end.

The Lord's Prayer
Our Father in heaven,
Hallowed be your name.
Your kingdom come,
Your will be done
on earth as it is in heaven.
Give us this day our daily bread.
And forgive us our debts,
as we also have forgiven our debtors.
And lead us not into temptation
But deliver us from the evil one.
For yours is the kingdom and the power and the glory forever.
Amen.

PRAYER OF THE CHURCH

Almighty God, heavenly Father, we ask you to work in us by your Holy Spirit, so that we may rightly know you, and sanctify, glorify, and praise you in all your works, in which shine forth your omnipotence, wisdom, goodness, righteousness, mercy, and truth. Grant us also that we may so direct our whole life— thoughts, words, and deeds—that your name is not blasphemed because of us, but honored and praised. Amen.
Zacharias Ursinus

BLESSING

The Lord Almighty grant us a peaceful night and a perfect end. Amen.

DAY 6 MORNING PRAYER

CALL TO PRAYER

Father, Son, and Holy Spirit, one God: O come, let us adore him.

CONFESSION OF FAITH

I believe there is one God, infinitely great and good, the creator and sustainer of all things visible and invisible, the one true source of light and life, who has life in himself and lives eternally in glorious light and sovereign love in three persons—Father, Son, and Holy Spirit—co-equal in nature, majesty, and glory. Everything God does in creating, sustaining, judging, and redeeming the world reflects who God is, the one whose perfections, including love, holiness, knowledge, wisdom, power, and righteousness, have been revealed in the history of salvation. God has freely purposed from before the foundation of the world to elect and form a people for himself to be his treasured possession, to the praise of his glory.
Adapted from the Reforming Catholic Confession

CANTICLE

I will exalt you, Lord,
because you have lifted me up
and have not allowed my enemies
to triumph over me.
Lord my God,
I cried to you for help, and you healed me.
Lord, you brought me up from Sheol;
you spared me from among those
going down to the Pit.
Sing to the Lord, you his faithful ones,
and praise his holy name.
For his anger lasts only a moment,
but his favor, a lifetime.

Weeping may stay overnight,
but there is joy in the morning.
Psalm 30:1–5

Morning Reading
John 5:1–23
After this, a Jewish festival took place, and Jesus went up to Jerusalem. By the Sheep Gate in Jerusalem there is a pool, called Bethesda in Aramaic, which has five colonnades. Within these lay a large number of the disabled—blind, lame, and paralyzed.

One man was there who had been disabled for thirty-eight years. When Jesus saw him lying there and realized he had already been there a long time, he said to him, "Do you want to get well?"

"Sir," the disabled man answered, "I have no one to put me into the pool when the water is stirred up, but while I'm coming, someone goes down ahead of me."

"Get up," Jesus told him, "pick up your mat and walk." Instantly the man got well, picked up his mat, and started to walk.

Now that day was the Sabbath, and so the Jews said to the man who had been healed, "This is the Sabbath. The law prohibits you from picking up your mat."

He replied, "The man who made me well told me, 'Pick up your mat and walk.'"

"Who is this man who told you, 'Pick up your mat and walk'?" they asked. But the man who was healed did not know who it was, because Jesus had slipped away into the crowd that was there.

After this, Jesus found him in the temple and said to him, "See, you are well. Do not sin anymore, so that something worse doesn't happen to you." The man went and reported to the Jews that it was Jesus who had made him well. Therefore, the Jews began persecuting Jesus because he was doing these things on the Sabbath.

Jesus responded to them, "My Father is still working, and I am working also." This is why the Jews began trying all the more to kill him: Not only was he breaking the Sabbath, but he was even calling God his own Father, making himself equal to God.

Jesus replied, "Truly I tell you, the Son is not able to do anything on his own, but only what he sees the Father doing. For whatever the Father does, the Son likewise does these things. For the Father loves the Son and shows him everything he is doing, and he will show him greater works than these so that you will be amazed. And just as the Father raises the dead and gives them life, so the Son also gives life to whom he wants. The Father, in fact, judges no one but has given all judgment to the Son, so that all people may honor the Son just as they honor the Father. Anyone who does not honor the Son does not honor the Father who sent him."

This is the Word of the Lord. Thanks be to God.

Gloria
Glory be to God the Father, God the Son, and God the Holy Spirit. As it was in the beginning, is now, and will be forever, world without end.

The Lord's Prayer
Our Father in heaven,
Hallowed be your name.
Your kingdom come,
Your will be done
on earth as it is in heaven.
Give us this day our daily bread.
And forgive us our debts,
as we also have forgiven our debtors.
And lead us not into temptation
But deliver us from the evil one.
For yours is the kingdom and the power and the glory forever.
Amen.

PRAYER OF THE CHURCH

Almighty and everlasting God, you have given to us your servants grace, by the confession of a true faith, to acknowledge the glory of the eternal Trinity, and in the power of your divine Majesty to worship the Unity: Keep us steadfast in this faith and worship, and bring us at last to see you in your one and eternal glory, O Father; who with the Son and the Holy Spirit live and reign, one God, for ever and ever. Amen.

The Book of Common Prayer

BLESSING

Now may the God of hope fill you with all joy and peace as you believe, so that you may overflow with hope by the power of the Holy Spirit.

Romans 15:13

DAY 6 MIDDAY PRAYER

CALL TO PRAYER

Grace to you and peace from God our Father and the Lord Jesus Christ.

Philippians 1:2

MIDDAY READING

John 5:24–47

"Truly I tell you, anyone who hears my word and believes him who sent me has eternal life and will not come under judgment but has passed from death to life.

"Truly I tell you, an hour is coming, and is now here, when the dead will hear the voice of the Son of God, and those who hear will live. For just as the Father has life in himself, so also he has granted to the Son to have life in himself. And he has granted him the right to pass judgment, because he is the Son of Man. Do not be amazed at this, because a time is coming when all who are in the graves will hear his voice and come out—those who have done good things, to the resurrection of life, but those who have done wicked things, to the resurrection of condemnation.

"I can do nothing on my own. I judge only as I hear, and my judgment is just, because I do not seek my own will, but the will of him who sent me.

"If I testify about myself, my testimony is not true. There is another who testifies about me, and I know that the testimony he gives about me is true. You sent messengers to John, and he testified to the truth. I don't receive human testimony, but I say these things so that you may be saved. John was a burning and shining lamp, and you were willing to rejoice for a while in his light.

"But I have a greater testimony than John's because of the works that the Father has given me to accomplish. These very works I am doing testify about me that the Father has sent me. The Father who sent me has himself testified about me. You have not heard his voice at any time, and you haven't seen his form. You don't have his word residing in you, because you don't believe the one he sent. You pore over the Scriptures because you think you have eternal life in them, and yet they testify about me. But you are not willing to come to me so that you may have life.

"I do not accept glory from people, but I know you—that you have no love for God within you. I have come in my Father's name, and yet you don't accept me. If someone else comes in his own name, you will accept him. How can you believe, since you accept glory from one another but don't seek the glory that comes from the only God? Do not think that I will accuse you to the Father. Your accuser is Moses, on whom you have set your hope. For if you believed Moses, you would believe me, because he wrote about me. But if you don't believe what he wrote, how will you believe my words?"

This is the Word of the Lord. Thanks be to God.

Glory be to God the Father, God the Son, and God the Holy Spirit. As it was in the beginning, is now, and will be forever, world without end.

THE LORD'S PRAYER
Our Father in heaven,
Hallowed be your name.
Your kingdom come,
Your will be done
on earth as it is in heaven.
Give us this day our daily bread.
And forgive us our debts,
as we also have forgiven our debtors.
And lead us not into temptation
But deliver us from the evil one.
For yours is the kingdom and the power and the glory forever.
Amen.

BLESSING
May [the LORD] give you what your heart desires and fulfill your whole purpose. May the LORD fulfill all your requests.
Psalm 20:4-5

DAY 6 EVENING PRAYER

CALL TO PRAYER
Come, let's go up to the mountain of the LORD, to the house of the God of Jacob. He will teach us about his ways so we may walk in his paths.
Micah 4:2

Confession of Sin

O Lord, as long as I am apart from you, I am self-satisfied, because I have no standard by which to measure my low stature. But when I come near to you, there for the first time I see myself. In your light I behold my darkness. In your purity I behold my corruption. My very confession of sin is the fruit of holiness. Oh, let me gaze on you more and more until, in the vision of your brightness, I loathe the sight of my impurity; until, in the blaze of that glory which human eye has not seen, I fall prostrate, blinded, broken, to rise again a new creation in you. Amen.
George Matheson

If we confess our sins, he is faithful and righteous to forgive us our sins and to cleanse us from all unrighteousness.
1 John 1:9

Canticle

Pay attention, heavens, and I will speak;
listen, earth, to the words from my mouth.
Let my teaching fall like rain
and my word settle like dew,
like gentle rain on new grass
and showers on tender plants.
For I will proclaim the LORD's name.
Declare the greatness of our God!
The Rock—his work is perfect;
all his ways are just.
A faithful God, without bias,
he is righteous and true.
Deuteronomy 32:1–4

Evening Reading

Matthew 5:1–20
When he saw the crowds, he went up on the mountain, and after he sat down, his disciples came to him. Then he began to teach them, saying:

"Blessed are the poor in spirit,
    for the kingdom of heaven is theirs.
Blessed are those who mourn,
    for they will be comforted.
Blessed are the humble,
    for they will inherit the earth.
Blessed are those who hunger and thirst for righteousness,
    for they will be filled.
Blessed are the merciful,
    for they will be shown mercy.
Blessed are the pure in heart,
    for they will see God.
Blessed are the peacemakers,
    for they will be called sons of God.
Blessed are those who are persecuted because
        of righteousness,
    for the kingdom of heaven is theirs.

"You are blessed when they insult you and persecute you and falsely say every kind of evil against you because of me. Be glad and rejoice, because your reward is great in heaven. For that is how they persecuted the prophets who were before you.

"You are the salt of the earth. But if the salt should lose its taste, how can it be made salty? It's no longer good for anything but to be thrown out and trampled under people's feet.

"You are the light of the world. A city situated on a hill cannot be hidden. No one lights a lamp and puts it under a basket, but rather on a lampstand, and it gives light for all who are in the house. In the same way, let your light shine before others, so that they may see your good works and give glory to your Father in heaven.

"Don't think that I came to abolish the Law or the Prophets. I did not come to abolish but to fulfill. For truly I tell you, until heaven and earth pass away, not the smallest letter or one stroke of a letter will pass away from the law until all things are accomplished. Therefore, whoever breaks one of the least of these commands and teaches others to do the same will be called least in the kingdom of heaven. But whoever does and teaches these commands will be called great in the kingdom of heaven. For I tell you, unless your righteousness surpasses that of the scribes and Pharisees, you will never get into the kingdom of heaven."

This is the Word of the Lord. Thanks be to God.

Gloria
Glory be to God the Father, God the Son, and God the Holy Spirit. As it was in the beginning, is now, and will be forever, world without end.

The Lord's Prayer
Our Father in heaven,
Hallowed be your name.
Your kingdom come,
Your will be done
on earth as it is in heaven.
Give us this day our daily bread.
And forgive us our debts,
as we also have forgiven our debtors.
And lead us not into temptation
But deliver us from the evil one.
For yours is the kingdom and the power and the glory forever.
Amen.

Intercessions and Personal Requests

Prayer of the Church
May God the Father, and the Eternal High Priest Jesus Christ, build us up in faith and truth and love, and grant to us our portion among the saints with all those who believe on our Lord Jesus Christ. We pray for all saints, for kings and rulers, for the enemies of the Cross of Christ, and for ourselves we pray that

our fruit may abound and we may be made perfect in Christ
Jesus our Lord. Amen.
Polycarp

Blessing

The Almighty and merciful Lord, Father, Son, and Holy Spirit,
bless us and keep us, this night and evermore. Amen.

DAY 7 MORNING PRAYER

CALL TO PRAYER

May the words of my mouth and the meditation of my heart be
acceptable to you, LORD my rock and my redeemer.
Psalm 19:14

CONFESSION OF FAITH

I believe that God has spoken and continues to speak in
and through Scripture, the only infallible and sufficiently
clear rule and authority for Christian faith, thought, and life.
Scripture is God's inspired and illuminating Word in the words
of his servants, the prophets and apostles, a gracious self-
communication of God's own light and life, a means of grace for
growing in knowledge and holiness. The Bible is to be believed
in all that it teaches, obeyed in all that it commands, trusted in
all that it promises, and revered in all that it reveals.
Adapted from the Reforming Catholic Confession

CANTICLE

The instruction of the LORD is perfect,
renewing one's life;
the testimony of the LORD is trustworthy,
making the inexperienced wise.
The precepts of the LORD are right,
making the heart glad;
the command of the LORD is radiant,
making the eyes light up.
The fear of the LORD is pure,
enduring forever;
the ordinances of the LORD are reliable
and altogether righteous.
They are more desirable than gold—
than an abundance of pure gold;
and sweeter than honey

dripping from a honeycomb.
In addition, your servant is warned by them,
and in keeping them there is an abundant reward.
Psalm 19:7–11

Morning Reading
Matthew 5:20–48

"You have heard that it was said to our ancestors, **Do not murder**, and whoever murders will be subject to judgment. But I tell you, everyone who is angry with his brother or sister will be subject to judgment. Whoever insults his brother or sister will be subject to the court. Whoever says, 'You fool!' will be subject to hellfire. So if you are offering your gift on the altar, and there you remember that your brother or sister has something against you, leave your gift there in front of the altar. First go and be reconciled with your brother or sister, and then come and offer your gift. Reach a settlement quickly with your adversary while you're on the way with him to the court, or your adversary will hand you over to the judge, and the judge to the officer, and you will be thrown into prison. Truly I tell you, you will never get out of there until you have paid the last penny.

"You have heard that it was said, **Do not commit adultery**. But I tell you, everyone who looks at a woman lustfully has already committed adultery with her in his heart. If your right eye causes you to sin, gouge it out and throw it away. For it is better that you lose one of the parts of your body than for your whole body to be thrown into hell. And if your right hand causes you to sin, cut it off and throw it away. For it is better that you lose one of the parts of your body than for your whole body to go into hell.

"It was also said, **Whoever divorces his wife must give her a written notice of divorce.** But I tell you, everyone who divorces his wife, except in a case of sexual immorality, causes her to commit adultery. And whoever marries a divorced woman commits adultery.

"Again, you have heard that it was said to our ancestors, **You must not break your oath, but you must keep your oaths**

to the Lord. But I tell you, don't take an oath at all: either by heaven, because it is God's throne; or by the earth, because it is his footstool; or by Jerusalem, because it is the city of the great King. Do not swear by your head, because you cannot make a single hair white or black. But let your 'yes' mean 'yes,' and your 'no' mean 'no.' Anything more than this is from the evil one.

"You have heard that it was said, **An eye for an eye** and **a tooth for a tooth.** But I tell you, don't resist an evildoer. On the contrary, if anyone slaps you on your right cheek, turn the other to him also. As for the one who wants to sue you and take away your shirt, let him have your coat as well. And if anyone forces you to go one mile, go with him two. Give to the one who asks you, and don't turn away from the one who wants to borrow from you.

"You have heard that it was said, **Love your neighbor** and hate your enemy. But I tell you, love your enemies and pray for those who persecute you, so that you may be children of your Father in heaven. For he causes his sun to rise on the evil and the good, and sends rain on the righteous and the unrighteous. For if you love those who love you, what reward will you have? Don't even the tax collectors do the same? And if you greet only your brothers and sisters, what are you doing out of the ordinary? Don't even the Gentiles do the same? Be perfect, therefore, as your heavenly Father is perfect."

This is the Word of the Lord. Thanks be to God.

Gloria

Glory be to God the Father, God the Son, and God the Holy Spirit. As it was in the beginning, is now, and will be forever, world without end.

The Lord's Prayer

Our Father in heaven,
Hallowed be your name.
Your kingdom come,

Your will be done
on earth as it is in heaven.
Give us this day our daily bread.
And forgive us our debts,
as we also have forgiven our debtors.
And lead us not into temptation
But deliver us from the evil one.
For yours is the kingdom and the power and the glory forever.
Amen.

Intercessions and Personal Requests

Prayer of the Church

Lord, you have given us your Word for a light to shine upon our path; grant us so to meditate on that Word, and to follow its teaching, that we may find in it the light that shines more and more until the perfect day; through Jesus Christ our Lord. Amen.

Jerome

Blessing

The grace of the Lord Jesus Christ, and the love of God, and the fellowship of the Holy Spirit be with us all.

2 Corinthians 13:14

DAY 7 MIDDAY PRAYER

Call to Prayer

Not to us, Lord, not to us, but to your name give glory because of your faithful love, because of your truth.

Psalm 115:1

Midday Reading

Matthew 6:1–18

"Be careful not to practice your righteousness in front of others to be seen by them. Otherwise, you have no reward with your Father in heaven. So whenever you give to the poor, don't sound a trumpet before you, as the hypocrites do in the synagogues and on the streets, to be applauded by people. Truly I tell you, they have their reward. But when you give to the poor, don't let your left hand know what your right hand is doing, so that your giving may be in secret. And your Father who sees in secret will reward you.

"Whenever you pray, you must not be like the hypocrites, because they love to pray standing in the synagogues and on the street corners to be seen by people. Truly I tell you, they have their reward. But when you pray, go into your private room, shut your door, and pray to your Father who is in secret. And your Father who sees in secret will reward you. When you pray, don't babble like the Gentiles, since they imagine they'll be heard for their many words. Don't be like them, because your Father knows the things you need before you ask him.

"Therefore, you should pray like this:

Our Father in heaven,
your name be honored as holy.
Your kingdom come.
Your will be done
on earth as it is in heaven.
Give us today our daily bread.
And forgive us our debts,
as we also have forgiven our debtors.
And do not bring us into temptation,
but deliver us from the evil one.

"For if you forgive others their offenses, your heavenly Father will forgive you as well. But if you don't forgive others, your Father will not forgive your offenses.

"Whenever you fast, don't be gloomy like the hypocrites. For they disfigure their faces so that their fasting is obvious to people. Truly I tell you, they have their reward. But when you fast, put oil on your head and wash your face, so that your fasting isn't obvious to others but to your Father who is in secret. And your Father who sees in secret will reward you."

This is the Word of the Lord. Thanks be to God.

Gloria

Glory be to God the Father, God the Son, and God the Holy Spirit. As it was in the beginning, is now, and will be forever, world without end.

Blessing

May the Lord cause you to increase and overflow with love for one another and for everyone. . . . May he make your hearts blameless in holiness before our God and Father at the coming of our Lord Jesus with all his saints. Amen.
1 Thessalonians 2:12–13

DAY 7 EVENING PRAYER

Call to Prayer

Send your light and your truth; let them lead me. Let them bring me to your holy mountain, to your dwelling place.
Psalm 43:3

Confession of Sin

O Word of our God, I betrayed you, the Truth, with my falsehood. I betrayed you when I promised to hallow the hours that vanish away. In overtaking me, night does not find me undarkened by sin. I did indeed pray, and I thought to stand blameless at evening. But someway and somewhere my feet have stumbled and fallen; for a storm-cloud swooped on me, envious lest I be saved. Kindle for me your light, O Christ, restore me by your presence.
Gregory of Nazianzus

How joyful is the one whose transgression is forgiven, whose
sin is covered!
Psalm 32:1

Canticle

May the name of God
be praised forever and ever,
for wisdom and power belong to him.
He changes the times and seasons;
he removes kings and establishes kings.
He gives wisdom to the wise
and knowledge to those
who have understanding.
He reveals the deep and hidden things;
he knows what is in the darkness,
and light dwells with him.
Daniel 2:20–23

Evening Reading

Matthew 6:19–7:12
"Don't store up for yourselves treasures on earth, where moth
and rust destroy and where thieves break in and steal. But store
up for yourselves treasures in heaven, where neither moth nor
rust destroys, and where thieves don't break in and steal. For
where your treasure is, there your heart will be also.

"The eye is the lamp of the body. If your eye is healthy, your
whole body will be full of light. But if your eye is bad, your
whole body will be full of darkness. So if the light within you is
darkness, how deep is that darkness!

"No one can serve two masters, since either he will hate one
and love the other, or he will be devoted to one and despise the
other. You cannot serve both God and money.

"Therefore I tell you: Don't worry about your life, what you
will eat or what you will drink; or about your body, what you
will wear. Isn't life more than food and the body more than
clothing? Consider the birds of the sky: They don't sow or reap
or gather into barns, yet your heavenly Father feeds them. Aren't

you worth more than they? Can any of you add one moment to his life span by worrying? And why do you worry about clothes? Observe how the wildflowers of the field grow: They don't labor or spin thread. Yet I tell you that not even Solomon in all his splendor was adorned like one of these. If that's how God clothes the grass of the field, which is here today and thrown into the furnace tomorrow, won't he do much more for you— you of little faith? So don't worry, saying, 'What will we eat?' or 'What will we drink?' or 'What will we wear?' For the Gentiles eagerly seek all these things, and your heavenly Father knows that you need them. But seek first the kingdom of God and his righteousness, and all these things will be provided for you. Therefore don't worry about tomorrow, because tomorrow will worry about itself. Each day has enough trouble of its own.

"Do not judge, so that you won't be judged. For you will be judged by the same standard with which you judge others, and you will be measured by the same measure you use. Why do you look at the splinter in your brother's eye but don't notice the beam of wood in your own eye? Or how can you say to your brother, 'Let me take the splinter out of your eye,' and look, there's a beam of wood in your own eye? Hypocrite! First take the beam of wood out of your eye, and then you will see clearly to take the splinter out of your brother's eye. Don't give what is holy to dogs or toss your pearls before pigs, or they will trample them under their feet, turn, and tear you to pieces.

"Ask, and it will be given to you. Seek, and you will find. Knock, and the door will be opened to you. For everyone who asks receives, and the one who seeks finds, and to the one who knocks, the door will be opened. Who among you, if his son asks him for bread, will give him a stone? Or if he asks for a fish, will give him a snake? If you then, who are evil, know how to give good gifts to your children, how much more will your Father in heaven give good things to those who ask him. Therefore, whatever you want others to do for you, do also the same for them, for this is the Law and the Prophets."

This is the Word of the Lord. Thanks be to God.

Gloria

Glory be to God the Father, God the Son, and God the Holy Spirit. As it was in the beginning, is now, and will be forever, world without end.

The Lord's Prayer

Our Father in heaven,
Hallowed be your name.
Your kingdom come,
Your will be done
on earth as it is in heaven.
Give us this day our daily bread.
And forgive us our debts,
as we also have forgiven our debtors.
And lead us not into temptation
But deliver us from the evil one.
For yours is the kingdom and the power and the glory forever.
Amen.

Intercessions and Personal Requests

Prayer of the Church

I ask you, my most gracious God, preserve me from the cares of this life, lest I should be too much entangled in them; and from the many necessities of the body, lest I should be ensnared by pleasure; and from whatever is an obstacle to the soul, lest, broken with troubles, I should be overthrown. Amen.
Thomas à Kempis

Blessing

The Lord Almighty grant us a peaceful night and a perfect end.
Amen.

DAY 8 MORNING PRAYER

CALL TO PRAYER

Exalt the LORD our God; bow in worship at his holy mountain,
for the LORD our God is holy.
Psalm 99:9

CONFESSION OF FAITH

I believe in God, the Father almighty,
creator of heaven and earth;
I believe in Jesus Christ, his only Son, our Lord.
He was conceived by the power of the Holy Spirit
and born of the Virgin Mary.
He suffered under Pontius Pilate,
was crucified, died, and was buried.
He descended to the dead.
On the third day he rose again.
He ascended into heaven,
and is seated at the right hand of the Father.
He will come again to judge the living and the dead.
I believe in the Holy Spirit,
the holy catholic Church,
the communion of saints,
the forgiveness of sins
the resurrection of the body,
and the life everlasting. Amen.
The Apostles' Creed

CANTICLE

LORD, I seek refuge in you;
let me never be disgraced.
Save me by your righteousness.
Listen closely to me; rescue me quickly.
Be a rock of refuge for me,
a mountain fortress to save me.

For you are my rock and my fortress;
you lead and guide me
for your name's sake.
Psalm 31:1–3

Morning Reading

Matthew 7:13–29

"Enter through the narrow gate. For the gate is wide and the
road broad that leads to destruction, and there are many who
go through it. How narrow is the gate and difficult the road that
leads to life, and few find it.

"Be on your guard against false prophets who come to you
in sheep's clothing but inwardly are ravaging wolves. You'll
recognize them by their fruit. Are grapes gathered from
thornbushes or figs from thistles? In the same way, every good
tree produces good fruit, but a bad tree produces bad fruit.
A good tree can't produce bad fruit; neither can a bad tree
produce good fruit. Every tree that doesn't produce good fruit is
cut down and thrown into the fire. So you'll recognize them by
their fruit.

"Not everyone who says to me, 'Lord, Lord,' will enter the
kingdom of heaven, but only the one who does the will of
my Father in heaven. On that day many will say to me, 'Lord,
Lord, didn't we prophesy in your name, drive out demons in
your name, and do many miracles in your name?' Then I will
announce to them, 'I never knew you. **Depart from me, you
lawbreakers!**'

"Therefore, everyone who hears these words of mine and acts
on them will be like a wise man who built his house on the rock.
The rain fell, the rivers rose, and the winds blew and pounded
that house. Yet it didn't collapse, because its foundation was
on the rock. But everyone who hears these words of mine and
doesn't act on them will be like a foolish man who built his
house on the sand. The rain fell, the rivers rose, the winds blew
and pounded that house, and it collapsed. It collapsed with a
great crash."

When Jesus had finished saying these things, the crowds were astonished at his teaching, because he was teaching them like one who had authority, and not like their scribes.

This is the Word of the Lord. Thanks be to God.

Gloria

Glory be to God the Father, God the Son, and God the Holy Spirit. As it was in the beginning, is now, and will be forever, world without end.

The Lord's Prayer

Our Father in heaven,
Hallowed be your name.
Your kingdom come,
Your will be done
on earth as it is in heaven.
Give us this day our daily bread.
And forgive us our debts,
as we also have forgiven our debtors.
And lead us not into temptation
But deliver us from the evil one.
For yours is the kingdom and the power and the glory forever.
Amen.

Intercessions and Personal Requests

Prayer of the Church

Blessed Lord, who caused all Holy Scriptures to be written for our learning: Grant us so to hear them, read, mark, learn, and inwardly digest them, that by patience and the comfort of your holy Word we may embrace and ever hold fast the blessed hope of everlasting life, which you have given us in our Savior Jesus

Christ; who lives and reigns with you and the Holy Spirit, one
God, forever and ever. Amen.
The Book of Common Prayer

Blessing

The grace of the Lord Jesus Christ, and the love of God, and the
fellowship of the Holy Spirit be with us all.
2 Corinthians 13:14

DAY 8 MIDDAY PRAYER

Call to Prayer

The Lord is full of compassion and mercy: O come, let us adore
him.

Midday Readings

Luke 7:2–17

A centurion's servant, who was highly valued by him, was sick
and about to die. When the centurion heard about Jesus, he sent
some Jewish elders to him, requesting him to come and save
the life of his servant. When they reached Jesus, they pleaded
with him earnestly, saying, "He is worthy for you to grant this,
because he loves our nation and has built us a synagogue."

Jesus went with them, and when he was not far from the
house, the centurion sent friends to tell him, "Lord, don't
trouble yourself, since I am not worthy to have you come under
my roof. That is why I didn't even consider myself worthy to
come to you. But say the word, and my servant will be healed.
For I too am a man placed under authority, having soldiers
under my command. I say to this one, 'Go,' and he goes; and to
another, 'Come,' and he comes; and to my servant, 'Do this,' and
he does it."

Jesus heard this and was amazed at him, and turning to the
crowd following him, he said, "I tell you, I have not found so

great a faith even in Israel." When those who had been sent returned to the house, they found the servant in good health.

Afterward he was on his way to a town called Nain. His disciples and a large crowd were traveling with him. Just as he neared the gate of the town, a dead man was being carried out. He was his mother's only son, and she was a widow. A large crowd from the town was also with her. When the Lord saw her, he had compassion on her and said, "Don't weep." Then he came up and touched the open coffin, and the pallbearers stopped. And he said, "Young man, I tell you, get up!"

The dead man sat up and began to speak, and Jesus gave him to his mother. Then fear came over everyone, and they glorified God, saying, "A great prophet has risen among us," and "God has visited his people." This report about him went throughout Judea and all the vicinity.

Luke 7:36–50

Then one of the Pharisees invited him to eat with him. He entered the Pharisee's house and reclined at the table. And a woman in the town who was a sinner found out that Jesus was reclining at the table in the Pharisee's house. She brought an alabaster jar of perfume and stood behind him at his feet, weeping, and began to wash his feet with her tears. She wiped his feet with her hair, kissing them and anointing them with the perfume.

When the Pharisee who had invited him saw this, he said to himself, "This man, if he were a prophet, would know who and what kind of woman this is who is touching him—she's a sinner!"

Jesus replied to him, "Simon, I have something to say to you."

He said, "Say it, teacher."

"A creditor had two debtors. One owed five hundred denarii, and the other fifty. Since they could not pay it back, he graciously forgave them both. So, which of them will love him more?"

Simon answered, "I suppose the one he forgave more."

"You have judged correctly," he told him. Turning to the woman, he said to Simon, "Do you see this woman? I entered your house; you gave me no water for my feet, but she, with her tears, has washed my feet and wiped them with her hair. You gave me no kiss, but she hasn't stopped kissing my feet since I came in. You didn't anoint my head with olive oil, but she has anointed my feet with perfume. Therefore I tell you, her many sins have been forgiven; that's why she loved much. But the one who is forgiven little, loves little." Then he said to her, "Your sins are forgiven."

Those who were at the table with him began to say among themselves, "Who is this man who even forgives sins?"

And he said to the woman, "Your faith has saved you. Go in peace."

Luke 8:1–3
Afterward he was traveling from one town and village to another, preaching and telling the good news of the kingdom of God. The Twelve were with him, and also some women who had been healed of evil spirits and sicknesses: Mary, called Magdalene (seven demons had come out of her); Joanna the wife of Chuza, Herod's steward; Susanna; and many others who were supporting them from their possessions.

This is the Word of the Lord. Thanks be to God.

GLORIA
Glory be to God the Father, God the Son, and God the Holy Spirit. As it was in the beginning, is now, and will be forever, world without end.

THE LORD'S PRAYER
Our Father in heaven,
Hallowed be your name.
Your kingdom come,
Your will be done
on earth as it is in heaven.
Give us this day our daily bread.
And forgive us our debts,
as we also have forgiven our debtors.

And lead us not into temptation
But deliver us from the evil one.
For yours is the kingdom and the power and the glory forever.
Amen.

Blessing

May your faithful love rest on us, LORD, for we put our hope
in you.
Psalm 33:22

DAY 8 EVENING PRAYER

Call to Prayer

Now bless the LORD, all you servants of the LORD who stand in
the LORD's house at night!
Psalm 134:1

Confession of Sin

Most merciful God,
we confess that we have sinned against you
in thought, word, and deed,
by what we have done,
and by what we have left undone.
We have not loved you with our whole heart;
we have not loved our neighbors as ourselves.
We are truly sorry and we humbly repent.
For the sake of your Son Jesus Christ,
have mercy on us and forgive us;
that we may delight in your will,
and walk in your ways,
to the glory of your Name. Amen.
The Book of Common Prayer

If we confess our sins, he is faithful and righteous to forgive us
our sins and to cleanse us from all unrighteousness.
1 John 1:9

CANTICLE

We have a strong city.
Salvation is established as walls and ramparts.
Open the gates
so a righteous nation can come in—one that remains faithful.
You will keep the mind that is dependent on you
in perfect peace,
for it is trusting in you.
Trust in the LORD forever,
because in the LORD, the LORD himself, is an everlasting rock!
Isaiah 26:1–4

EVENING READINGS

Matthew 11:20–30
Then he proceeded to denounce the towns where most of his
miracles were done, because they did not repent: "Woe to you,
Chorazin! Woe to you, Bethsaida! For if the miracles that were
done in you had been done in Tyre and Sidon, they would have
repented in sackcloth and ashes long ago. But I tell you, it will
be more tolerable for Tyre and Sidon on the day of judgment
than for you. And you, Capernaum, will you be exalted to
heaven? No, you will go down to Hades. For if the miracles
that were done in you had been done in Sodom, it would have
remained until today. But I tell you, it will be more tolerable for
the land of Sodom on the day of judgment than for you."

At that time Jesus said, "I praise you, Father, Lord of heaven
and earth, because you have hidden these things from the
wise and intelligent and revealed them to infants. Yes, Father,
because this was your good pleasure. All things have been
entrusted to me by my Father. No one knows the Son except the
Father, and no one knows the Father except the Son and anyone
to whom the Son desires to reveal him.

"Come to me, all of you who are weary and burdened, and I will give you rest. Take up my yoke and learn from me, because I am lowly and humble in heart, and you will find rest for your souls. For my yoke is easy and my burden is light."

Matthew 12:22–37
Then a demon-possessed man who was blind and unable to speak was brought to him. He healed him, so that the man could both speak and see. All the crowds were astounded and said, "Could this be the Son of David?"

When the Pharisees heard this, they said, "This man drives out demons only by Beelzebul, the ruler of the demons."

Knowing their thoughts, he told them, "Every kingdom divided against itself is headed for destruction, and no city or house divided against itself will stand. If Satan drives out Satan, he is divided against himself. How then will his kingdom stand? And if I drive out demons by Beelzebul, by whom do your sons drive them out? For this reason they will be your judges. If I drive out demons by the Spirit of God, then the kingdom of God has come upon you. How can someone enter a strong man's house and steal his possessions unless he first ties up the strong man? Then he can plunder his house. Anyone who is not with me is against me, and anyone who does not gather with me scatters. Therefore, I tell you, people will be forgiven every sin and blasphemy, but the blasphemy against the Spirit will not be forgiven. Whoever speaks a word against the Son of Man, it will be forgiven him; but whoever speaks against the Holy Spirit, it will not be forgiven him, either in this age or in the one to come.

"Either make the tree good and its fruit will be good, or make the tree bad and its fruit will be bad; for a tree is known by its fruit. Brood of vipers! How can you speak good things when you are evil? For the mouth speaks from the overflow of the heart. A good person produces good things from his storeroom of good, and an evil person produces evil things from his storeroom of evil. I tell you that on the day of judgment people will have to account for every careless word they speak. For by your words you will be acquitted, and by your words you will be condemned."

This is the Word of the Lord. Thanks be to God.

GLORIA

Glory be to God the Father, God the Son, and God the Holy
Spirit. As it was in the beginning, is now, and will be forever,
world without end.

THE LORD'S PRAYER

Our Father in heaven,
Hallowed be your name.
Your kingdom come,
Your will be done
on earth as it is in heaven.
Give us this day our daily bread.
And forgive us our debts,
as we also have forgiven our debtors.
And lead us not into temptation
But deliver us from the evil one.
For yours is the kingdom and the power and the glory forever.
Amen.

INTERCESSIONS AND PERSONAL REQUESTS

PRAYER OF THE CHURCH

Precious Lord, take my hand. Lead me on, let me stand. I'm
tired, I'm weak, I'm lone. Through the storm, through the night,
lead me on to the light. Take my hand precious Lord, lead me
home.
Thomas Dorsey

BLESSING

The Almighty and merciful Lord, Father, Son, and Holy Spirit,
bless us and keep us, this night and evermore. Amen.

DAY 9 MORNING PRAYER

The earth is the Lord's for he made it: O come, let us adore him.

We believe in one God,
the Father, the Almighty,
maker of heaven and earth,
of all that is, seen and unseen.
From the Nicene Creed

I called to the Lord in my distress,
and he answered me.
I cried out for help from deep inside Sheol;
you heard my voice.
When you threw me into the depths,
into the heart of the seas,
the current overcame me.
All your breakers and your billows swept over me.
And I said, "I have been banished
from your sight,
yet I will look once more
toward your holy temple."
The water engulfed me up to the neck;
the watery depths overcame me;
seaweed was wrapped around my head.
I sank to the foundations of the mountains,
the earth's gates shut behind me forever!
Then you raised my life from the Pit, Lord my God!
As my life was fading away,
I remembered the Lord,
and my prayer came to you,
to your holy temple.

Those who cherish worthless idols
abandon their faithful love,
but as for me, I will sacrifice to you
with a voice of thanksgiving.
I will fulfill what I have vowed.
Salvation belongs to the LORD.
Jonah 2:2–10

Morning Reading

Matthew 12:38–50

Then some of the scribes and Pharisees said to him, "Teacher, we want to see a sign from you."

He answered them, "An evil and adulterous generation demands a sign, but no sign will be given to it except the sign of the prophet Jonah. For as Jonah was in the belly of the huge fish three days and three nights, so the Son of Man will be in the heart of the earth three days and three nights. The men of Nineveh will stand up at the judgment with this generation and condemn it, because they repented at Jonah's preaching; and look—something greater than Jonah is here. The queen of the south will rise up at the judgment with this generation and condemn it, because she came from the ends of the earth to hear the wisdom of Solomon; and look—something greater than Solomon is here.

"When an unclean spirit comes out of a person, it roams through waterless places looking for rest but doesn't find any. Then it says, 'I'll go back to my house that I came from.' Returning, it finds the house vacant, swept, and put in order. Then it goes and brings with it seven other spirits more evil than itself, and they enter and settle down there. As a result, that person's last condition is worse than the first. That's how it will also be with this evil generation."

While he was still speaking with the crowds, his mother and brothers were standing outside wanting to speak to him. Someone told him, "Look, your mother and your brothers are standing outside, wanting to speak to you."

He replied to the one who was speaking to him, "Who is my mother and who are my brothers?" Stretching out his hand toward his disciples, he said, "Here are my mother and my brothers! For whoever does the will of my Father in heaven is my brother and sister and mother."

This is the Word of the Lord. Thanks be to God.

Gloria

Glory be to God the Father, God the Son, and God the Holy Spirit. As it was in the beginning, is now, and will be forever, world without end.

The Lord's Prayer

Our Father in heaven,
Hallowed be your name.
Your kingdom come,
Your will be done
on earth as it is in heaven.
Give us this day our daily bread.
And forgive us our debts,
as we also have forgiven our debtors.
And lead us not into temptation
But deliver us from the evil one.
For yours is the kingdom and the power and the glory forever.
Amen.

Intercessions and Personal Requests

Prayer of the Church

Lord God, almighty and everlasting Father, you have brought me in safety to this new day: Preserve me with your mighty power, that I may not fall into sin, nor be overcome by adversity; and in all I do direct me to the fulfilling of your purpose; through Jesus Christ my Lord. Amen.
The Book of Common Prayer

DAY 9 MIDDAY PRAYER

CALL TO PRAYER

Love the LORD, all his faithful ones. The LORD protects the
loyal, but fully repays the arrogant.
Psalm 31:23

MIDDAY READING

Mark 7:1–23

The Pharisees and some of the scribes who had come from
Jerusalem gathered around him. They observed that some of his
disciples were eating bread with unclean—that is, unwashed—
hands. (For the Pharisees and all the Jews do not eat unless they
give their hands a ceremonial washing, keeping the tradition of
the elders. When they come from the marketplace, they do not
eat unless they have washed. And there are many other customs
they have received and keep, like the washing of cups, pitchers,
kettles, and dining couches.) So the Pharisees and the scribes
asked him, "Why don't your disciples live according to the
tradition of the elders, instead of eating bread with ceremonially
unclean hands?"

He answered them, "Isaiah prophesied correctly about you
hypocrites, as it is written:

> **This people honors me with their lips,**
> **but their heart is far from me.**
> **They worship me in vain,**
> **teaching as doctrines human commands.**

Abandoning the command of God, you hold on to human
tradition." He also said to them, "You have a fine way of

invalidating God's command in order to set up your tradition! For Moses said: **Honor your father and your mother;** and Whoever speaks evil of father or mother must be put to death. But you say, 'If anyone tells his father or mother: Whatever benefit you might have received from me is corban'" (that is, an offering devoted to God), "you no longer let him do anything for his father or mother. You nullify the word of God by your tradition that you have handed down. And you do many other similar things."

Summoning the crowd again, he told them, "Listen to me, all of you, and understand: Nothing that goes into a person from outside can defile him but the things that come out of a person are what defile him."

When he went into the house away from the crowd, his disciples asked him about the parable. He said to them, "Are you also as lacking in understanding? Don't you realize that nothing going into a person from the outside can defile him? For it doesn't go into his heart but into the stomach and is eliminated" (thus he declared all foods clean). And he said, "What comes out of a person is what defiles him. For from within, out of people's hearts, come evil thoughts, sexual immoralities, thefts, murders, adulteries, greed, evil actions, deceit, self-indulgence, envy, slander, pride, and foolishness. All these evil things come from within and defile a person."

This is the Word of the Lord. Thanks be to God.

GLORIA

Glory be to God the Father, God the Son, and God the Holy Spirit. As it was in the beginning, is now, and will be forever, world without end.

THE LORD'S PRAYER

Our Father in heaven,
Hallowed be your name.
Your kingdom come,

Your will be done
on earth as it is in heaven.
Give us this day our daily bread.
And forgive us our debts,
as we also have forgiven our debtors.
And lead us not into temptation
But deliver us from the evil one.
For yours is the kingdom and the power and the glory forever.
Amen.

Blessing

The grace of the Lord Jesus Christ, and the love of God, and the
fellowship of the Holy Spirit be with us all.
2 Corinthians 13:14

DAY 9 EVENING PRAYER

Call to Prayer

The Lord founded the earth by wisdom and established the
heavens by understanding. By his knowledge the watery depths
broke open, and the clouds dripped with dew.
Proverbs 3:19–20

Confession of Sin

Dear God, I cast myself at the foot of the cross, mourning my
exceeding sinfulness, deeply moved by the infinity of your
mercies. I plead your precious promises, and earnestly pray to
you to shed abroad in my heart more love, more humility, more
faith, more hope, more peace and joy; in short, to fill me with
all the fullness of God, and make me worthy to be a partaker of
the inheritance of the saints in light. Then I shall also be better
in all the relations of life in which I am now so defective, and
my light will shine before others, that I shall adorn the doctrine
of my Savior in all things. Amen.
William Wilberforce

The sacrifice pleasing to God is a broken spirit. You will not despise a broken and humbled heart, God.
Psalm 51:17

CANTICLE

The path of the righteous is level;
you clear a straight path for the righteous.
Yes, LORD, we wait for you
in the path of your judgments.
Our desire is for your name and renown.
I long for you in the night;
yes, my spirit within me diligently seeks you,
for when your judgments are in the land,
the inhabitants of the world will learn righteousness.
Isaiah 26:7–9

EVENING READINGS

Mark 7:24–37
He got up and departed from there to the region of Tyre. He entered a house and did not want anyone to know it, but he could not escape notice. Instead, immediately after hearing about him, a woman whose little daughter had an unclean spirit came and fell at his feet. The woman was a Gentile, a Syrophoenician by birth, and she was asking him to cast the demon out of her daughter. He said to her, "Let the children be fed first, because it isn't right to take the children's bread and throw it to the dogs."

But she replied to him, "Lord, even the dogs under the table eat the children's crumbs."

Then he told her, "Because of this reply, you may go. The demon has left your daughter." When she went back to her home, she found her child lying on the bed, and the demon was gone.

Again, leaving the region of Tyre, he went by way of Sidon to the Sea of Galilee, through the region of the Decapolis. They brought to him a deaf man who had difficulty speaking and begged Jesus to lay his hand on him. So he took him away from the crowd in private. After putting his fingers in the man's ears and spitting, he touched his tongue. Looking up to heaven, he sighed deeply and said to him, "Ephphatha!" (that is, "Be opened!"). Immediately his ears were opened, his tongue was loosened, and he began to speak clearly. He ordered them to tell no one, but the more he ordered them, the more they proclaimed it.

They were extremely astonished and said, "He has done everything well. He even makes the deaf hear and the mute speak."

Luke 10:25–42
Then an expert in the law stood up to test him, saying, "Teacher, what must I do to inherit eternal life?"

"What is written in the law?" he asked him. "How do you read it?"

He answered, **"Love the Lord your God with all your heart, with all your soul, with all your strength, and with all your mind,"** and **"your neighbor as yourself."**

"You've answered correctly," he told him. "Do this and you will live."

But wanting to justify himself, he asked Jesus, "And who is my neighbor?"

Jesus took up the question and said, "A man was going down from Jerusalem to Jericho and fell into the hands of robbers. They stripped him, beat him up, and fled, leaving him half dead. A priest happened to be going down that road. When he saw him, he passed by on the other side. In the same way, a Levite, when he arrived at the place and saw him, passed by on the other side. But a Samaritan on his journey came up to him, and when he saw the man, he had compassion. He went over to him and bandaged his wounds, pouring on olive oil and wine. Then he put him on his own animal, brought him to an inn, and took care of him. The next day he took out two denarii, gave them to the innkeeper, and said, 'Take care of him. When I come back I'll reimburse you for whatever extra you spend.'

"Which of these three do you think proved to be a neighbor to the man who fell into the hands of the robbers?"

"The one who showed mercy to him," he said.

Then Jesus told him, "Go and do the same."

While they were traveling, he entered a village, and a woman named Martha welcomed him into her home. She had a sister named Mary, who also sat at the Lord's feet and was listening to what he said. But Martha was distracted by her many tasks, and she came up and asked, "Lord, don't you care that my sister has left me to serve alone? So tell her to give me a hand."

The Lord answered her, "Martha, Martha, you are worried and upset about many things, but one thing is necessary. Mary has made the right choice, and it will not be taken away from her."

This is the Word of the Lord. Thanks be to God.

GLORIA

Glory be to God the Father, God the Son, and God the Holy Spirit. As it was in the beginning, is now, and will be forever, world without end.

THE LORD'S PRAYER

Our Father in heaven,
Hallowed be your name.
Your kingdom come,
Your will be done
on earth as it is in heaven.
Give us this day our daily bread.
And forgive us our debts,
as we also have forgiven our debtors.
And lead us not into temptation
But deliver us from the evil one.
For yours is the kingdom and the power and the glory forever.
Amen.

PRAYER OF THE CHURCH

Stay with us, O Christ! It is toward evening, and the day is now far spent. Abide with us, O Jesus, abide with us. For where you are not, there everything is darkness, night and shadow, but you are the true Sun, light and shining brightness. The one whose way you illuminate cannot go astray.

Balthasar Hubmaier

BLESSING

The Lord Almighty grant us a peaceful night and a perfect end. Amen.

DAY 10 MORNING PRAYER

My life is down in the dust; give me life through your word.
Psalm 119:25

Confession of Faith

We believe in one Lord, Jesus Christ,
the only Son of God,
eternally begotten of the Father,
God from God, Light from Light,
true God from true God,
begotten, not made,
of one Being with the Father.
Through him all things were made.
For us and for our salvation
he came down from heaven:
by the power of the Holy Spirit
he became incarnate from the Virgin Mary,
and was made man.
For our sake he was crucified under Pontius Pilate;
he suffered death and was buried.
On the third day he rose again
in accordance with the Scriptures;
he ascended into heaven
and is seated at the right hand of the Father.
He will come again in glory to judge the living and the dead,
and his kingdom will have no end.
From the Nicene Creed

Canticle

My people, hear my instruction;
listen to the words from my mouth.
I will declare wise sayings;
I will speak mysteries from the past—

things we have heard and known
and that our ancestors have passed down to us.
We will not hide them from their children,
but will tell a future generation
the praiseworthy acts of the LORD,
his might, and the wondrous works
he has performed.
Psalm 78:1–4

MORNING READING

Matthew 13:1–23

Jesus went out of the house and was sitting by the sea. Such
large crowds gathered around him that he got into a boat and
sat down, while the whole crowd stood on the shore.

Then he told them many things in parables, saying, "Consider
the sower who went out to sow. As he sowed, some seed fell
along the path, and the birds came and devoured them. Other
seed fell on rocky ground where it didn't have much soil, and
it grew up quickly since the soil wasn't deep. But when the sun
came up, it was scorched, and since it had no root, it withered
away. Other seed fell among thorns, and the thorns came
up and choked it. Still other seed fell on good ground and
produced fruit: some a hundred, some sixty, and some thirty
times what was sown. Let anyone who has ears listen."

Then the disciples came up and asked him, "Why are you
speaking to them in parables?"

He answered, "Because the secrets of the kingdom of heaven
have been given for you to know, but it has not been given to
them. For whoever has, more will be given to him, and he will
have more than enough; but whoever does not have, even what
he has will be taken away from him. That is why I speak to
them in parables, because looking they do not see, and hearing
they do not listen or understand. Isaiah's prophecy is fulfilled in
them, which says:

You will listen and listen,
but never understand;
you will look and look,
but never perceive.

For this people's heart has grown callous;
their ears are hard of hearing,
and they have shut their eyes;
otherwise they might see with their eyes,
and hear with their ears, and
understand with their hearts,
and turn back—and I would heal them.

"Blessed are your eyes because they do see, and your ears because they do hear. For truly I tell you, many prophets and righteous people longed to see the things you see but didn't see them, to hear the things you hear but didn't hear them.

"So listen to the parable of the sower: When anyone hears the word about the kingdom and doesn't understand it, the evil one comes and snatches away what was sown in his heart. This is the one sown along the path. And the one sown on rocky ground—this is one who hears the word and immediately receives it with joy. But he has no root and is short-lived. When distress or persecution comes because of the word, immediately he falls away. Now the one sown among the thorns—this is one who hears the word, but the worries of this age and the deceitfulness of wealth choke the word, and it becomes unfruitful. But the one sown on the good ground—this is one who hears and understands the word, who does produce fruit and yields: some a hundred, some sixty, some thirty times what was sown."

This is the Word of the Lord. Thanks be to God.

Gloria

Glory be to God the Father, God the Son, and God the Holy Spirit. As it was in the beginning, is now, and will be forever, world without end.

The Lord's Prayer

Our Father in heaven,
Hallowed be your name.
Your kingdom come,

Your will be done
on earth as it is in heaven.
Give us this day our daily bread.
And forgive us our debts,
as we also have forgiven our debtors.
And lead us not into temptation
But deliver us from the evil one.
For yours is the kingdom and the power and the glory forever.
Amen.

INTERCESSIONS AND PERSONAL REQUESTS

PRAYER OF THE CHURCH

Almighty God, and most merciful Father, we humbly submit ourselves and fall down before your Majesty, asking you from the bottom of our hearts, that this seed of your Word now sown among us, may take such deep root, that neither the burning heat of persecution cause it to wither, nor the thorny cares of this life choke it. But that, as seed sown in good ground, it may bring forth thirty, sixty, or a hundredfold, as your heavenly wisdom has appointed. Amen.
Middelburg Liturgy

BLESSING

May God be gracious to us and bless us; may he make his face shine upon us so that your way may be known on earth, your salvation among all nations.
Psalm 67:1–2

DAY 10 MIDDAY PRAYER

Call to Prayer

Help me understand the meaning of your precepts so that I can meditate on your wonders.
Psalm 119:27

Midday Readings

Mark 4:26–29

"The kingdom of God is like this," he said. "A man scatters seed on the ground. He sleeps and rises night and day; the seed sprouts and grows, although he doesn't know how. The soil produces a crop by itself—first the blade, then the head, and then the full grain on the head. As soon as the crop is ready, he sends for the sickle, because the harvest has come."

Matthew 13:24–43

He presented another parable to them: "The kingdom of heaven may be compared to a man who sowed good seed in his field. But while people were sleeping, his enemy came, sowed weeds among the wheat, and left. When the plants sprouted and produced grain, then the weeds also appeared. The landowner's servants came to him and said, 'Master, didn't you sow good seed in your field? Then where did the weeds come from?'

"'An enemy did this,' he told them.

"'So, do you want us to go and pull them up?' the servants asked him.

"'No,' he said. 'When you pull up the weeds, you might also uproot the wheat with them. Let both grow together until the harvest. At harvest time I'll tell the reapers: Gather the weeds first and tie them in bundles to burn them, but collect the wheat in my barn.'"

He presented another parable to them: "The kingdom of heaven is like a mustard seed that a man took and sowed in his field. It's the smallest of all the seeds, but when grown, it's taller than the garden plants and becomes a tree, so that the birds of the sky come and nest in its branches."

He told them another parable: "The kingdom of heaven is like leaven that a woman took and mixed into fifty pounds of flour until all of it was leavened."

Jesus told the crowds all these things in parables, and he did not tell them anything without a parable, so that what was spoken through the prophet might be fulfilled:

I will open my mouth in parables;
I will declare things kept secret
from the foundation of the world.

Then he left the crowds and went into the house. His disciples approached him and said, "Explain to us the parable of the weeds in the field."

He replied, "The one who sows the good seed is the Son of Man; the field is the world; and the good seed—these are the children of the kingdom. The weeds are the children of the evil one, and the enemy who sowed them is the devil. The harvest is the end of the age, and the harvesters are angels. Therefore, just as the weeds are gathered and burned in the fire, so it will be at the end of the age. The Son of Man will send out his angels, and they will gather from his kingdom all who cause sin and those guilty of lawlessness. They will throw them into the blazing furnace where there will be weeping and gnashing of teeth. Then the righteous will shine like the sun in their Father's kingdom. Let anyone who has ears listen."

This is the Word of the Lord. Thanks be to God.

GLORIA

Glory be to God the Father, God the Son, and God the Holy Spirit. As it was in the beginning, is now, and will be forever, world without end.

The Lord's Prayer

Our Father in heaven,
Hallowed be your name.
Your kingdom come,
Your will be done
on earth as it is in heaven.
Give us this day our daily bread.
And forgive us our debts,
as we also have forgiven our debtors.
And lead us not into temptation
But deliver us from the evil one.
For yours is the kingdom and the power and the glory forever.
Amen.

Blessing

May the LORD bless you and protect you; may the LORD make
his face shine on you and be gracious to you; may the LORD
look with favor on you and give you peace.
Numbers 6:24–26

DAY 10 EVENING PRAYER

Call to Prayer

Come and see the wonders of God; his acts for humanity are
awe-inspiring.
Psalm 66:5

Confession of Sin

Lord Jesus Christ, who stretched out your hands on the cross,
and redeemed us by your blood: forgive me, a sinner, for none
of my thoughts are hidden from you. Pardon I ask, pardon I
hope for, pardon I trust to have. You who are full of pity and
mercy: spare me, and forgive.
Ambrose

As far as the east is from the west, so far has he removed our
transgressions from us.
Psalm 103:12

Blessed be your glorious name,
and may it be exalted above all blessing and praise.
You, LORD, are the only God.
You created the heavens,
the highest heavens with all their stars,
the earth and all that is on it,
the seas and all that is in them.
You give life to all of them,
and all the stars of heaven worship you.
Nehemiah 9:5–6

EVENING READINGS

Matthew 13:44–52
"The kingdom of heaven is like treasure, buried in a field, that
a man found and reburied. Then in his joy he goes and sells
everything he has and buys that field.

"Again, the kingdom of heaven is like a merchant in search
of fine pearls. When he found one priceless pearl, he went and
sold everything he had and bought it.

"Again, the kingdom of heaven is like a large net thrown into
the sea. It collected every kind of fish, and when it was full, they
dragged it ashore, sat down, and gathered the good fish into
containers, but threw out the worthless ones. So it will be at the
end of the age. The angels will go out, separate the evil people
from the righteous, and throw them into the blazing furnace,
where there will be weeping and gnashing of teeth.

"Have you understood all these things?"

They answered him, "Yes."

"Therefore," he said to them, "every teacher of the law who
has become a disciple in the kingdom of heaven is like the

owner of a house who brings out of his storeroom treasures new and old."

Mark 4:35–41
On that day, when evening had come, he told them, "Let's cross over to the other side of the sea." So they left the crowd and took him along since he was in the boat. And other boats were with him. A great windstorm arose, and the waves were breaking over the boat, so that the boat was already being swamped. He was in the stern, sleeping on the cushion. So they woke him up and said to him, "Teacher! Don't you care that we're going to die?"

He got up, rebuked the wind, and said to the sea, "Silence! Be still!" The wind ceased, and there was a great calm. Then he said to them, "Why are you afraid? Do you still have no faith?"

And they were terrified and asked one another, "Who then is this? Even the wind and the sea obey him!"

This is the Word of the Lord. Thanks be to God.

GLORIA
Glory be to God the Father, God the Son, and God the Holy Spirit. As it was in the beginning, is now, and will be forever, world without end.

THE LORD'S PRAYER
Our Father in heaven,
Hallowed be your name.
Your kingdom come,
Your will be done
on earth as it is in heaven.
Give us this day our daily bread.
And forgive us our debts,
as we also have forgiven our debtors.
And lead us not into temptation
But deliver us from the evil one.

For yours is the kingdom and the power and the glory forever. Amen.

Intercessions and Personal Requests

Prayer of the Church

O Lord, the Helper of the helpless, the Hope of those who are past hope, the Savior of the tempest-tossed, the Harbor of the voyagers, the Physician of the sick. . . . You know each soul and our prayer, each home and its need. Become to each one of us what we most dearly require, receiving us all into your kingdom, making us children of light, and pour on us your peace and love, O Lord our God. Amen.
Basil the Great

Blessing

The Almighty and merciful Lord, Father, Son, and Holy Spirit, bless us and keep us, this night and evermore. Amen.

DAY 11 MORNING PRAYER

CALL TO PRAYER

Be strong, and let your heart be courageous, all you who put
your hope in the LORD.
Psalm 31:24

CONFESSION OF FAITH

We believe in the Holy Spirit, the Lord, the giver of life,
who proceeds from the Father and the Son.
With the Father and the Son he is worshiped and glorified.
He has spoken through the Prophets.
We believe in one holy catholic and apostolic Church.
We acknowledge one baptism for the forgiveness of sins.
We look for the resurrection of the dead,
and the life of the world to come. Amen.
From the Nicene Creed

CANTICLE

Let the redeemed of the LORD proclaim
that he has redeemed them from the power of the foe
and has gathered them from the lands—
from the east and the west,
from the north and the south.
Others sat in darkness and gloom—prisoners in cruel chains—
He brought them out of darkness and gloom
and broke their chains apart.
Let them give thanks to the LORD
for his faithful love
and his wondrous works for all humanity.
For he has broken down the bronze gates
and cut through the iron bars.
Psalm 107:2–3,10,14–16

Mark 5:1–20

They came to the other side of the sea, to the region of the Gerasenes. As soon as he got out of the boat, a man with an unclean spirit came out of the tombs and met him. He lived in the tombs, and no one was able to restrain him anymore—not even with a chain—because he often had been bound with shackles and chains, but had torn the chains apart and smashed the shackles. No one was strong enough to subdue him. Night and day among the tombs and on the mountains, he was always crying out and cutting himself with stones.

When he saw Jesus from a distance, he ran and knelt down before him. And he cried out with a loud voice, "What do you have to do with me, Jesus, Son of the Most High God? I beg you before God, don't torment me!" For he had told him, "Come out of the man, you unclean spirit!"

"What is your name?" he asked him.

"My name is Legion," he answered him, "because we are many." And he begged him earnestly not to send them out of the region.

A large herd of pigs was there, feeding on the hillside. The demons begged him, "Send us to the pigs, so that we may enter them." So he gave them permission, and the unclean spirits came out and entered the pigs. The herd of about two thousand rushed down the steep bank into the sea and drowned there.

The men who tended them ran off and reported it in the town and the countryside, and people went to see what had happened. They came to Jesus and saw the man who had been demon-possessed, sitting there, dressed and in his right mind; and they were afraid. Those who had seen it described to them what had happened to the demon-possessed man and told about the pigs. Then they began to beg him to leave their region.

As he was getting into the boat, the man who had been demon-possessed begged him earnestly that he might remain with him. Jesus did not let him but told him, "Go home to your own people, and report to them how much the Lord has done for you and how he has had mercy on you." So he went out and began to proclaim in the Decapolis how much Jesus had done for him, and they were all amazed.

This is the Word of the Lord. Thanks be to God.

Gloria

Glory be to God the Father, God the Son, and God the Holy Spirit. As it was in the beginning, is now, and will be forever, world without end.

The Lord's Prayer

Our Father in heaven,
Hallowed be your name.
Your kingdom come,
Your will be done
on earth as it is in heaven.
Give us this day our daily bread.
And forgive us our debts,
as we also have forgiven our debtors.
And lead us not into temptation
But deliver us from the evil one.
For yours is the kingdom and the power and the glory forever.
Amen.

Intercessions and Personal Requests

Prayer of the Church

O my God, teach my heart where and how to seek you, where and how to find you. You are my God and you are my all and I have never seen you. You have made me and remade me, you have showered upon me all the good things I possess, still I do not know you. I have not yet done that for which I was made. Teach me to seek you. I cannot seek you unless you teach me or find you unless you show yourself to me. Let me seek you in

my desire, let me desire you in my seeking. Let me find you by loving you, let me love you when I find you.
Anselm

BLESSING

May the Lord cause you to increase and overflow with love for one another and for everyone. . . . May he make your hearts blameless in holiness before our God and Father at the coming of our Lord Jesus with all his saints. Amen.
1 Thessalonians 2:12–13

DAY 11 MIDDAY PRAYER

CALL TO PRAYER

My soul, bless the LORD, and all that is within me, bless his holy name. My soul, bless the LORD, and do not forget all his benefits.
Psalm 103:1–2

MIDDAY READING

Mark 5:21–43

When Jesus had crossed over again by boat to the other side, a large crowd gathered around him while he was by the sea. One of the synagogue leaders, named Jairus, came, and when he saw Jesus, he fell at his feet and begged him earnestly, "My little daughter is dying. Come and lay your hands on her so that she can get well and live." So Jesus went with him, and a large crowd was following and pressing against him.

Now a woman suffering from bleeding for twelve years had endured much under many doctors. She had spent everything she had and was not helped at all. On the contrary, she became worse. Having heard about Jesus, she came up behind him in the crowd and touched his clothing. For she said, "If I just touch his clothes, I'll be made well." Instantly her flow of blood ceased, and she sensed in her body that she was healed of her affliction.

Immediately Jesus realized that power had gone out from him. He turned around in the crowd and said, "Who touched my clothes?"

His disciples said to him, "You see the crowd pressing against you, and yet you say, 'Who touched me?'"

But he was looking around to see who had done this. The woman, with fear and trembling, knowing what had happened to her, came and fell down before him, and told him the whole truth. "Daughter," he said to her, "your faith has saved you. Go in peace and be healed from your affliction."

While he was still speaking, people came from the synagogue leader's house and said, "Your daughter is dead. Why bother the teacher anymore?"

When Jesus overheard what was said, he told the synagogue leader, "Don't be afraid. Only believe." He did not let anyone accompany him except Peter, James, and John, James's brother. They came to the leader's house, and he saw a commotion—people weeping and wailing loudly. He went in and said to them, "Why are you making a commotion and weeping? The child is not dead but asleep." They laughed at him, but he put them all outside. He took the child's father, mother, and those who were with him, and entered the place where the child was. Then he took the child by the hand and said to her, "Talitha koum" (which is translated, "Little girl, I say to you, get up"). Immediately the girl got up and began to walk. (She was twelve years old.) At this they were utterly astounded. Then he gave them strict orders that no one should know about this and told them to give her something to eat.

This is the Word of the Lord. Thanks be to God.

GLORIA

Glory be to God the Father, God the Son, and God the Holy Spirit. As it was in the beginning, is now, and will be forever, world without end.

Our Father in heaven,
Hallowed be your name.
Your kingdom come,
Your will be done
on earth as it is in heaven.
Give us this day our daily bread.
And forgive us our debts,
as we also have forgiven our debtors.
And lead us not into temptation
But deliver us from the evil one.
For yours is the kingdom and the power and the glory forever.
Amen.

BLESSING

The grace of the Lord Jesus Christ, and the love of God, and the
fellowship of the Holy Spirit be with us all.
2 Corinthians 13:14

DAY 11 EVENING PRAYER

CALL TO PRAYER

Say among the nations, "The LORD reigns. The world is firmly
established; it cannot be shaken. He judges the peoples fairly."
Psalm 96:10

CONFESSION OF SIN

O Lord, no day of my life has passed that has not proved me
guilty in your sight. All things in me call for my rejection. All
things in you call for my acceptance. Grant me to hear your
voice assuring me: that by your stripes I am healed, that you
were bruised for my iniquities, that you have been made sin
for me that I might be righteous in you, that my grievous sins,
my many sins, are all forgiven, buried in the ocean of your

concealing blood. Keep me always clinging to your cross. Flood me every moment with descending grace.
The Valley of Vision

If we confess our sins, he is faithful and righteous to forgive us our sins and to cleanse us from all unrighteousness.
1 John 1:9

CANTICLE
Shout for joy, you heavens!
Earth, rejoice!
Mountains break into joyful shouts!
For the LORD has comforted his people,
and will have compassion on his afflicted ones.
Isaiah 49:13

EVENING READING
Matthew 10:5–42
Jesus sent out these twelve after giving them instructions: "Don't take the road that leads to the Gentiles, and don't enter any Samaritan town. Instead, go to the lost sheep of the house of Israel. As you go, proclaim, 'The kingdom of heaven has come near.' Heal the sick, raise the dead, cleanse those with leprosy, drive out demons. Freely you received, freely give. Don't acquire gold, silver, or copper for your money-belts. Don't take a traveling bag for the road, or an extra shirt, sandals, or a staff, for the worker is worthy of his food. When you enter any town or village, find out who is worthy, and stay there until you leave. Greet a household when you enter it, and if the household is worthy, let your peace be on it; but if it is unworthy, let your peace return to you. If anyone does not welcome you or listen to your words, shake the dust off your feet when you leave that house or town. Truly I tell you, it will be more tolerable on the day of judgment for the land of Sodom and Gomorrah than for that town.

"Look, I'm sending you out like sheep among wolves. Therefore be as shrewd as serpents and as innocent as doves.

Beware of them, because they will hand you over to local courts and flog you in their synagogues. You will even be brought before governors and kings because of me, to bear witness to them and to the Gentiles. But when they hand you over, don't worry about how or what you are to speak. For you will be given what to say at that hour, because it isn't you speaking, but the Spirit of your Father is speaking through you.

"Brother will betray brother to death, and a father his child. Children will rise up against parents and have them put to death. You will be hated by everyone because of my name. But the one who endures to the end will be saved. When they persecute you in one town, flee to another. For truly I tell you, you will not have gone through the towns of Israel before the Son of Man comes. A disciple is not above his teacher, or a slave above his master. It is enough for a disciple to become like his teacher and a slave like his master. If they called the head of the house 'Beelzebul,' how much more the members of his household!

"Therefore, don't be afraid of them, since there is nothing covered that won't be uncovered and nothing hidden that won't be made known. What I tell you in the dark, speak in the light. What you hear in a whisper, proclaim on the housetops. Don't fear those who kill the body but are not able to kill the soul; rather, fear him who is able to destroy both soul and body in hell. Aren't two sparrows sold for a penny? Yet not one of them falls to the ground without your Father's consent. But even the hairs of your head have all been counted. So don't be afraid; you are worth more than many sparrows.

"Therefore, everyone who will acknowledge me before others, I will also acknowledge him before my Father in heaven. But whoever denies me before others, I will also deny him before my Father in heaven. Don't assume that I came to bring peace on the earth. I did not come to bring peace, but a sword. For I came to turn

a man against his father,
a daughter against her mother,
a daughter-in-law against her mother-in-law;
and a man's enemies will be
the members of his household.

The one who loves a father or mother more than me is not worthy of me; the one who loves a son or daughter more than me is not worthy of me. And whoever doesn't take up his cross and follow me is not worthy of me. Anyone who finds his life will lose it, and anyone who loses his life because of me will find it.

"The one who welcomes you welcomes me, and the one who welcomes me welcomes him who sent me. Anyone who welcomes a prophet because he is a prophet will receive a prophet's reward. And anyone who welcomes a righteous person because he's righteous will receive a righteous person's reward. And whoever gives even a cup of cold water to one of these little ones because he is a disciple, truly I tell you, he will never lose his reward."

This is the Word of the Lord. Thanks be to God.

GLORIA

Glory be to God the Father, God the Son, and God the Holy Spirit. As it was in the beginning, is now, and will be forever, world without end.

THE LORD'S PRAYER

Our Father in heaven,
Hallowed be your name.
Your kingdom come,
Your will be done
on earth as it is in heaven.
Give us this day our daily bread.
And forgive us our debts,
as we also have forgiven our debtors.
And lead us not into temptation
But deliver us from the evil one.
For yours is the kingdom and the power and the glory forever.
Amen.

PRAYER OF THE CHURCH

O God, you have made of one blood all the peoples of the earth, and sent your blessed Son to preach peace to those who are far off and to those who are near. Grant that people everywhere may seek after you and find you; bring the nations into your fold; pour out your Spirit upon all flesh; and hasten the coming of your kingdom; through Jesus Christ our Lord.
The Book of Common Prayer

BLESSING

The Lord Almighty grant us a peaceful night and a perfect end. Amen.

DAY 12 MORNING PRAYER

CALL TO PRAYER

Turn your face from all my sins and blot out all my guilt.
Psalm 51:9

CONFESSION OF FAITH

I believe that God, who is rich in mercy towards the
undeserving, has made gracious provision for human
wrongdoing, corruption, and guilt, provisionally and
typologically through Israel's Temple and sin offerings, then
definitively and gloriously in the gift of Jesus's once-for-all
sufficient and perfect sacrificial death on the cross in the temple
of his human flesh. By his death in our stead, he revealed God's
love and upheld God's justice, removing our guilt, vanquishing
the powers that held us captive, and reconciling us to God. It
is wholly by grace, not our own works or merits, that we have
been forgiven; it is wholly by Jesus's shed blood, not by our own
sweat and tears, that we have been cleansed.
Adapted from the Reforming Catholic Confession

CANTICLE

Listen, LORD, and answer me,
for I am poor and needy.
Protect my life, for I am faithful.
You are my God; save your servant who trusts in you.
Be gracious to me, Lord,
for I call to you all day long.
Bring joy to your servant's life,
because I appeal to you, Lord.
For you, Lord, are kind and ready to forgive,
abounding in faithful love to all who call on you.
LORD, hear my prayer;
listen to my cries for mercy.

I call on you in the day of my distress,
for you will answer me.
Psalm 86:1–7

Morning Reading
Matthew 18:15–35

"If your brother sins against you, go tell him his fault, between you and him alone. If he listens to you, you have won your brother. But if he won't listen, take one or two others with you, so that **by the testimony of two or three witnesses every fact may be established.** If he doesn't pay attention to them, tell the church. If he doesn't pay attention even to the church, let him be like a Gentile and a tax collector to you. Truly I tell you, whatever you bind on earth will have been bound in heaven, and whatever you loose on earth will have been loosed in heaven. Again, truly I tell you, if two of you on earth agree about any matter that you pray for, it will be done for you by my Father in heaven. For where two or three are gathered together in my name, I am there among them."

Then Peter approached him and asked, "Lord, how many times must I forgive my brother or sister who sins against me? As many as seven times?"

"I tell you, not as many as seven," Jesus replied, "but seventy times seven.

"For this reason, the kingdom of heaven can be compared to a king who wanted to settle accounts with his servants. When he began to settle accounts, one who owed ten thousand talents was brought before him. Since he did not have the money to pay it back, his master commanded that he, his wife, his children, and everything he had be sold to pay the debt.

"At this, the servant fell facedown before him and said, 'Be patient with me, and I will pay you everything.' Then the master of that servant had compassion, released him, and forgave him the loan.

"That servant went out and found one of his fellow servants who owed him a hundred denarii. He grabbed him, started choking him, and said, 'Pay what you owe!'

"At this, his fellow servant fell down and began begging him, 'Be patient with me, and I will pay you back.' But he wasn't willing. Instead, he went and threw him into prison until he could pay what was owed. When the other servants saw what had taken place, they were deeply distressed and went and reported to their master everything that had happened. Then, after he had summoned him, his master said to him, 'You wicked servant! I forgave you all that debt because you begged me. Shouldn't you also have had mercy on your fellow servant, as I had mercy on you?' And because he was angry, his master handed him over to the jailers to be tortured until he could pay everything that was owed. So also my heavenly Father will do to you unless every one of you forgives his brother or sister from your heart."

This is the Word of the Lord. Thanks be to God.

Gloria

Glory be to God the Father, God the Son, and God the Holy Spirit. As it was in the beginning, is now, and will be forever, world without end.

The Lord's Prayer

Our Father in heaven,
Hallowed be your name.
Your kingdom come,
Your will be done
on earth as it is in heaven.
Give us this day our daily bread.
And forgive us our debts,
as we also have forgiven our debtors.
And lead us not into temptation
But deliver us from the evil one.
For yours is the kingdom and the power and the glory forever.
Amen.

PRAYER OF THE CHURCH

Almighty God, you have given us grace at this time with one accord to make our common supplication to you; and you have promised through your well-beloved Son that when two or three are gathered together in his Name you will be in the midst of them: Fulfill now, O Lord, our desires and petitions as may be best for us; granting us in this world knowledge of your truth, and in the age to come life everlasting. Amen.
The Book of Common Prayer

BLESSING

Now to him who is able to do above and beyond all that we ask or think according to the power that works in us—to him be glory in the church and in Christ Jesus to all generations, forever and ever. Amen.
Ephesians 3:20–21

DAY 12 MIDDAY PRAYER

CALL TO PRAYER

We will bless the LORD both now and forever. Hallelujah!
Psalm 115:18

MIDDAY READINGS

Matthew 19:3–15
Some Pharisees approached him to test him. They asked, "Is it lawful for a man to divorce his wife on any grounds?"

"Haven't you read," he replied, "that he who created them in the beginning **made them male and female**, and he also said, **'For this reason a man will leave his father and mother and be joined to his wife, and the two will become one flesh'**? So they are no longer two, but one flesh. Therefore, what God has joined together, let no one separate."

"Why then," they asked him, "did Moses command us to give divorce papers and to send her away?"

He told them, "Moses permitted you to divorce your wives because of the hardness of your hearts, but it was not like that from the beginning. I tell you, whoever divorces his wife, except for sexual immorality, and marries another commits adultery."

His disciples said to him, "If the relationship of a man with his wife is like this, it's better not to marry."

He responded, "Not everyone can accept this saying, but only those to whom it has been given. For there are eunuchs who were born that way from their mother's womb, there are eunuchs who were made by men, and there are eunuchs who have made themselves that way because of the kingdom of heaven. The one who is able to accept it should accept it."

Then little children were brought to Jesus for him to place his hands on them and pray, but the disciples rebuked them. Jesus said, "Leave the little children alone, and don't try to keep them from coming to me, because the kingdom of heaven belongs to such as these." After placing his hands on them, he went on from there.

Matthew 20:1–16
"The kingdom of heaven is like a landowner who went out early in the morning to hire workers for his vineyard. After agreeing with the workers on one denarius, he sent them into his vineyard for the day. When he went out about nine in the morning, he saw others standing in the marketplace doing nothing. He said to them, 'You also go into my vineyard, and I'll give you whatever is right.' So off they went. About noon and about three, he went out again and did the same thing. Then about five he went and found others standing around and said to them, 'Why have you been standing here all day doing nothing?'

"'Because no one hired us,' they said to him.

"'You also go into my vineyard,' he told them. When evening came, the owner of the vineyard told his foreman, 'Call the workers and give them their pay, starting with the last and ending with the first.'

"When those who were hired about five came, they each received one denarius. So when the first ones came, they assumed they would get more, but they also received a denarius each. When they received it, they began to complain to the landowner: 'These last men put in one hour, and you made them equal to us who bore the burden of the day's work and the burning heat.'

"He replied to one of them, 'Friend, I'm doing you no wrong. Didn't you agree with me on a denarius? Take what's yours and go. I want to give this last man the same as I gave you. Don't I have the right to do what I want with what is mine? Are you jealous because I'm generous?'

"So the last will be first, and the first last."

This is the Word of the Lord. Thanks be to God.

Gloria

Glory be to God the Father, God the Son, and God the Holy Spirit. As it was in the beginning, is now, and will be forever, world without end.

The Lord's Prayer

Our Father in heaven,
Hallowed be your name.
Your kingdom come,
Your will be done
on earth as it is in heaven.
Give us this day our daily bread.
And forgive us our debts,
as we also have forgiven our debtors.
And lead us not into temptation
But deliver us from the evil one.
For yours is the kingdom and the power and the glory forever.
Amen.

May your faithful love rest on us, Lord, for we put our hope in you.
Psalm 33:22

DAY 12 EVENING PRAYER

Call to Prayer

I will bless the Lord who counsels me—even at night when my thoughts trouble me. I always let the Lord guide me. Because he is at my right hand, I will not be shaken.
Psalm 16:7–8

Confession of Sin

Lord Jesus Christ, Son of God, have mercy on me, a sinner.

How joyful is the one whose transgression is forgiven, whose sin is covered!
Psalm 32:1

Canticle

God, your way is holy.
What god is great like God?
You are the God who works wonders;
you revealed your strength among the peoples.
With power you redeemed your people,
the descendants of Jacob and Joseph. *Selah*
The water saw you, God.
The water saw you; it trembled.
Even the depths shook.
The clouds poured down water.
The storm clouds thundered;
your arrows flashed back and forth.
The sound of your thunder was in the whirlwind;
lightning lit up the world.

The earth shook and quaked.
Your way went through the sea
and your path through the vast water,
but your footprints were unseen.
You led your people like a flock
by the hand of Moses and Aaron.
Psalm 77:13–20

Evening Readings

John 6:1–14

After this, Jesus crossed the Sea of Galilee (or Tiberias). A huge crowd was following him because they saw the signs that he was performing by healing the sick. Jesus went up a mountain and sat down there with his disciples.

Now the Passover, a Jewish festival, was near. So when Jesus looked up and noticed a huge crowd coming toward him, he asked Philip, "Where will we buy bread so that these people can eat?" He asked this to test him, for he himself knew what he was going to do.

Philip answered him, "Two hundred denarii worth of bread wouldn't be enough for each of them to have a little."

One of his disciples, Andrew, Simon Peter's brother, said to him, "There's a boy here who has five barley loaves and two fish—but what are they for so many?"

Jesus said, "Have the people sit down."

There was plenty of grass in that place; so they sat down. The men numbered about five thousand. Then Jesus took the loaves, and after giving thanks he distributed them to those who were seated—so also with the fish, as much as they wanted.

When they were full, he told his disciples, "Collect the leftovers so that nothing is wasted." So they collected them and filled twelve baskets with the pieces from the five barley loaves that were left over by those who had eaten.

When the people saw the sign he had done, they said, "This truly is the Prophet who is to come into the world."

Matthew 14:22–33
Immediately he made the disciples get into the boat and go ahead of him to the other side, while he dismissed the crowds. After dismissing the crowds, he went up on the mountain by himself to pray. Well into the night, he was there alone. Meanwhile, the boat was already some distance from land, battered by the waves, because the wind was against them. Jesus came toward them walking on the sea very early in the morning. When the disciples saw him walking on the sea, they were terrified. "It's a ghost!" they said, and they cried out in fear.

Immediately Jesus spoke to them. "Have courage! It is I. Don't be afraid."

"Lord, if it's you," Peter answered him, "command me to come to you on the water."

He said, "Come."

And climbing out of the boat, Peter started walking on the water and came toward Jesus. But when he saw the strength of the wind, he was afraid, and beginning to sink he cried out, "Lord, save me!"

Immediately Jesus reached out his hand, caught hold of him, and said to him, "You of little faith, why did you doubt?"

When they got into the boat, the wind ceased. Then those in the boat worshiped him and said, "Truly you are the Son of God."

This is the Word of the Lord. Thanks be to God.

Gloria

Glory be to God the Father, God the Son, and God the Holy Spirit. As it was in the beginning, is now, and will be forever, world without end.

The Lord's Prayer

Our Father in heaven,
Hallowed be your name.
Your kingdom come,
Your will be done
on earth as it is in heaven.
Give us this day our daily bread.
And forgive us our debts,
as we also have forgiven our debtors.
And lead us not into temptation
But deliver us from the evil one.
For yours is the kingdom and the power and the glory forever.
Amen.

Intercessions and Personal Requests

Prayer of the Church

O crucified Jesus, in whom I live and without whom I die,
mortify in me all wrong desires, inflame my heart with your
holy love that I may no longer esteem the vanities of this world
but place my affections entirely on you. Let my last breath,
when my soul shall leave my body, breathe forth love to you,
my God. I entered into life without acknowledging you; let me
therefore finish it in loving you. O let the last act of life be love,
remembering that God is love. Amen.
Richard Allen

Blessing

The Almighty and merciful Lord, Father, Son, and Holy Spirit,
bless us and keep us, this night and evermore. Amen.

DAY 13 MORNING PRAYER

CALL TO PRAYER

Let us give thanks to the LORD for his faithful love and his
wondrous works for all humanity. For he has satisfied the
thirsty and filled the hungry with good things.
Adapted from Psalm 107:8–9

CONFESSION OF FAITH

I believe that through participating in baptism and the Lord's
Supper, as well as prayer, the ministry of the Word, and other
forms of corporate worship, we grow into our new reality as
God's people, a holy nation, called to put on Christ through
his indwelling Spirit. It is through the Spirit's enlivening power
that we live in imitation of Christ as his disciples, individually
and corporately, a royal priesthood that proclaims his excellent
deeds and offers our bodies as spiritual sacrifices in right
worship of God and sacrificial service to the world through
works of love, compassion for the poor, and justice for the
oppressed, always, everywhere and to everyone bearing wise
witness to the way, truth, and life of Jesus Christ.
Adapted from the Reforming Catholic Confession

CANTICLE

The LORD has chosen Zion;
he has desired it for his home:
"This is my resting place forever;
I will make my home here
because I have desired it.
I will abundantly bless its food;
I will satisfy its needy with bread.
I will clothe its priests with salvation,
and its faithful people will shout for joy.
There I will make a horn grow for David;
I have prepared a lamp for my anointed one.

I will clothe his enemies with shame,
but the crown he wears will be glorious."
Psalm 132:13–18

Morning Reading

John 6:22–40

The next day, the crowd that had stayed on the other side of
the sea saw there had been only one boat. They also saw that
Jesus had not boarded the boat with his disciples, but that his
disciples had gone off alone. Some boats from Tiberias came
near the place where they had eaten the bread after the Lord
had given thanks. When the crowd saw that neither Jesus nor
his disciples were there, they got into the boats and went to
Capernaum looking for Jesus. When they found him on the
other side of the sea, they said to him, "Rabbi, when did you get
here?"

Jesus answered, "Truly I tell you, you are looking for me, not
because you saw the signs, but because you ate the loaves and
were filled. Don't work for the food that perishes but for the
food that lasts for eternal life, which the Son of Man will give
you, because God the Father has set his seal of approval on
him."

"What can we do to perform the works of God?" they asked.

Jesus replied, "This is the work of God—that you believe in
the one he has sent."

"What sign, then, are you going to do so that we may see and
believe you?" they asked. "What are you going to perform? Our
ancestors ate the manna in the wilderness, just as it is written:
He gave them bread from heaven to eat."

Jesus said to them, "Truly I tell you, Moses didn't give you the
bread from heaven, but my Father gives you the true bread from
heaven. For the bread of God is the one who comes down from
heaven and gives life to the world."

Then they said, "Sir, give us this bread always."

"I am the bread of life," Jesus told them. "No one who comes
to me will ever be hungry, and no one who believes in me will
ever be thirsty again. But as I told you, you've seen me, and yet
you do not believe. Everyone the Father gives me will come to

me, and the one who comes to me I will never cast out. For I have come down from heaven, not to do my own will, but the will of him who sent me. This is the will of him who sent me: that I should lose none of those he has given me but should raise them up on the last day. For this is the will of my Father: that everyone who sees the Son and believes in him will have eternal life, and I will raise him up on the last day."

This is the Word of the Lord. Thanks be to God.

Gloria

Glory be to God the Father, God the Son, and God the Holy Spirit. As it was in the beginning, is now, and will be forever, world without end.

The Lord's Prayer

Our Father in heaven,
Hallowed be your name.
Your kingdom come,
Your will be done
on earth as it is in heaven.
Give us this day our daily bread.
And forgive us our debts,
as we also have forgiven our debtors.
And lead us not into temptation
But deliver us from the evil one.
For yours is the kingdom and the power and the glory forever.
Amen.

Intercessions and Personal Requests

Prayer of the Church

Gracious Father, whose blessed Son Jesus Christ came down from heaven to be the true bread which gives life to the world: Evermore give us this bread, that he may live in us, and we in

him; who lives and reigns with you and the Holy Spirit, one
God, now and for ever. Amen.
The Book of Common Prayer

BLESSING

Now may the God of hope fill you with all joy and peace as you
believe, so that you may overflow with hope by the power of the
Holy Spirit.
Romans 15:13

DAY 13 MIDDAY PRAYER

CALL TO PRAYER

My mouth will tell about your righteousness and your salvation
all day long, though I cannot sum them up.
Psalm 71:15

MIDDAY READING

John 6:41–71
Therefore the Jews started grumbling about him because he
said, "I am the bread that came down from heaven." They were
saying, "Isn't this Jesus the son of Joseph, whose father and
mother we know? How can he now say, 'I have come down from
heaven'?"

Jesus answered them, "Stop grumbling among yourselves.
No one can come to me unless the Father who sent me draws
him, and I will raise him up on the last day. It is written in the
Prophets: **And they will all be taught by God.** Everyone who
has listened to and learned from the Father comes to me—not
that anyone has seen the Father except the one who is from
God. He has seen the Father.

"Truly I tell you, anyone who believes has eternal life. I
am the bread of life. Your ancestors ate the manna in the
wilderness, and they died. This is the bread that comes down
from heaven so that anyone may eat of it and not die. I am the

living bread that came down from heaven. If anyone eats of this bread he will live forever. The bread that I will give for the life of the world is my flesh."

At that, the Jews argued among themselves, "How can this man give us his flesh to eat?"

So Jesus said to them, "Truly I tell you, unless you eat the flesh of the Son of Man and drink his blood, you do not have life in yourselves. The one who eats my flesh and drinks my blood has eternal life, and I will raise him up on the last day, because my flesh is true food and my blood is true drink. The one who eats my flesh and drinks my blood remains in me, and I in him. Just as the living Father sent me and I live because of the Father, so the one who feeds on me will live because of me. This is the bread that came down from heaven; it is not like the manna your ancestors ate—and they died. The one who eats this bread will live forever."

He said these things while teaching in the synagogue in Capernaum.

Therefore, when many of his disciples heard this, they said, "This teaching is hard. Who can accept it?"

Jesus, knowing in himself that his disciples were grumbling about this, asked them, "Does this offend you? Then what if you were to observe the Son of Man ascending to where he was before? The Spirit is the one who gives life. The flesh doesn't help at all. The words that I have spoken to you are spirit and are life. But there are some among you who don't believe." (For Jesus knew from the beginning those who did not believe and the one who would betray him.) He said, "This is why I told you that no one can come to me unless it is granted to him by the Father."

From that moment many of his disciples turned back and no longer accompanied him. So Jesus said to the Twelve, "You don't want to go away too, do you?"

Simon Peter answered, "Lord, to whom will we go? You have the words of eternal life. We have come to believe and know that you are the Holy One of God."

Jesus replied to them, "Didn't I choose you, the Twelve? Yet one of you is a devil." He was referring to Judas, Simon Iscariot's son, one of the Twelve, because he was going to betray him.

This is the Word of the Lord. Thanks be to God.

Glory be to God the Father, God the Son, and God the Holy Spirit. As it was in the beginning, is now, and will be forever, world without end.

THE LORD'S PRAYER

Our Father in heaven,
Hallowed be your name.
Your kingdom come,
Your will be done
on earth as it is in heaven.
Give us this day our daily bread.
And forgive us our debts,
as we also have forgiven our debtors.
And lead us not into temptation
But deliver us from the evil one.
For yours is the kingdom and the power and the glory forever.
Amen.

BLESSING

May [the LORD] give you what your heart desires and fulfill your whole purpose. May the LORD fulfill all your requests.
Psalm 20:4–5

DAY 13 EVENING PRAYER

CALL TO PRAYER

If anyone wants to follow after me, let him deny himself, take up his cross and follow me.
Mark 8:34

CONFESSION OF SIN

Lord, have mercy on us.
Christ, have mercy on us.

Lord, have mercy on us.

If we confess our sins, he is faithful and righteous to forgive us
our sins and to cleanse us from all unrighteousness.
1 John 1:9

CANTICLE

Born as a Son,
led forth as a lamb,
sacrificed as a sheep,
buried as a man,
he rose from the dead as God,
for he was by nature God and man.
He is all things:
he judges, and so he is law;
he teaches, and so he is wisdom;
he saves, and so he is grace;
he is begotten, and so he is Son;
he suffers, and so he is sacrifice;
he is buried, and so he is man;
he rises again, and so he is God.
This is Jesus Christ,
to whom belongs glory for all ages.
Melito of Sardis

EVENING READING

Matthew 16:13–28
When Jesus came to the region of Caesarea Philippi, he asked
his disciples, "Who do people say that the Son of Man is?"

They replied, "Some say John the Baptist; others, Elijah; still
others, Jeremiah or one of the prophets."

"But you," he asked them, "who do you say that I am?"

Simon Peter answered, "You are the Messiah, the Son of the
living God."

Jesus responded, "Blessed are you, Simon son of Jonah,
because flesh and blood did not reveal this to you, but my
Father in heaven. And I also say to you that you are Peter, and

on this rock I will build my church, and the gates of Hades will not overpower it. I will give you the keys of the kingdom of heaven, and whatever you bind on earth will have been bound in heaven, and whatever you loose on earth will have been loosed in heaven." Then he gave the disciples orders to tell no one that he was the Messiah.

From then on Jesus began to point out to his disciples that it was necessary for him to go to Jerusalem and suffer many things from the elders, chief priests, and scribes, be killed, and be raised the third day. Peter took him aside and began to rebuke him, "Oh no, Lord! This will never happen to you!"

Jesus turned and told Peter, "Get behind me, Satan! You are a hindrance to me because you're not thinking about God's concerns but human concerns."

Then Jesus said to his disciples, "If anyone wants to follow after me, let him deny himself, take up his cross, and follow me. For whoever wants to save his life will lose it, but whoever loses his life because of me will find it. For what will it benefit someone if he gains the whole world yet loses his life? Or what will anyone give in exchange for his life? For the Son of Man is going to come with his angels in the glory of his Father, and then he will reward each according to what he has done. Truly I tell you, there are some standing here who will not taste death until they see the Son of Man coming in his kingdom."

This is the Word of the Lord. Thanks be to God.

GLORIA
Glory be to God the Father, God the Son, and God the Holy Spirit. As it was in the beginning, is now, and will be forever, world without end.

THE LORD'S PRAYER
Our Father in heaven,
Hallowed be your name.
Your kingdom come,

Your will be done
on earth as it is in heaven.
Give us this day our daily bread.
And forgive us our debts,
as we also have forgiven our debtors.
And lead us not into temptation
But deliver us from the evil one.
For yours is the kingdom and the power and the glory forever.
Amen.

Intercessions and Personal Requests

Prayer of the Church

Father, keep us from vain strife of words. Grant to us constant profession of the truth! Preserve us in a true and undefiled faith so that we may hold fast to what we professed when we were baptized in the name of the Father, Son and Holy Spirit, that we may have you for our Father, that we may abide in your Son and in the fellowship of the Holy Spirit. Through Jesus Christ, Our Lord.
Hilary of Poitiers

Blessing

The Lord Almighty grant us a peaceful night and a perfect end. Amen.

DAY 14 MORNING PRAYER

The Lord has shown forth his glory: O come, let us adore him.

CONFESSION OF FAITH

I believe that the one, holy, catholic, and apostolic church is
God's new society, the first fruit of the new creation, the whole
company of the redeemed through the ages, of which Christ is
Lord and head. The truth that Jesus is the Christ, the Son of the
living God, is the church's firm foundation. The local church is
both embassy and parable of the kingdom of heaven, an earthly
place where his will is done and he is now present, existing
visibly everywhere two or three gather in his name to proclaim
and spread the gospel in word and works of love, and by
obeying the Lord's command to baptize disciples and celebrate
the Lord's Supper.
Adapted from the Reforming Catholic Confession

CANTICLE

The LORD reigns! Let the peoples tremble.
He is enthroned between the cherubim.
Let the earth quake.
The LORD is great in Zion;
he is exalted above all the peoples.
Let them praise your great
and awe-inspiring name.
He is holy.
The mighty King loves justice.
You have established fairness;
you have administered justice
and righteousness in Jacob.
Exalt the LORD our God;

bow in worship at his holy mountain,
for the LORD our God is holy.
Psalm 99:1–4,9

MORNING READINGS

Luke 9:28–36

About eight days after this conversation, he took along Peter,
John, and James and went up on the mountain to pray. As he
was praying, the appearance of his face changed, and his clothes
became dazzling white. Suddenly, two men were talking with
him—Moses and Elijah. They appeared in glory and were
speaking of his departure, which he was about to accomplish in
Jerusalem.

Peter and those with him were in a deep sleep, and when they
became fully awake, they saw his glory and the two men who
were standing with him. As the two men were departing from
him, Peter said to Jesus, "Master, it's good for us to be here. Let's
set up three shelters: one for you, one for Moses, and one for
Elijah"—not knowing what he was saying.

While he was saying this, a cloud appeared and
overshadowed them. They became afraid as they entered the
cloud. Then a voice came from the cloud, saying, "This is my
Son, the Chosen One; listen to him!"

After the voice had spoken, Jesus was found alone. They kept
silent, and at that time told no one what they had seen.

Mark 9:14–29

When they came to the disciples, they saw a large crowd around
them and scribes disputing with them. When the whole crowd
saw him, they were amazed and ran to greet him. He asked
them, "What are you arguing with them about?"

Someone from the crowd answered him, "Teacher, I brought
my son to you. He has a spirit that makes him unable to speak.
Whenever it seizes him, it throws him down, and he foams at
the mouth, grinds his teeth, and becomes rigid. I asked your
disciples to drive it out, but they couldn't."

He replied to them, "You unbelieving generation, how long
will I be with you? How long must I put up with you? Bring

him to me." So they brought the boy to him. When the spirit saw him, it immediately threw the boy into convulsions. He fell to the ground and rolled around, foaming at the mouth. "How long has this been happening to him?" Jesus asked his father.

"From childhood," he said. "And many times it has thrown him into fire or water to destroy him. But if you can do anything, have compassion on us and help us."

Jesus said to him, "'If you can'? Everything is possible for the one who believes."

Immediately the father of the boy cried out, "I do believe; help my unbelief!"

When Jesus saw that a crowd was quickly gathering, he rebuked the unclean spirit, saying to it, "You mute and deaf spirit, I command you: Come out of him and never enter him again."

Then it came out, shrieking and throwing him into terrible convulsions. The boy became like a corpse, so that many said, "He's dead." But Jesus, taking him by the hand, raised him, and he stood up.

After he had gone into the house, his disciples asked him privately, "Why couldn't we drive it out?"

And he told them, "This kind can come out by nothing but prayer."

This is the Word of the Lord. Thanks be to God.

Gloria

Glory be to God the Father, God the Son, and God the Holy Spirit. As it was in the beginning, is now, and will be forever, world without end.

The Lord's Prayer

Our Father in heaven,
Hallowed be your name.
Your kingdom come,
Your will be done
on earth as it is in heaven.

Give us this day our daily bread.
And forgive us our debts,
as we also have forgiven our debtors.
And lead us not into temptation
But deliver us from the evil one.
For yours is the kingdom and the power and the glory forever.
Amen.

Intercessions and Personal Requests

Prayer of the Church

O God, who on the holy mount revealed to chosen witnesses
your well-beloved Son, wonderfully transfigured, in raiment
white and glistening: Mercifully grant that we, being delivered
from the disquietude of this world, may by faith behold the
King in his beauty; who with you and the Holy Spirit lives and
reigns, one God for ever and ever. Amen.
The Book of Common Prayer

Blessing

The grace of the Lord Jesus Christ, and the love of God, and the
fellowship of the Holy Spirit be with us all.
2 Corinthians 13:14

DAY 14 MIDDAY PRAYER

Call to Prayer

I will boast in the Lord; the humble will hear and be glad.
Psalm 34:2

Matthew 17:22–27

As they were gathering together in Galilee, Jesus told them, "The Son of Man is about to be betrayed into the hands of men. They will kill him, and on the third day he will be raised up." And they were deeply distressed.

When they came to Capernaum, those who collected the temple tax approached Peter and said, "Doesn't your teacher pay the temple tax?"

"Yes," he said.

When he went into the house, Jesus spoke to him first, "What do you think, Simon? From whom do earthly kings collect tariffs or taxes? From their sons or from strangers?"

"From strangers," he said.

"Then the sons are free," Jesus told him. "But, so we won't offend them, go to the sea, cast in a fishhook, and take the first fish that you catch. When you open its mouth you'll find a coin. Take it and give it to them for me and you."

Mark 9:33–42

They came to Capernaum. When he was in the house, he asked them, "What were you arguing about on the way?" But they were silent, because on the way they had been arguing with one another about who was the greatest. Sitting down, he called the Twelve and said to them, "If anyone wants to be first, he must be last and servant of all." He took a child, had him stand among them, and taking him in his arms, he said to them, "Whoever welcomes one little child such as this in my name welcomes me. And whoever welcomes me does not welcome me, but him who sent me."

John said to him, "Teacher, we saw someone driving out demons in your name, and we tried to stop him because he wasn't following us."

"Don't stop him," said Jesus, "because there is no one who will perform a miracle in my name who can soon afterward speak evil of me. For whoever is not against us is for us. And whoever gives you a cup of water to drink in my name, because you belong to Christ—truly I tell you, he will never lose his reward.

"But whoever causes one of these little ones who believe in me to fall away—it would be better for him if a heavy millstone were hung around his neck and he were thrown into the sea."

Luke 9:51–62
When the days were coming to a close for him to be taken up, he determined to journey to Jerusalem. He sent messengers ahead of himself, and on the way they entered a village of the Samaritans to make preparations for him. But they did not welcome him, because he determined to journey to Jerusalem. When the disciples James and John saw this, they said, "Lord, do you want us to call down fire from heaven to consume them?"

But he turned and rebuked them, and they went to another village.

As they were traveling on the road someone said to him, "I will follow you wherever you go."

Jesus told him, "Foxes have dens, and birds of the sky have nests, but the Son of Man has no place to lay his head." Then he said to another, "Follow me."

"Lord," he said, "first let me go bury my father."

But he told him, "Let the dead bury their own dead, but you go and spread the news of the kingdom of God."

Another said, "I will follow you, Lord, but first let me go and say good-bye to those at my house."

But Jesus said to him, "No one who puts his hand to the plow and looks back is fit for the kingdom of God."

This is the Word of the Lord. Thanks be to God.

GLORIA

Glory be to God the Father, God the Son, and God the Holy Spirit. As it was in the beginning, is now, and will be forever, world without end.

Our Father in heaven,
Hallowed be your name.
Your kingdom come,
Your will be done
on earth as it is in heaven.
Give us this day our daily bread.
And forgive us our debts,
as we also have forgiven our debtors.
And lead us not into temptation
But deliver us from the evil one.
For yours is the kingdom and the power and the glory forever.
Amen.

Blessing

The peace of God, which passes all understanding, keep your
hearts and minds in the knowledge and love of God, and of his
Son Jesus Christ our Lord; and the blessing of God Almighty,
the Father, the Son, and the Holy Spirit, be among you, and
remain with you always. Amen.

DAY 14 EVENING PRAYER

Call to Prayer

Be alert, since you don't know when the master of the house
is coming—whether in the evening or at midnight or at the
crowing of the rooster or early in the morning. Otherwise,
when he comes suddenly he might find you sleeping.
Mark 13:35–36

Confession of Sin

Holy Spirit, grant us each a true conviction leading to a
true repentance. Indeed it was our desire to serve you well
in this day, O God, but we have again fallen short of your
righteousness in our thoughts, our intentions, our actions, and

our utterances. We have responded at times without grace. We have chosen sometimes that which is unprofitable and which leads neither to our own flourishing nor to the proclamation of your glory. Forgive us, O King, for treasons both known and unknown. Forgive us for the harms we have done this day, and for the goods we might have done but failed to do; forgive us also for the constant condition of our hearts, for the self-serving impulses, inclinations, and desires which stand us every moment in need of a savior.
Every Moment Holy

The sacrifice pleasing to God is a broken spirit. You will not despise a broken and humbled heart, God.
Psalm 51:17

Canticle

How can a young man keep his way pure?
By keeping your word.
I have sought you with all my heart;
don't let me wander from your commands.
I have treasured your word in my heart
so that I may not sin against you.
Psalm 119:9–11

Evening Readings

Luke 12:13–21
Someone from the crowd said to him, "Teacher, tell my brother to divide the inheritance with me."

"Friend," he said to him, "who appointed me a judge or arbitrator over you?" He then told them, "Watch out and be on guard against all greed, because one's life is not in the abundance of his possessions."

Then he told them a parable: "A rich man's land was very productive. He thought to himself, 'What should I do, since I don't have anywhere to store my crops? I will do this,' he said. 'I'll tear down my barns and build bigger ones and store all my grain and my goods there. Then I'll say to myself, "You have many goods stored up for many years. Take it easy; eat, drink, and enjoy yourself." '

"But God said to him, 'You fool! This very night your life is demanded of you. And the things you have prepared—whose will they be?'

"That's how it is with the one who stores up treasure for himself and is not rich toward God."

Luke 12:35–48
"Be ready for service and have your lamps lit. You are to be like people waiting for their master to return from the wedding banquet so that when he comes and knocks, they can open the door for him at once. Blessed will be those servants the master finds alert when he comes. Truly I tell you, he will get ready, have them recline at the table, then come and serve them. If he comes in the middle of the night, or even near dawn, and finds them alert, blessed are those servants. But know this: If the homeowner had known at what hour the thief was coming, he would not have let his house be broken into. You also be ready, because the Son of Man is coming at an hour you do not expect."

"Lord," Peter asked, "are you telling this parable to us or to everyone?"

The Lord said, "Who then is the faithful and sensible manager his master will put in charge of his household servants to give them their allotted food at the proper time? Blessed is that servant whom the master finds doing his job when he comes. Truly I tell you, he will put him in charge of all his possessions. But if that servant says in his heart, 'My master is delaying his coming,' and starts to beat the male and female servants, and to eat and drink and get drunk, that servant's master will come on a day he does not expect him and at an hour he does not know. He will cut him to pieces and assign him a place with the unfaithful. And that servant who knew his master's will and didn't prepare himself or do it will be severely beaten. But the one who did not know and did what deserved punishment will receive a light beating. From everyone who has been given much, much will be required; and from the one who has been entrusted with much, even more will be expected."

This is the Word of the Lord. Thanks be to God.

GLORIA
Glory be to God the Father, God the Son, and God the Holy Spirit. As it was in the beginning, is now, and will be forever, world without end.

THE LORD'S PRAYER
Our Father in heaven,
Hallowed be your name.
Your kingdom come,
Your will be done
on earth as it is in heaven.
Give us this day our daily bread.
And forgive us our debts,
as we also have forgiven our debtors.
And lead us not into temptation
But deliver us from the evil one.
For yours is the kingdom and the power and the glory forever.
Amen.

INTERCESSIONS AND PERSONAL REQUESTS

PRAYER OF THE CHURCH
Almighty God, it is the glorious hope of a blessed immortality beyond the grave, that supports your children through this vale of tears. Forever blessed be your name, for you have implanted this hope in my heart. If you have plucked my soul as a brand from the burning, it is not because you have seen any worth in me, but it is because of your distinguishing mercy, for mercy is your darling attribute. Clothe my soul with humility as with a garment. Let not a murmuring thought enter my heart, but may

I cheerfully bear with all the trials of life. Clothe me with the pure robes of Christ's righteousness, that when he shall come in flaming fire to judge the world, I may appear before him with joy and not with grief. Amen.
Maria W. Stewart

The Almighty and merciful Lord, Father, Son, and Holy Spirit, bless us and keep us, this night and evermore. Amen.

DAY 15 MORNING PRAYER

Call to Prayer

Both the Spirit and the bride say, "Come!" Let anyone who
hears, say, "Come!" Let the one who is thirsty come. Let the one
who desires take the water of life freely.
Revelation 22:17

Confession of Faith

I believe in God, the Father almighty,
creator of heaven and earth;
I believe in Jesus Christ, his only Son, our Lord.
He was conceived by the power of the Holy Spirit
and born of the Virgin Mary.
He suffered under Pontius Pilate,
was crucified, died, and was buried.
He descended to the dead.
On the third day he rose again.
He ascended into heaven,
and is seated at the right hand of the Father.
He will come again to judge the living and the dead.
I believe in the Holy Spirit,
the holy catholic Church,
the communion of saints,
the forgiveness of sins
the resurrection of the body,
and the life everlasting. Amen.
The Apostles' Creed

Canticle

The poor and the needy seek water, but there is none;
their tongues are parched with thirst.
I will answer them.
I am the Lord, the God of Israel. I will not abandon them.
I will open rivers on the barren heights,

and springs in the middle of the plains.
I will turn the desert into a pool
and dry land into springs.
I will plant cedar, acacia, myrtle, and olive trees
in the wilderness.
I will put juniper, elm, and cypress trees together
in the desert,
so that all may see and know,
consider and understand,
that the hand of the LORD has done this,
the Holy One of Israel has created it.
Isaiah 41:17–20

MORNING READING

John 7:10–39
After his brothers had gone up to the festival, then he also went up, not openly but secretly. The Jews were looking for him at the festival and saying, "Where is he?" And there was a lot of murmuring about him among the crowds. Some were saying, "He's a good man." Others were saying, "No, on the contrary, he's deceiving the people." Still, nobody was talking publicly about him for fear of the Jews.

When the festival was already half over, Jesus went up into the temple and began to teach. Then the Jews were amazed and said, "How is this man so learned, since he hasn't been trained?"

Jesus answered them, "My teaching isn't mine but is from the one who sent me. If anyone wants to do his will, he will know whether the teaching is from God or whether I am speaking on my own. The one who speaks on his own seeks his own glory; but he who seeks the glory of the one who sent him is true, and there is no unrighteousness in him. Didn't Moses give you the law? Yet none of you keeps the law. Why are you trying to kill me?"

"You have a demon!" the crowd responded. "Who is trying to kill you?"

"I performed one work, and you are all amazed," Jesus answered. "This is why Moses has given you circumcision— not that it comes from Moses but from the fathers—and you circumcise a man on the Sabbath. If a man receives circumcision on the Sabbath so that the law of Moses won't be broken, are you angry at me because I made a man entirely well on the Sabbath? Stop judging according to outward appearances; rather judge according to righteous judgment."

Some of the people of Jerusalem were saying, "Isn't this the man they are trying to kill? Yet, look, he's speaking publicly and they're saying nothing to him. Can it be true that the authorities know he is the Messiah? But we know where this man is from. When the Messiah comes, nobody will know where he is from."

As he was teaching in the temple, Jesus cried out, "You know me and you know where I am from. Yet I have not come on my own, but the one who sent me is true. You don't know him; I know him because I am from him, and he sent me."

Then they tried to seize him. Yet no one laid a hand on him because his hour had not yet come. However, many from the crowd believed in him and said, "When the Messiah comes, he won't perform more signs than this man has done, will he?" The Pharisees heard the crowd murmuring these things about him, and so the chief priests and the Pharisees sent servants to arrest him.

Then Jesus said, "I am only with you for a short time. Then I'm going to the one who sent me. You will look for me, but you will not find me; and where I am, you cannot come."

Then the Jews said to one another, "Where does he intend to go that we won't find him? He doesn't intend to go to the Jewish people dispersed among the Greeks and teach the Greeks, does he? What is this remark he made: 'You will look for me, and you will not find me; and where I am, you cannot come'?"

On the last and most important day of the festival, Jesus stood up and cried out, "If anyone is thirsty, let him come to me and drink. The one who believes in me, as the Scripture has said, will have streams of living water flow from deep within him." He said this about the Spirit. Those who believed in Jesus were going to receive the Spirit, for the Spirit had not yet been given because Jesus had not yet been glorified.

This is the Word of the Lord. Thanks be to God.

Gloria

Glory be to God the Father, God the Son, and God the Holy Spirit. As it was in the beginning, is now, and will be forever, world without end.

The Lord's Prayer

Our Father in heaven,
Hallowed be your name.
Your kingdom come,
Your will be done
on earth as it is in heaven.
Give us this day our daily bread.
And forgive us our debts,
as we also have forgiven our debtors.
And lead us not into temptation
But deliver us from the evil one.
For yours is the kingdom and the power and the glory forever.
Amen.

Intercessions and Personal Requests

Prayer of the Church

Merciful God, allow me to drink from the stream which flows from your fountain of life. May I taste the sweet beauty of its waters, which sprang from the very depths of your truth. O Lord, you are that fountain from which I desire with all my heart to drink. Give me, Lord Jesus, this water, that it may quench the burning spiritual thirst within my soul, and purify me from all sin. I know, King of Glory, that I am asking from you a great gift. But you give to your faithful people without counting the cost, and you promise even greater things in the future. Indeed, nothing is greater than yourself, and you have given yourself to mankind on the cross. Therefore, in praying for the waters of life, I am praying that you, the source of those

waters, will give yourself to me. You are my light, my salvation, my food, my drink, my God.
Columbanus

The grace of the Lord Jesus Christ, and the love of God, and the fellowship of the Holy Spirit be with us all.
2 Corinthians 13:14

DAY 15 MIDDAY PRAYER

CALL TO PRAYER

Holy, holy, holy, Lord God, the Almighty, who was, who is, and who is to come.
Revelation 4:8

MIDDAY READING

John 8:2–30

At dawn he went to the temple again, and all the people were coming to him. He sat down and began to teach them.

Then the scribes and the Pharisees brought a woman caught in adultery, making her stand in the center. "Teacher," they said to him, "this woman was caught in the act of committing adultery. In the law Moses commanded us to stone such women. So what do you say?" They asked this to trap him, in order that they might have evidence to accuse him.

Jesus stooped down and started writing on the ground with his finger. When they persisted in questioning him, he stood up and said to them, "The one without sin among you should be the first to throw a stone at her." Then he stooped down again and continued writing on the ground. When they heard this, they left one by one, starting with the older men. Only he was left, with the woman in the center. When Jesus stood up, he said to her, "Woman, where are they? Has no one condemned you?"

"No one, Lord," she answered.

"Neither do I condemn you," said Jesus. "Go, and from now on do not sin anymore."

Jesus spoke to them again: "I am the light of the world. Anyone who follows me will never walk in the darkness but will have the light of life."

So the Pharisees said to him, "You are testifying about yourself. Your testimony is not valid."

"Even if I testify about myself," Jesus replied, "My testimony is true, because I know where I came from and where I'm going. But you don't know where I come from or where I'm going. You judge by human standards. I judge no one. And if I do judge, my judgment is true, because it is not I alone who judge, but I and the Father who sent me. Even in your law it is written that the testimony of two witnesses is true. I am the one who testifies about myself, and the Father who sent me testifies about me."

Then they asked him, "Where is your Father?"

"You know neither me nor my Father," Jesus answered. "If you knew me, you would also know my Father." He spoke these words by the treasury, while teaching in the temple. But no one seized him, because his hour had not yet come.

Then he said to them again, "I'm going away; you will look for me, and you will die in your sin. Where I'm going, you cannot come."

So the Jews said again, "He won't kill himself, will he, since he says, 'Where I'm going, you cannot come'?"

"You are from below," he told them, "I am from above. You are of this world; I am not of this world. Therefore I told you that you will die in your sins. For if you do not believe that I am he, you will die in your sins."

"Who are you?" they questioned.

"Exactly what I've been telling you from the very beginning," Jesus told them. "I have many things to say and to judge about you, but the one who sent me is true, and what I have heard from him—these things I tell the world."

They did not know he was speaking to them about the Father. So Jesus said to them, "When you lift up the Son of Man, then you will know that I am he, and that I do nothing on my own. But just as the Father taught me, I say these things. The one who

sent me is with me. He has not left me alone, because I always
do what pleases him."

As he was saying these things, many believed in him.

This is the Word of the Lord. Thanks be to God.

Gloria

Glory be to God the Father, God the Son, and God the Holy
Spirit. As it was in the beginning, is now, and will be forever,
world without end.

The Lord's Prayer

Our Father in heaven,
Hallowed be your name.
Your kingdom come,
Your will be done
on earth as it is in heaven.
Give us this day our daily bread.
And forgive us our debts,
as we also have forgiven our debtors.
And lead us not into temptation
But deliver us from the evil one.
For yours is the kingdom and the power and the glory forever.
Amen.

Blessing

May the Lord bless you and protect you; may the Lord make
his face shine on you and be gracious to you; may the Lord
look with favor on you and give you peace.
Numbers 6:24–26

DAY 15 EVENING PRAYER

CALL TO PRAYER

As for me, I will tell about him forever; I will sing praise to the
God of Jacob.
Psalm 75:9

CONFESSION OF SIN

Most merciful God,
we confess that we have sinned against you
in thought, word, and deed,
by what we have done,
and by what we have left undone.
We have not loved you with our whole heart;
we have not loved our neighbors as ourselves.
We are truly sorry and we humbly repent.
For the sake of your Son Jesus Christ,
have mercy on us and forgive us;
that we may delight in your will,
and walk in your ways,
to the glory of your Name. Amen.
The Book of Common Prayer

If we confess our sins, he is faithful and righteous to forgive us
our sins and to cleanse us from all unrighteousness.
1 John 1:9

CANTICLE

But you, Israel, my servant,
Jacob, whom I have chosen,
descendant of Abraham, my friend—
I brought you from the ends of the earth
and called you from its farthest corners.
I said to you: You are my servant;
I have chosen you; I haven't rejected you.

Do not fear, for I am with you;
do not be afraid, for I am your God.
I will strengthen you; I will help you;
I will hold on to you with my righteous right hand.
Isaiah 41:8–10

Evening Reading

John 8:31–59

Then Jesus said to the Jews who had believed him, "If you continue in my word, you really are my disciples. You will know the truth, and the truth will set you free."

"We are descendants of Abraham," they answered him, "and we have never been enslaved to anyone. How can you say, 'You will become free'?"

Jesus responded, "Truly I tell you, everyone who commits sin is a slave of sin. A slave does not remain in the household forever, but a son does remain forever. So if the Son sets you free, you really will be free. I know you are descendants of Abraham, but you are trying to kill me because my word has no place among you. I speak what I have seen in the presence of the Father; so then, you do what you have heard from your father."

"Our father is Abraham," they replied.

"If you were Abraham's children," Jesus told them, "you would do what Abraham did. But now you are trying to kill me, a man who has told you the truth that I heard from God. Abraham did not do this. You're doing what your father does."

"We weren't born of sexual immorality," they said. "We have one Father—God."

Jesus said to them, "If God were your Father, you would love me, because I came from God and I am here. For I didn't come on my own, but he sent me. Why don't you understand what I say? Because you cannot listen to my word. You are of your father the devil, and you want to carry out your father's desires. He was a murderer from the beginning and does not stand in the truth, because there is no truth in him. When he tells a lie, he speaks from his own nature, because he is a liar and the father of lies. Yet because I tell the truth, you do not believe me. Who among you can convict me of sin? If I am telling the truth, why don't you believe me? The one who is from God listens to God's words. This is why you don't listen, because you are not from God."

The Jews responded to him, "Aren't we right in saying that you're a Samaritan and have a demon?"

"I do not have a demon," Jesus answered. "On the contrary, I honor my Father and you dishonor me. I do not seek my own glory; there is one who seeks it and judges. Truly I tell you, if anyone keeps my word, he will never see death."

Then the Jews said, "Now we know you have a demon. Abraham died and so did the prophets. You say, 'If anyone keeps my word, he will never taste death.' Are you greater than our father Abraham who died? And the prophets died. Who do you claim to be?"

"If I glorify myself," Jesus answered, "my glory is nothing. My Father—about whom you say, 'He is our God'—he is the one who glorifies me. You do not know him, but I know him. If I were to say I don't know him, I would be a liar like you. But I do know him, and I keep his word. Your father Abraham rejoiced to see my day; he saw it and was glad."

The Jews replied, "You aren't fifty years old yet, and you've seen Abraham?"

Jesus said to them, "Truly I tell you, before Abraham was, I am."

So they picked up stones to throw at him. But Jesus was hidden and went out of the temple.

This is the Word of the Lord. Thanks be to God.

Gloria

Glory be to God the Father, God the Son, and God the Holy Spirit. As it was in the beginning, is now, and will be forever, world without end.

The Lord's Prayer

Our Father in heaven,
Hallowed be your name.

Your kingdom come,
Your will be done
on earth as it is in heaven.
Give us this day our daily bread.
And forgive us our debts,
as we also have forgiven our debtors.
And lead us not into temptation
But deliver us from the evil one.
For yours is the kingdom and the power and the glory forever.
Amen.

INTERCESSIONS AND PERSONAL REQUESTS

PRAYER OF THE CHURCH

Lord God, of might inconceivable, of glory incomprehensible,
of mercy immeasurable, of goodness ineffable; O Master,
look down upon us in your tender love, and show forth,
toward us and those who pray with us, your rich mercies and
compassions. Amen.
John Chrysostom

BLESSING

The Lord Almighty grant us a peaceful night and a perfect end.
Amen.

DAY 16 MORNING PRAYER

Call to Prayer

Open my eyes so that I may contemplate wondrous things from
your instruction.
Psalm 119:18

Confession of Faith

I believe that God has spoken and continues to speak in
and through Scripture, the only infallible and sufficiently
clear rule and authority for Christian faith, thought, and life.
Scripture is God's inspired and illuminating Word in the words
of his servants, the prophets and apostles, a gracious self-
communication of God's own light and life, a means of grace for
growing in knowledge and holiness. The Bible is to be believed
in all that it teaches, obeyed in all that it commands, trusted in
all that it promises, and revered in all that it reveals.
Adapted from the Reforming Catholic Confession

Canticle

This is what God, the LORD, says—
who created the heavens and stretched them out,
who spread out the earth and what comes from it,
who gives breath to the people on it
and spirit to those who walk on it—
"I am the LORD. I have called you
for a righteous purpose,
and I will hold you by your hand.
I will watch over you, and I will appoint you
to be a covenant for the people
and a light to the nations,
in order to open blind eyes,
to bring out prisoners from the dungeon,
and those sitting in darkness from the prison house.
Isaiah 42:5–7

John 9:1–16

As he was passing by, he saw a man blind from birth. His disciples asked him, "Rabbi, who sinned, this man or his parents, that he was born blind?"

"Neither this man nor his parents sinned," Jesus answered. "This came about so that God's works might be displayed in him. We must do the works of him who sent me while it is day. Night is coming when no one can work. As long as I am in the world, I am the light of the world."

After he said these things he spit on the ground, made some mud from the saliva, and spread the mud on his eyes. "Go," he told him, "wash in the pool of Siloam" (which means "Sent"). So he left, washed, and came back seeing.

His neighbors and those who had seen him before as a beggar said, "Isn't this the one who used to sit begging?" Some said, "He's the one." Others were saying, "No, but he looks like him."

He kept saying, "I'm the one."

So they asked him, "Then how were your eyes opened?"

He answered, "The man called Jesus made mud, spread it on my eyes, and told me, 'Go to Siloam and wash.' So when I went and washed I received my sight."

"Where is he?" they asked.

"I don't know," he said.

They brought the man who used to be blind to the Pharisees. The day that Jesus made the mud and opened his eyes was a Sabbath. Then the Pharisees asked him again how he received his sight.

"He put mud on my eyes," he told them. "I washed and I can see."

Some of the Pharisees said, "This man is not from God, because he doesn't keep the Sabbath." But others were saying, "How can a sinful man perform such signs?" And there was a division among them.

This is the Word of the Lord. Thanks be to God.

GLORIA

Glory be to God the Father, God the Son, and God the Holy
Spirit. As it was in the beginning, is now, and will be forever,
world without end.

THE LORD'S PRAYER

Our Father in heaven,
Hallowed be your name.
Your kingdom come,
Your will be done
on earth as it is in heaven.
Give us this day our daily bread.
And forgive us our debts,
as we also have forgiven our debtors.
And lead us not into temptation
But deliver us from the evil one.
For yours is the kingdom and the power and the glory forever.
Amen.

INTERCESSIONS AND PERSONAL REQUESTS

PRAYER OF THE CHURCH

To you, O God of my fathers, I give thanks! I am the work
of your hands, the price of your blood, the image of your
countenance, the servant of your purchase, the seal of your
name, the child of your adoption, a temple of your spirit, a
member of your church.
Lancelot Andrewes

BLESSING

Now to him who is able to do above and beyond all that we
ask or think according to the power that works in us—to him
be glory in the church and in Christ Jesus to all generations,
forever and ever. Amen.
Ephesians 3:20–21

DAY 16 MIDDAY PRAYER

CALL TO PRAYER

Lord, open my lips, and my mouth will declare your praise.
Psalm 51:15

MIDDAY READING

John 9:17–41
Again they asked the blind man, "What do you say about him,
since he opened your eyes?"

"He's a prophet," he said.

The Jews did not believe this about him—that he was blind
and received sight—until they summoned the parents of the one
who had received his sight.

They asked them, "Is this your son, the one you say was born
blind? How then does he now see?"

"We know this is our son and that he was born blind," his
parents answered. "But we don't know how he now sees, and we
don't know who opened his eyes. Ask him; he's of age. He will
speak for himself." His parents said these things because they
were afraid of the Jews, since the Jews had already agreed that
if anyone confessed him as the Messiah, he would be banned
from the synagogue. This is why his parents said, "He's of age;
ask him."

So a second time they summoned the man who had been
blind and told him, "Give glory to God. We know that this man
is a sinner."

He answered, "Whether or not he's a sinner, I don't know.
One thing I do know: I was blind, and now I can see!"

Then they asked him, "What did he do to you? How did he
open your eyes?"

"I already told you," he said, "and you didn't listen. Why
do you want to hear it again? You don't want to become his
disciples too, do you?"

They ridiculed him: "You're that man's disciple, but we're Moses's disciples. We know that God has spoken to Moses. But this man—we don't know where he's from."

"This is an amazing thing!" the man told them. "You don't know where he is from, and yet he opened my eyes. We know that God doesn't listen to sinners, but if anyone is God-fearing and does his will, he listens to him. Throughout history no one has ever heard of someone opening the eyes of a person born blind. If this man were not from God, he wouldn't be able to do anything."

"You were born entirely in sin," they replied, "and are you trying to teach us?" Then they threw him out.

Jesus heard that they had thrown the man out, and when he found him, he asked, "Do you believe in the Son of Man?"

"Who is he, Sir, that I may believe in him?" he asked.

Jesus answered, "You have seen him; in fact, he is the one speaking with you."

"I believe, Lord!" he said, and he worshiped him.

Jesus said, "I came into this world for judgment, in order that those who do not see will see and those who do see will become blind."

Some of the Pharisees who were with him heard these things and asked him, "We aren't blind too, are we?"

"If you were blind," Jesus told them, "you wouldn't have sin. But now that you say, 'We see,' your sin remains."

This is the Word of the Lord. Thanks be to God.

Gloria

Glory be to God the Father, God the Son, and God the Holy Spirit. As it was in the beginning, is now, and will be forever, world without end.

The Lord's Prayer

Our Father in heaven,
Hallowed be your name.
Your kingdom come,

Your will be done
on earth as it is in heaven.
Give us this day our daily bread.
And forgive us our debts,
as we also have forgiven our debtors.
And lead us not into temptation
But deliver us from the evil one.
For yours is the kingdom and the power and the glory forever.
Amen.

BLESSING

The grace of the Lord Jesus Christ, and the love of God, and the
fellowship of the Holy Spirit be with us all.
2 Corinthians 13:14

DAY 16 EVENING PRAYER

CALL TO PRAYER

Come, let's worship and bow down; let's kneel before the LORD
our Maker. For he is our God, and we are the people of his
pasture, the sheep under his care.
Psalm 95:6–7

CONFESSION OF SIN

O Lord, the house of my soul is narrow; enlarge it that you
may enter in. It is ruined, O repair it! It displeases your sight;
I confess it, I know. But who shall cleanse it, or to whom shall
I cry but unto you? Cleanse me from my secret faults, O Lord,
and spare your servant from sin.
Augustine

The sacrifice pleasing to God is a broken spirit. You will not
despise a broken and humbled heart, God.
Psalm 51:17

CANTICLE

The LORD is my shepherd;
I have what I need.
He lets me lie down in green pastures;
he leads me beside quiet waters.
He renews my life;
he leads me along the right paths
for his name's sake.
Even when I go through the darkest valley,
I fear no danger,
for you are with me;
your rod and your staff—they comfort me.
You prepare a table before me
in the presence of my enemies;
you anoint my head with oil;
my cup overflows.
Only goodness and faithful love will pursue me
all the days of my life,
and I will dwell in the house of the LORD
as long as I live.
Psalm 23

EVENING READING

John 10:1–21

"Truly I tell you, anyone who doesn't enter the sheep pen
by the gate but climbs in some other way is a thief and a
robber. The one who enters by the gate is the shepherd of the
sheep. The gatekeeper opens it for him, and the sheep hear
his voice. He calls his own sheep by name and leads them out.
When he has brought all his own outside, he goes ahead of
them. The sheep follow him because they know his voice. They
will never follow a stranger; instead they will run away from
him, because they don't know the voice of strangers." Jesus gave
them this figure of speech, but they did not understand what he
was telling them.

Jesus said again, "Truly I tell you, I am the gate for the sheep.
All who came before me are thieves and robbers, but the sheep
didn't listen to them. I am the gate. If anyone enters by me, he

will be saved and will come in and go out and find pasture. A thief comes only to steal and kill and destroy. I have come so that they may have life and have it in abundance.

"I am the good shepherd. The good shepherd lays down his life for the sheep. The hired hand, since he is not the shepherd and doesn't own the sheep, leaves them and runs away when he sees a wolf coming. The wolf then snatches and scatters them. This happens because he is a hired hand and doesn't care about the sheep.

"I am the good shepherd. I know my own, and my own know me, just as the Father knows me, and I know the Father. I lay down my life for the sheep. But I have other sheep that are not from this sheep pen; I must bring them also, and they will listen to my voice. Then there will be one flock, one shepherd. This is why the Father loves me, because I lay down my life so that I may take it up again. No one takes it from me, but I lay it down on my own. I have the right to lay it down, and I have the right to take it up again. I have received this command from my Father."

Again the Jews were divided because of these words. Many of them were saying, "He has a demon and he's crazy. Why do you listen to him?" Others were saying, "These aren't the words of someone who is demon-possessed. Can a demon open the eyes of the blind?"

This is the Word of the Lord. Thanks be to God.

Gloria

Glory be to God the Father, God the Son, and God the Holy Spirit. As it was in the beginning, is now, and will be forever, world without end.

The Lord's Prayer

Our Father in heaven,
Hallowed be your name.
Your kingdom come,

Your will be done
on earth as it is in heaven.
Give us this day our daily bread.
And forgive us our debts,
as we also have forgiven our debtors.
And lead us not into temptation
But deliver us from the evil one.
For yours is the kingdom and the power and the glory forever.
Amen.

Intercessions and Personal Requests

Prayer of the Church

O God, whose Son Jesus is the good shepherd of your people;
Grant that when we hear his voice we may know him who calls
us each by name, and follow where he leads; who, with you
and the Holy Spirit, lives and reigns, one God, for ever and
ever. Amen.
The Book of Common Prayer

Blessing

The Almighty and merciful Lord, Father, Son, and Holy Spirit,
bless us and keep us, this night and evermore. Amen.

DAY 17 MORNING PRAYER

CALL TO PRAYER

Israel, put your hope in the LORD. For there is faithful love with
the LORD, and with him is redemption in abundance.
Psalm 130:7

CONFESSION OF FAITH

I believe that Jesus Christ is the eternal Son of God become
human for us and our salvation, the only Mediator between
God and humanity, born of the virgin Mary, the Son of David
and servant of the house of Israel, one person with two natures,
truly God and truly man. He lived a fully human life, having
entered into the disorder and brokenness of fallen existence,
yet without sin, and in his words, deeds, attitude, and suffering
embodied the free and loving communication of God's own
light and life.
Adapted from the Reforming Catholic Confession

CANTICLE

Let the peoples praise you, God;
let all the peoples praise you.
Let the nations rejoice and shout for joy,
for you judge the peoples with fairness
and lead the nations on earth.
Let the peoples praise you, God,
let all the peoples praise you.
Psalm 67:3–5

MORNING READING

John 10:22–42
Then the Festival of Dedication took place in Jerusalem, and
it was winter. Jesus was walking in the temple in Solomon's
Colonnade. The Jews surrounded him and asked, "How long

are you going to keep us in suspense? If you are the Messiah, tell us plainly."

"I did tell you and you don't believe," Jesus answered them. "The works that I do in my Father's name testify about me. But you don't believe because you are not of my sheep. My sheep hear my voice, I know them, and they follow me. I give them eternal life, and they will never perish. No one will snatch them out of my hand. My Father, who has given them to me, is greater than all. No one is able to snatch them out of the Father's hand. I and the Father are one."

Again the Jews picked up rocks to stone him.

Jesus replied, "I have shown you many good works from the Father. For which of these works are you stoning me?"

"We aren't stoning you for a good work," the Jews answered, "but for blasphemy, because you—being a man—make yourself God."

Jesus answered them, "Isn't it written in your law, **I said, you are gods**? If he called those to whom the word of God came 'gods'—and the Scripture cannot be broken—do you say, 'You are blaspheming' to the one the Father set apart and sent into the world, because I said: I am the Son of God? If I am not doing my Father's works, don't believe me. But if I am doing them and you don't believe me, believe the works. This way you will know and understand that the Father is in me and I in the Father." Then they were trying again to seize him, but he escaped their grasp.

So he departed again across the Jordan to the place where John had been baptizing earlier, and he remained there. Many came to him and said, "John never did a sign, but everything John said about this man was true." And many believed in him there.

This is the Word of the Lord. Thanks be to God.

Gloria

Glory be to God the Father, God the Son, and God the Holy Spirit. As it was in the beginning, is now, and will be forever, world without end.

The Lord's Prayer

Our Father in heaven,
Hallowed be your name.
Your kingdom come,
Your will be done
on earth as it is in heaven.
Give us this day our daily bread.
And forgive us our debts,
as we also have forgiven our debtors.
And lead us not into temptation
But deliver us from the evil one.
For yours is the kingdom and the power and the glory forever.
Amen.

Intercessions and Personal Requests

Prayer of the Church

Meet me, O Christ, in the stillness of this morning. Move me, O
Spirit, to quiet my heart. Mend me, O Father, from yesterday's
harms. From the discords of yesterday, resurrect my peace.
From the discouragements of yesterday, resurrect my hope.
From the weariness of yesterday, resurrect my strength. From
the doubts of yesterday, resurrect my faith. From the wounds of
yesterday, resurrect my love. Let me enter this new day, aware of
my need, and awake to your grace, O Lord. Amen.
Every Moment Holy

Blessing

May God be gracious to us and bless us; may he make his face
shine upon us so that your way may be known on earth, your
salvation among all nations.
Psalm 67:1–2

DAY 17 MIDDAY PRAYER

Call to Prayer

Blessed be the Lord from Zion; he dwells in Jerusalem.
Hallelujah!
Psalm 135:21

Midday Readings

Luke 13:1–17

At that time, some people came and reported to him about the
Galileans whose blood Pilate had mixed with their sacrifices.
And he responded to them, "Do you think that these Galileans
were more sinful than all the other Galileans because they
suffered these things? No, I tell you; but unless you repent, you
will all perish as well. Or those eighteen that the tower in Siloam
fell on and killed—do you think they were more sinful than all
the other people who live in Jerusalem? No, I tell you; but unless
you repent, you will all perish as well."

And he told this parable: "A man had a fig tree that was
planted in his vineyard. He came looking for fruit on it and
found none. He told the vineyard worker, 'Listen, for three years
I have come looking for fruit on this fig tree and haven't found
any. Cut it down! Why should it even waste the soil?'

"But he replied to him, 'Sir, leave it this year also, until I dig
around it and fertilize it. Perhaps it will produce fruit next year,
but if not, you can cut it down.'"

As he was teaching in one of the synagogues on the Sabbath,
a woman was there who had been disabled by a spirit for over
eighteen years. She was bent over and could not straighten up
at all. When Jesus saw her, he called out to her, "Woman, you
are free of your disability." Then he laid his hands on her, and
instantly she was restored and began to glorify God.

But the leader of the synagogue, indignant because Jesus had
healed on the Sabbath, responded by telling the crowd, "There
are six days when work should be done; therefore come on
those days and be healed and not on the Sabbath day."

But the Lord answered him and said, "Hypocrites! Doesn't each one of you untie his ox or donkey from the feeding trough on the Sabbath and lead it to water? Satan has bound this woman, a daughter of Abraham, for eighteen years—shouldn't she be untied from this bondage on the Sabbath day?"

When he had said these things, all his adversaries were humiliated, but the whole crowd was rejoicing over all the glorious things he was doing.

Luke 13:22–35

He went through one town and village after another, teaching and making his way to Jerusalem. "Lord," someone asked him, "are only a few people going to be saved?"

He said to them, "Make every effort to enter through the narrow door, because I tell you, many will try to enter and won't be able once the homeowner gets up and shuts the door. Then you will stand outside and knock on the door, saying, 'Lord, open up for us!' He will answer you, 'I don't know you or where you're from.' Then you will say, 'We ate and drank in your presence, and you taught in our streets.' But he will say, 'I tell you, I don't know you or where you're from. Get away from me, all you evildoers!' There will be weeping and gnashing of teeth in that place, when you see Abraham, Isaac, Jacob, and all the prophets in the kingdom of God, but yourselves thrown out. They will come from east and west, from north and south, to share the banquet in the kingdom of God. Note this: Some who are last will be first, and some who are first will be last."

At that time some Pharisees came and told him, "Go, get out of here. Herod wants to kill you."

He said to them, "Go tell that fox, 'Look, I'm driving out demons and performing healings today and tomorrow, and on the third day I will complete my work.' Yet it is necessary that I travel today, tomorrow, and the next day, because it is not possible for a prophet to perish outside of Jerusalem.

"Jerusalem, Jerusalem, who kills the prophets and stones those who are sent to her. How often I wanted to gather your children together, as a hen gathers her chicks under her wings, but you were not willing! See, your house is abandoned to you. I

tell you, you will not see me until the time comes when you say,
'Blessed is he who comes in the name of the Lord'! "

This is the Word of the Lord. Thanks be to God.

GLORIA
Glory be to God the Father, God the Son, and God the Holy
Spirit. As it was in the beginning, is now, and will be forever,
world without end.

THE LORD'S PRAYER
Our Father in heaven,
Hallowed be your name.
Your kingdom come,
Your will be done
on earth as it is in heaven.
Give us this day our daily bread.
And forgive us our debts,
as we also have forgiven our debtors.
And lead us not into temptation
But deliver us from the evil one.
For yours is the kingdom and the power and the glory forever.
Amen.

BLESSING
May your faithful love rest on us, LORD, for we put our hope
in you.
Psalm 33:22

DAY 17 EVENING PRAYER

Call to Prayer

Save us, LORD our God, and gather us from the nations, so
that we may give thanks to your holy name and rejoice in your
praise.
Psalm 106:47

Confession of Sin

O Almighty and merciful Father, you pour your benefits upon
us—forgive the unthankfulness with which we have responded
to your goodness. We have remained before you with dead
and senseless hearts, unkindled with love of your gentle and
enduring goodness. Turn us, O merciful Father, and so shall we
be turned. Make us with our whole heart to hunger and thirst
after you, and with all our longing to desire you. Amen.
Anselm

As far as the east is from the west, so far has he removed our
transgressions from us.
Psalm 103:12

Canticle

Great and awe-inspiring are your works,
Lord God, the Almighty;
just and true are your ways,
King of the nations.
Lord, who will not fear
and glorify your name?
For you alone are holy.
All the nations will come
and worship before you
because your righteous acts
have been revealed.
Revelation 15:3–4

Luke 14:7–33

He told a parable to those who were invited, when he noticed how they would choose the best places for themselves: "When you are invited by someone to a wedding banquet, don't sit in the place of honor, because a more distinguished person than you may have been invited by your host. The one who invited both of you may come and say to you, 'Give your place to this man,' and then in humiliation, you will proceed to take the lowest place.

"But when you are invited, go and sit in the lowest place, so that when the one who invited you comes, he will say to you, 'Friend, move up higher.' You will then be honored in the presence of all the other guests. For everyone who exalts himself will be humbled, and the one who humbles himself will be exalted."

He also said to the one who had invited him, "When you give a lunch or a dinner, don't invite your friends, your brothers or sisters, your relatives, or your rich neighbors, because they might invite you back, and you would be repaid. On the contrary, when you host a banquet, invite those who are poor, maimed, lame, or blind. And you will be blessed, because they cannot repay you; for you will be repaid at the resurrection of the righteous."

When one of those who reclined at the table with him heard these things, he said to him, "Blessed is the one who will eat bread in the kingdom of God!"

Then he told him, "A man was giving a large banquet and invited many. At the time of the banquet, he sent his servant to tell those who were invited, 'Come, because everything is now ready.'

"But without exception they all began to make excuses. The first one said to him, 'I have bought a field, and I must go out and see it. I ask you to excuse me.'

"Another said, 'I have bought five yoke of oxen, and I'm going to try them out. I ask you to excuse me.'

"And another said, 'I just got married, and therefore I'm unable to come.'

"So the servant came back and reported these things to his master. Then in anger, the master of the house told his servant, 'Go out quickly into the streets and alleys of the city, and bring in here the poor, maimed, blind, and lame.'

"'Master,' the servant said, 'what you ordered has been done, and there's still room.'

"Then the master told the servant, 'Go out into the highways and hedges and make them come in, so that my house may be filled. For I tell you, not one of those people who were invited will enjoy my banquet.'"

Now great crowds were traveling with him. So he turned and said to them, "If anyone comes to me and does not hate his own father and mother, wife and children, brothers and sisters—yes, and even his own life—he cannot be my disciple. Whoever does not bear his own cross and come after me cannot be my disciple.

"For which of you, wanting to build a tower, doesn't first sit down and calculate the cost to see if he has enough to complete it? Otherwise, after he has laid the foundation and cannot finish it, all the onlookers will begin to ridicule him, saying, 'This man started to build and wasn't able to finish.'

"Or what king, going to war against another king, will not first sit down and decide if he is able with ten thousand to oppose the one who comes against him with twenty thousand? If not, while the other is still far off, he sends a delegation and asks for terms of peace. In the same way, therefore, every one of you who does not renounce all his possessions cannot be my disciple."

This is the Word of the Lord. Thanks be to God.

Gloria

Glory be to God the Father, God the Son, and God the Holy Spirit. As it was in the beginning, is now, and will be forever, world without end.

The Lord's Prayer

Our Father in heaven,
Hallowed be your name.
Your kingdom come,
Your will be done
on earth as it is in heaven.
Give us this day our daily bread.
And forgive us our debts,
as we also have forgiven our debtors.
And lead us not into temptation
But deliver us from the evil one.
For yours is the kingdom and the power and the glory forever.
Amen.

Intercessions and Personal Requests

Prayer of the Church

Give us grace, O Lord, to answer readily the call of our Savior
Jesus Christ and proclaim to all people the Good News of his
salvation, that we and the whole world may perceive the glory
of his marvelous works; who lives and reigns with you and the
Holy Spirit, one God, for ever and ever.
The Book of Common Prayer

Blessing

The Lord Almighty grant us a peaceful night and a perfect end.
Amen.

DAY 18 MORNING PRAYER

CALL TO PRAYER

The Lord is full of compassion and mercy: O come, let us adore him.

CONFESSION OF FAITH

We believe in one God,
the Father, the Almighty,
maker of heaven and earth,
of all that is, seen and unseen.
From the Nicene Creed

CANTICLE

Zion, herald of good news,
go up on a high mountain.
Jerusalem, herald of good news,
raise your voice loudly.
Raise it, do not be afraid!
Say to the cities of Judah,
"Here is your God!"
See, the Lord GOD comes with strength,
and his power establishes his rule.
His wages are with him,
and his reward accompanies him.
He protects his flock like a shepherd;
he gathers the lambs in his arms
and carries them in the fold of his garment.
He gently leads those that are nursing.
Isaiah 40:9–11

Luke 15:1–32

All the tax collectors and sinners were approaching to listen to him. And the Pharisees and scribes were complaining, "This man welcomes sinners and eats with them."

So he told them this parable: "What man among you, who has a hundred sheep and loses one of them, does not leave the ninety-nine in the open field and go after the lost one until he finds it? When he has found it, he joyfully puts it on his shoulders, and coming home, he calls his friends and neighbors together, saying to them, 'Rejoice with me, because I have found my lost sheep!' I tell you, in the same way, there will be more joy in heaven over one sinner who repents than over ninety-nine righteous people who don't need repentance.

"Or what woman who has ten silver coins, if she loses one coin, does not light a lamp, sweep the house, and search carefully until she finds it? When she finds it, she calls her friends and neighbors together, saying, 'Rejoice with me, because I have found the silver coin I lost!' I tell you, in the same way, there is joy in the presence of God's angels over one sinner who repents."

He also said, "A man had two sons. The younger of them said to his father, 'Father, give me the share of the estate I have coming to me.' So he distributed the assets to them. Not many days later, the younger son gathered together all he had and traveled to a distant country, where he squandered his estate in foolish living. After he had spent everything, a severe famine struck that country, and he had nothing. Then he went to work for one of the citizens of that country, who sent him into his fields to feed pigs. He longed to eat his fill from the pods that the pigs were eating, but no one would give him anything. When he came to his senses, he said, 'How many of my father's hired workers have more than enough food, and here I am dying of hunger! I'll get up, go to my father, and say to him, "Father, I have sinned against heaven and in your sight. I'm no longer worthy to be called your son. Make me like one of your hired workers."' So he got up and went to his father. But while the son was still a long way off, his father saw him and was filled with compassion. He ran, threw his arms around his neck, and kissed him. The son said to him, 'Father, I have sinned against heaven and in your sight. I'm no longer worthy to be called your son.'

"But the father told his servants, 'Quick! Bring out the best robe and put it on him; put a ring on his finger and sandals on his feet. Then bring the fattened calf and slaughter it, and let's celebrate with a feast, because this son of mine was dead and is alive again; he was lost and is found!' So they began to celebrate.

"Now his older son was in the field; as he came near the house, he heard music and dancing. So he summoned one of the servants, questioning what these things meant. 'Your brother is here,' he told him, 'and your father has slaughtered the fattened calf because he has him back safe and sound.'

"Then he became angry and didn't want to go in. So his father came out and pleaded with him. But he replied to his father, 'Look, I have been slaving many years for you, and I have never disobeyed your orders, yet you never gave me a goat so that I could celebrate with my friends. But when this son of yours came, who has devoured your assets with prostitutes, you slaughtered the fattened calf for him.'

"'Son,' he said to him, 'you are always with me, and everything I have is yours. But we had to celebrate and rejoice, because this brother of yours was dead and is alive again; he was lost and is found.'"

This is the Word of the Lord. Thanks be to God.

Gloria

Glory be to God the Father, God the Son, and God the Holy Spirit. As it was in the beginning, is now, and will be forever, world without end.

The Lord's Prayer

Our Father in heaven,
Hallowed be your name.
Your kingdom come,

Your will be done
on earth as it is in heaven.
Give us this day our daily bread.
And forgive us our debts,
as we also have forgiven our debtors.
And lead us not into temptation
But deliver us from the evil one.
For yours is the kingdom and the power and the glory forever.
Amen.

INTERCESSIONS AND PERSONAL REQUESTS

PRAYER OF THE CHURCH

We beg you, Lord, to help and defend us. Deliver the oppressed. Pity the insignificant. Raise the fallen. Show yourself to the needy. Heal the sick. Bring back those of your people who have gone astray. Feed the hungry. Lift up the weak. Take off the prisoners' chains. May every nation come to know that you alone are God, that Jesus is your Child, that we are your people, the sheep that you pasture. Amen.
Clement of Rome

BLESSING

The peace of God, which passes all understanding, keep your hearts and minds in the knowledge and love of God, and of his Son Jesus Christ our Lord; and the blessing of God Almighty, the Father, the Son, and the Holy Spirit, be among you, and remain with you always. Amen.

DAY 18 MIDDAY PRAYER

Cast your burden on the LORD, and he will sustain you; he will never allow the righteous to be shaken.
Psalm 55:22

MIDDAY READING

Luke 16:1–16

Now he said to the disciples, "There was a rich man who received an accusation that his manager was squandering his possessions. So he called the manager in and asked, 'What is this I hear about you? Give an account of your management, because you can no longer be my manager.'

"Then the manager said to himself, 'What will I do since my master is taking the management away from me? I'm not strong enough to dig; I'm ashamed to beg. I know what I'll do so that when I'm removed from management, people will welcome me into their homes.'

"So he summoned each one of his master's debtors. 'How much do you owe my master?' he asked the first one.

"'A hundred measures of olive oil,' he said.

"'Take your invoice,' he told him, 'sit down quickly, and write fifty.'

"Next he asked another, 'How much do you owe?'

"'A hundred measures of wheat,' he said.

"'Take your invoice,' he told him, 'and write eighty.'

"The master praised the unrighteous manager because he had acted shrewdly. For the children of this age are more shrewd than the children of light in dealing with their own people. And I tell you, make friends for yourselves by means of worldly wealth so that when it fails, they may welcome you into eternal dwellings. Whoever is faithful in very little is also faithful in much, and whoever is unrighteous in very little is also unrighteous in much. So if you have not been faithful with worldly wealth, who will trust you with what is genuine? And if you have not been faithful with what belongs to someone else, who will give you what is your own? No servant can serve two masters, since either he will hate one and love the other, or he will be devoted to one and despise the other. You cannot serve both God and money."

The Pharisees, who were lovers of money, were listening to all these things and scoffing at him. And he told them, "You are the ones who justify yourselves in the sight of others, but God knows your hearts. For what is highly admired by people is revolting in God's sight.

"The Law and the Prophets were until John; since then, the good news of the kingdom of God has been proclaimed, and everyone is urgently invited to enter it."

This is the Word of the Lord. Thanks be to God.

Gloria

Glory be to God the Father, God the Son, and God the Holy Spirit. As it was in the beginning, is now, and will be forever, world without end.

The Lord's Prayer

Our Father in heaven,
Hallowed be your name.
Your kingdom come,
Your will be done
on earth as it is in heaven.
Give us this day our daily bread.
And forgive us our debts,
as we also have forgiven our debtors.
And lead us not into temptation
But deliver us from the evil one.
For yours is the kingdom and the power and the glory forever.
Amen.

May the LORD bless you and protect you; may the LORD make
his face shine on you and be gracious to you; may
the LORD look with favor on you and give you peace.
Numbers 6:24–26

DAY 18 EVENING PRAYER

CALL TO PRAYER

Enter his gates with thanksgiving and his courts with praise.
Give thanks to him and bless his name.
Psalm 100:4

CONFESSION OF SIN

O Lord and Master, I am unworthy both of heaven and of earth,
because I have surrendered myself to sin, and become the slave
of worldly pleasures. Yet, since you created me, and since you
can shape me as you want, I do not despair of salvation; but
made bold by your compassionate love, I come before you.
Receive me, dear Lord, as you received the harlot, the thief, the
tax collector, and even the prodigal son. You love all people, so
pour out your love upon me. Lift from me the heavy burden of
sin, cleanse every stain of unrighteousness from me, and wash
me white with the waters of holiness.
Basil of Caesarea

The sacrifice pleasing to God is a broken spirit. You will not
despise a broken and humbled heart, God.
Psalm 51:17

CANTICLE

As for me—poor and in pain—
let your salvation protect me, God.
I will praise God's name with song
and exalt him with thanksgiving.

That will please the LORD more than an ox,
more than a bull with horns and hooves.
The humble will see it and rejoice.
You who seek God, take heart!
For the LORD listens to the needy
and does not despise
his own who are prisoners.
Psalm 69:29–33

EVENING READINGS

Luke 16:19–31

"There was a rich man who would dress in purple and fine
linen, feasting lavishly every day. But a poor man named
Lazarus, covered with sores, was lying at his gate. He longed to
be filled with what fell from the rich man's table, but instead the
dogs would come and lick his sores. One day the poor man died
and was carried away by the angels to Abraham's side. The rich
man also died and was buried. And being in torment in Hades,
he looked up and saw Abraham a long way off, with Lazarus at
his side. 'Father Abraham!' he called out, 'Have mercy on me
and send Lazarus to dip the tip of his finger in water and cool
my tongue, because I am in agony in this flame!'

"'Son,' Abraham said, 'remember that during your life you
received your good things, just as Lazarus received bad things,
but now he is comforted here, while you are in agony. Besides
all this, a great chasm has been fixed between us and you, so
that those who want to pass over from here to you cannot;
neither can those from there cross over to us.'

"'Father,' he said, 'then I beg you to send him to my father's
house—because I have five brothers—to warn them, so that
they won't also come to this place of torment.'

"But Abraham said, 'They have Moses and the prophets; they
should listen to them.'

"'No, father Abraham,' he said. 'But if someone from the dead
goes to them, they will repent.'

"But he told him, 'If they don't listen to Moses and the prophets, they will not be persuaded if someone rises from the dead.'"

Luke 17:11–19
While traveling to Jerusalem, he passed between Samaria and Galilee. As he entered a village, ten men with leprosy met him. They stood at a distance and raised their voices, saying, "Jesus, Master, have mercy on us!"

When he saw them, he told them, "Go and show yourselves to the priests." And while they were going, they were cleansed.

But one of them, seeing that he was healed, returned and, with a loud voice, gave glory to God. He fell facedown at his feet, thanking him. And he was a Samaritan.

Then Jesus said, "Were not ten cleansed? Where are the nine? Didn't any return to give glory to God except this foreigner?" And he told him, "Get up and go on your way. Your faith has saved you."

This is the Word of the Lord. Thanks be to God.

Gloria

Glory be to God the Father, God the Son, and God the Holy Spirit. As it was in the beginning, is now, and will be forever, world without end.

The Lord's Prayer

Our Father in heaven,
Hallowed be your name.
Your kingdom come,
Your will be done
on earth as it is in heaven.
Give us this day our daily bread.
And forgive us our debts,
as we also have forgiven our debtors.
And lead us not into temptation
But deliver us from the evil one.

For yours is the kingdom and the power and the glory forever.
Amen.

INTERCESSIONS AND PERSONAL REQUESTS

PRAYER OF THE CHURCH

Behold, Lord, an empty vessel that needs to be filled. My
Lord, fill it. I am weak in the faith; strengthen me. I am cold
in love; warm me and make me fervent, that my love may go
out to my neighbor. I do not have a strong and firm faith; at
times I doubt and am unable to trust you altogether. O Lord,
help me. Strengthen my faith and trust in you. In you I have
sealed the treasure of all I have. I am poor; you are rich and
came to be merciful to the poor. I am a sinner; you are upright.
With me, there is an abundance of sin; in you is the fullness of
righteousness. Therefore, I will remain with you of whom I can
receive, but to whom I may not give.
Martin Luther

BLESSING

The Almighty and merciful Lord, Father, Son, and Holy Spirit,
bless us and keep us, this night and evermore. Amen.

DAY 19 MORNING PRAYER

CALL TO PRAYER

I call to God, and the LORD will save me. I complain and groan
morning, noon, and night, and he hears my voice.
Psalm 55:16–17

CONFESSION OF FAITH

We believe in one Lord, Jesus Christ,
the only Son of God,
eternally begotten of the Father,
God from God, Light from Light,
true God from true God,
begotten, not made,
of one Being with the Father.
Through him all things were made.
For us and for our salvation
he came down from heaven:
by the power of the Holy Spirit
he became incarnate from the Virgin Mary,
and was made man.
For our sake he was crucified under Pontius Pilate;
he suffered death and was buried.
On the third day he rose again
in accordance with the Scriptures;
he ascended into heaven
and is seated at the right hand of the Father.
He will come again in glory to judge the living and the dead,
and his kingdom will have no end.
From the Nicene Creed

CANTICLE

I cry aloud to the LORD;
I plead aloud to the LORD for mercy.
I pour out my complaint before him;

I reveal my trouble to him.
Although my spirit is weak within me,
you know my way.
Psalm 142:1–3

Morning Readings

Luke 11:5–8

He also said to them, "Suppose one of you has a friend and
goes to him at midnight and says to him, 'Friend, lend me
three loaves of bread, because a friend of mine on a journey has
come to me, and I don't have anything to offer him.' Then he
will answer from inside and say, 'Don't bother me! The door is
already locked, and my children and I have gone to bed. I can't
get up to give you anything.' I tell you, even though he won't get
up and give him anything because he is his friend, yet because
of his friend's shameless boldness, he will get up and give him as
much as he needs."

Luke 17:5–10

The apostles said to the Lord, "Increase our faith."

"If you have faith the size of a mustard seed," the Lord
said, "you can say to this mulberry tree, 'Be uprooted and
planted in the sea,' and it will obey you.

"Which one of you having a servant tending sheep or plowing
will say to him when he comes in from the field, 'Come at once
and sit down to eat'? Instead, will he not tell him, 'Prepare
something for me to eat, get ready, and serve me while I eat and
drink; later you can eat and drink'? Does he thank that servant
because he did what was commanded? In the same way, when
you have done all that you were commanded, you should say,
'We are unworthy servants; we've only done our duty.'"

Luke 18:1–14

Now he told them a parable on the need for them to pray
always and not give up. "There was a judge in a certain town
who didn't fear God or respect people. And a widow in that
town kept coming to him, saying, 'Give me justice against my
adversary.'

"For a while he was unwilling, but later he said to himself, 'Even though I don't fear God or respect people, yet because this widow keeps pestering me, I will give her justice, so that she doesn't wear me out by her persistent coming.'"

Then the Lord said, "Listen to what the unjust judge says. Will not God grant justice to his elect who cry out to him day and night? Will he delay helping them? I tell you that he will swiftly grant them justice. Nevertheless, when the Son of Man comes, will he find faith on earth?"

He also told this parable to some who trusted in themselves that they were righteous and looked down on everyone else: "Two men went up to the temple to pray, one a Pharisee and the other a tax collector. The Pharisee was standing and praying like this about himself: 'God, I thank you that I'm not like other people—greedy, unrighteous, adulterers, or even like this tax collector. I fast twice a week; I give a tenth of everything I get.'

"But the tax collector, standing far off, would not even raise his eyes to heaven but kept striking his chest and saying, 'God, have mercy on me, a sinner!' I tell you, this one went down to his house justified rather than the other, because everyone who exalts himself will be humbled, but the one who humbles himself will be exalted."

This is the Word of the Lord. Thanks be to God.

Gloria

Glory be to God the Father, God the Son, and God the Holy Spirit. As it was in the beginning, is now, and will be forever, world without end.

The Lord's Prayer

Our Father in heaven,
Hallowed be your name.
Your kingdom come,
Your will be done
on earth as it is in heaven.
Give us this day our daily bread.

And forgive us our debts,
as we also have forgiven our debtors.
And lead us not into temptation
But deliver us from the evil one.
For yours is the kingdom and the power and the glory forever.
Amen.

Intercessions and Personal Requests

Prayer of the Church

O Lord our God and heavenly Father! We, your unworthy children, come into your most holy and heavenly presence to give you praise and glory for your great mercies and blessings—especially that you have preserved us this night past and have given us quiet rest to our bodies, and brought us now safely to the beginning of this day. Lord, open our eyes every day more and more to see and consider your great and marvelous love to us, that our hearts may be drawn yet nearer to you—even more to love you, fear you, and obey you.

Arthur Dent

Blessing

Now to him who is able to do above and beyond all that we ask or think according to the power that works in us—to him be glory in the church and in Christ Jesus to all generations, forever and ever. Amen.

Ephesians 3:20–21

DAY 19 MIDDAY PRAYER

Call to Prayer

I will sing of faithful love and justice; I will sing praise to you, Lord.

Psalm 101:1

Luke 18:18–34

A ruler asked him, "Good teacher, what must I do to inherit eternal life?"

"Why do you call me good?" Jesus asked him. "No one is good except God alone. You know the commandments: **Do not commit adultery; do not murder; do not steal; do not bear false witness; honor your father and mother.**"

"I have kept all these from my youth," he said.

When Jesus heard this, he told him, "You still lack one thing: Sell all you have and distribute it to the poor, and you will have treasure in heaven. Then come, follow me."

After he heard this, he became extremely sad, because he was very rich.

Seeing that he became sad, Jesus said, "How hard it is for those who have wealth to enter the kingdom of God! For it is easier for a camel to go through the eye of a needle than for a rich person to enter the kingdom of God."

Those who heard this asked, "Then who can be saved?"

He replied, "What is impossible with man is possible with God."

Then Peter said, "Look, we have left what we had and followed you."

So he said to them, "Truly I tell you, there is no one who has left a house, wife or brothers or sisters, parents or children because of the kingdom of God, who will not receive many times more at this time, and eternal life in the age to come."

Then he took the Twelve aside and told them, "See, we are going up to Jerusalem. Everything that is written through the prophets about the Son of Man will be accomplished. For he will be handed over to the Gentiles, and he will be mocked, insulted, spit on; and after they flog him, they will kill him, and he will rise on the third day."

They understood none of these things. The meaning of the saying was hidden from them, and they did not grasp what was said.

This is the Word of the Lord. Thanks be to God.

Gloria

Glory be to God the Father, God the Son, and God the Holy Spirit. As it was in the beginning, is now, and will be forever, world without end.

The Lord's Prayer

Our Father in heaven,
Hallowed be your name.
Your kingdom come,
Your will be done
on earth as it is in heaven.
Give us this day our daily bread.
And forgive us our debts,
as we also have forgiven our debtors.
And lead us not into temptation
But deliver us from the evil one.
For yours is the kingdom and the power and the glory forever.
Amen.

Blessing

May your faithful love rest on us, Lord, for we put our hope in you.
Psalm 33:22

DAY 19 EVENING PRAYER

Call to Prayer

This is the Lord's declaration. I will look favorably on this kind of person: one who is humble, submissive in spirit, and trembles at my word.
Isaiah 66:2

Confession of Sin

Lord Jesus Christ, you carry the lost sheep back into the fold in your arms, and delight to hear the confession of the tax collector—graciously remit all my guilt and sin. Lord, you hear the penitent thief, you have set a heritage of mercy for your saints, and have not withheld pardon from the sinner—hear the prayers of your servants according to your mercy. Amen.
Wilhelm Loehe

If we confess our sins, he is faithful and righteous to forgive us our sins and to cleanse us from all unrighteousness.
1 John 1:9

Canticle

I will lead the blind by a way they did not know;
I will guide them on paths they have not known.
I will turn darkness to light in front of them
and rough places into level ground.
This is what I will do for them,
and I will not abandon them.
Isaiah 42:16

Evening Readings

Mark 10:35–52
James and John, the sons of Zebedee, approached him and said, "Teacher, we want you to do whatever we ask you."

"What do you want me to do for you?" he asked them.

They answered him, "Allow us to sit at your right and at your left in your glory."

Jesus said to them, "You don't know what you're asking. Are you able to drink the cup I drink or to be baptized with the baptism I am baptized with?"

"We are able," they told him.

Jesus said to them, "You will drink the cup I drink, and you will be baptized with the baptism I am baptized with. But to sit at my right or left is not mine to give; instead, it is for those for whom it has been prepared."

When the ten disciples heard this, they began to be indignant with James and John. Jesus called them over and said to them, "You know that those who are regarded as rulers of the Gentiles lord it over them, and those in high positions act as tyrants over them. But it is not so among you. On the contrary, whoever wants to become great among you will be your servant, and whoever wants to be first among you will be a slave to all. For even the Son of Man did not come to be served, but to serve, and to give his life as a ransom for many."

They came to Jericho. And as he was leaving Jericho with his disciples and a large crowd, Bartimaeus (the son of Timaeus), a blind beggar, was sitting by the road. When he heard that it was Jesus of Nazareth, he began to cry out, "Jesus, Son of David, have mercy on me!" Many warned him to keep quiet, but he was crying out all the more, "Have mercy on me, Son of David!"

Jesus stopped and said, "Call him."

So they called the blind man and said to him, "Have courage! Get up; he's calling for you." He threw off his coat, jumped up, and came to Jesus.

Then Jesus answered him, "What do you want me to do for you?"

"*Rabboni*," the blind man said to him, "I want to see."

Jesus said to him, "Go, your faith has saved you." Immediately he could see and began to follow Jesus on the road.

Luke 19:1–10

He entered Jericho and was passing through. There was a man named Zacchaeus who was a chief tax collector, and he was rich. He was trying to see who Jesus was, but he was not able because of the crowd, since he was a short man. So running ahead, he climbed up a sycamore tree to see Jesus, since he was about to pass that way. When Jesus came to the place, he looked up and said to him, "Zacchaeus, hurry and come down because today it is necessary for me to stay at your house."

So he quickly came down and welcomed him joyfully. All who saw it began to complain, "He's gone to stay with a sinful man."

But Zacchaeus stood there and said to the Lord, "Look, I'll give half of my possessions to the poor, Lord. And if I have extorted anything from anyone, I'll pay back four times as much."

"Today salvation has come to this house," Jesus told him, "because he too is a son of Abraham. For the Son of Man has come to seek and to save the lost."

This is the Word of the Lord. Thanks be to God.

GLORIA

Glory be to God the Father, God the Son, and God the Holy Spirit. As it was in the beginning, is now, and will be forever, world without end.

THE LORD'S PRAYER

Our Father in heaven,
Hallowed be your name.
Your kingdom come,
Your will be done
on earth as it is in heaven.
Give us this day our daily bread.
And forgive us our debts,
as we also have forgiven our debtors.
And lead us not into temptation
But deliver us from the evil one.
For yours is the kingdom and the power and the glory forever.
Amen.

INTERCESSIONS AND PERSONAL REQUESTS

PRAYER OF THE CHURCH

Father of heaven, whose goodness has brought us in safety to the close of this day, another day is now gone, and added to those, for which we were before accountable. Give us grace

to endeavor after a truly Christian spirit to seek to attain that temper of forbearance and patience of which our blessed Savior has set us the highest example; and which, while it prepares us for the spiritual happiness of the life to come, will secure to us the best enjoyment of what this world can give. Incline us, O God, to think humbly of ourselves, to be severe only in the examination of our own conduct, to consider our fellow-creatures with kindness, and to judge of all they say and do with that charity which we would desire from them ourselves.
Jane Austen

BLESSING
The Lord Almighty grant us a peaceful night and a perfect end. Amen.

DAY 20 MORNING PRAYER

CALL TO PRAYER

Wake up, my soul! Wake up, harp and lyre! I will wake up the dawn.
Psalm 57:8

CONFESSION OF FAITH

We believe in the Holy Spirit, the Lord, the giver of life,
who proceeds from the Father and the Son.
With the Father and the Son he is worshiped and glorified.
He has spoken through the Prophets.
We believe in one holy catholic and apostolic Church.
We acknowledge one baptism for the forgiveness of sins.
We look for the resurrection of the dead,
and the life of the world to come. Amen.
From the Nicene Creed

CANTICLE

I love the Lord, because he has heard
my voice and my pleas for mercy.
Because he inclined his ear to me,
therefore I will call on him as long as I live.
The snares of death encompassed me;
the pangs of Sheol laid hold on me;
I suffered distress and anguish.
Then I called on the name of the Lord:
"O Lord, I pray, deliver my soul!"
Psalm 116:1–4

MORNING READING

John 11:1–16
Now a man was sick, Lazarus from Bethany, the village of Mary and her sister Martha. Mary was the one who anointed the Lord

with perfume and wiped his feet with her hair, and it was her brother Lazarus who was sick. So the sisters sent a message to him: "Lord, the one you love is sick."

When Jesus heard it, he said, "This sickness will not end in death but is for the glory of God, so that the Son of God may be glorified through it." Now Jesus loved Martha, her sister, and Lazarus. So when he heard that he was sick, he stayed two more days in the place where he was. Then after that, he said to the disciples, "Let's go to Judea again."

"Rabbi," the disciples told him, "just now the Jews tried to stone you, and you're going there again?"

"Aren't there twelve hours in a day?" Jesus answered. "If anyone walks during the day, he doesn't stumble, because he sees the light of this world. But if anyone walks during the night, he does stumble, because the light is not in him."

He said this, and then he told them, "Our friend Lazarus has fallen asleep, but I'm on my way to wake him up."

Then the disciples said to him, "Lord, if he has fallen asleep, he will get well."

Jesus, however, was speaking about his death, but they thought he was speaking about natural sleep. So Jesus then told them plainly, "Lazarus has died. I'm glad for you that I wasn't there so that you may believe. But let's go to him."

Then Thomas (called "Twin") said to his fellow disciples, "Let's go too so that we may die with him."

This is the Word of the Lord. Thanks be to God.

Gloria

Glory be to God the Father, God the Son, and God the Holy Spirit. As it was in the beginning, is now, and will be forever, world without end.

The Lord's Prayer

Our Father in heaven,
Hallowed be your name.
Your kingdom come,

Your will be done
on earth as it is in heaven.
Give us this day our daily bread.
And forgive us our debts,
as we also have forgiven our debtors.
And lead us not into temptation
But deliver us from the evil one.
For yours is the kingdom and the power and the glory forever.
Amen.

INTERCESSIONS AND PERSONAL REQUESTS

PRAYER OF THE CHURCH

O God, you have made of one blood all the peoples of the earth, and sent your blessed Son to preach peace to those who are far off and to those who are near. Grant that people everywhere may seek after you and find you; bring the nations into your fold; pour out your Spirit upon all flesh; and hasten the coming of your kingdom; through Jesus Christ our Lord.
The Book of Common Prayer

BLESSING

Now may the God of hope fill you with all joy and peace as you believe, so that you may overflow with hope by the power of the Holy Spirit.
Romans 15:13

DAY 20 MIDDAY PRAYER

CALL TO PRAYER

Rest in God alone, my soul, for my hope comes from him.
Psalm 62:5

Midday Reading

John 11:17–46

When Jesus arrived, he found that Lazarus had already been in the tomb four days. Bethany was near Jerusalem (less than two miles away). Many of the Jews had come to Martha and Mary to comfort them about their brother.

As soon as Martha heard that Jesus was coming, she went to meet him, but Mary remained seated in the house. Then Martha said to Jesus, "Lord, if you had been here, my brother wouldn't have died. Yet even now I know that whatever you ask from God, God will give you."

"Your brother will rise again," Jesus told her.

Martha said to him, "I know that he will rise again in the resurrection at the last day."

Jesus said to her, "I am the resurrection and the life. The one who believes in me, even if he dies, will live. Everyone who lives and believes in me will never die. Do you believe this?"

"Yes, Lord," she told him, "I believe you are the Messiah, the Son of God, who comes into the world."

Having said this, she went back and called her sister Mary, saying in private, "The Teacher is here and is calling for you."

As soon as Mary heard this, she got up quickly and went to him. Jesus had not yet come into the village but was still in the place where Martha had met him. The Jews who were with her in the house consoling her saw that Mary got up quickly and went out. They followed her, supposing that she was going to the tomb to cry there.

As soon as Mary came to where Jesus was and saw him, she fell at his feet and told him, "Lord, if you had been here, my brother wouldn't have died!"

When Jesus saw her crying, and the Jews who had come with her crying, he was deeply moved in his spirit and troubled. "Where have you put him?" he asked.

"Lord," they told him, "come and see."

Jesus wept.

So the Jews said, "See how he loved him!" But some of them said, "Couldn't he who opened the blind man's eyes also have kept this man from dying?"

Then Jesus, deeply moved again, came to the tomb. It was a cave, and a stone was lying against it. "Remove the stone," Jesus said.

Martha, the dead man's sister, told him, "Lord, there is already a stench because he has been dead four days."

Jesus said to her, "Didn't I tell you that if you believed you would see the glory of God?"

So they removed the stone. Then Jesus raised his eyes and said, "Father, I thank you that you heard me. I know that you always hear me, but because of the crowd standing here I said this, so that they may believe you sent me." After he said this, he shouted with a loud voice, "Lazarus, come out!" The dead man came out bound hand and foot with linen strips and with his face wrapped in a cloth. Jesus said to them, "Unwrap him and let him go."

Therefore, many of the Jews who came to Mary and saw what he did believed in him. But some of them went to the Pharisees and told them what Jesus had done.

This is the Word of the Lord. Thanks be to God.

Gloria

Glory be to God the Father, God the Son, and God the Holy Spirit. As it was in the beginning, is now, and will be forever, world without end.

The Lord's Prayer

Our Father in heaven,
Hallowed be your name.
Your kingdom come,
Your will be done
on earth as it is in heaven.
Give us this day our daily bread.
And forgive us our debts,
as we also have forgiven our debtors.
And lead us not into temptation
But deliver us from the evil one.

For yours is the kingdom and the power and the glory forever.
Amen.

May [the Lord] give you what your heart desires and fulfill
your whole purpose. May the Lord fulfill all your requests.
Psalm 20:4–5

DAY 20 EVENING PRAYER

Call to Prayer

Blessed be the Lord God, the God of Israel, who alone does
wonders.
Psalm 72:18

Confession of Sin

O Lord, as long as I am apart from you, I am self-satisfied,
because I have no standard by which to measure my low stature.
But when I come near to you, there for the first time I see myself.
In your light I behold my darkness. In your purity I behold my
corruption. My very confession of sin is the fruit of holiness.
Oh, let me gaze on you more and more until, in the vision of
your brightness, I loathe the sight of my impurity; until, in the
blaze of that glory which human eye has not seen, I fall prostrate,
blinded, broken, to rise again a new creation in you. Amen.
George Matheson

How joyful is the one whose transgression is forgiven, whose
sin is covered!
Psalm 32:1

Canticle

This is the declaration of the Lord
to my Lord:

"Sit at my right hand
until I make your enemies your footstool."
The LORD will extend your mighty scepter from Zion.
Rule over your surrounding enemies.
Your people will volunteer
on your day of battle.
In holy splendor, from the womb of the dawn,
the dew of your youth belongs to you.
The LORD has sworn an oath and will not take it back:
"You are a priest forever
according to the pattern of Melchizedek."
Psalm 110:1–4

EVENING READINGS

John 12:1–11

Six days before the Passover, Jesus came to Bethany where
Lazarus was, the one Jesus had raised from the dead. So they
gave a dinner for him there; Martha was serving them, and
Lazarus was one of those reclining at the table with him. Then
Mary took a pound of perfume, pure and expensive nard,
anointed Jesus's feet, and wiped his feet with her hair. So the
house was filled with the fragrance of the perfume.

Then one of his disciples, Judas Iscariot (who was about
to betray him), said, "Why wasn't this perfume sold for three
hundred denarii and given to the poor?" He didn't say this
because he cared about the poor but because he was a thief. He
was in charge of the money-bag and would steal part of what
was put in it.

Jesus answered, "Leave her alone; she has kept it for the day
of my burial. For you always have the poor with you, but you do
not always have me."

Then a large crowd of the Jews learned he was there. They
came not only because of Jesus but also to see Lazarus, the one
he had raised from the dead. But the chief priests had decided

to kill Lazarus also, because he was the reason many of the Jews were deserting them and believing in Jesus.

Matthew 26:14–16
Then one of the Twelve, the man called Judas Iscariot, went to the chief priests and said, "What are you willing to give me if I hand him over to you?" So they weighed out thirty pieces of silver for him. And from that time he started looking for a good opportunity to betray him.

This is the Word of the Lord. Thanks be to God.

GLORIA
Glory be to God the Father, God the Son, and God the Holy Spirit. As it was in the beginning, is now, and will be forever, world without end.

THE LORD'S PRAYER
Our Father in heaven,
Hallowed be your name.
Your kingdom come,
Your will be done
on earth as it is in heaven.
Give us this day our daily bread.
And forgive us our debts,
as we also have forgiven our debtors.
And lead us not into temptation
But deliver us from the evil one.
For yours is the kingdom and the power and the glory forever.
Amen.

Prayer of the Church

Grant, most sweet and loving Jesus, that I may seek my repose in you above every creature; above all health and beauty; above every honor and glory; every power and dignity; above all knowledge and cleverness, all riches and arts, all joy and gladness; above all fame and praise, all sweetness and consolation; above every hope and promise, every merit and desire; above all the gifts and favors that you can give or pour down on me; above all the joy and exultation that the mind can receive and feel; and finally, above the angels and archangels and all the heavenly host; above all things visible and invisible; and may I seek my repose in you above everything that is not you, my God. For you, O Lord my God, are above all things the best. You alone are most high, you alone most powerful. You alone are most sufficient and most satisfying, you alone most sweet and consoling. You alone are most beautiful and loving, you alone most noble and glorious above all things. In you is every perfection that has been or ever will be. Therefore, whatever you give me besides yourself, whatever you reveal to me concerning yourself, and whatever you promise, is too small and insufficient when I do not see and fully enjoy you alone. For my heart cannot rest or be fully content until, rising above all gifts and every created thing, it rests in you.
Thomas à Kempis

Blessing

The Almighty and merciful Lord, Father, Son, and Holy Spirit, bless us and keep us, this night and evermore. Amen.

DAY 21 MORNING PRAYER

CALL TO PRAYER

Lift up your heads, you gates! Rise up, ancient doors! Then
the King of glory will come in. Who is this King of glory?
The LORD, strong and mighty, the LORD, mighty in battle.
Psalm 24:7–8

CONFESSION OF FAITH

I believe in Jesus Christ, who, existing in the form of God,
did not consider equality with God
as something to be exploited.
Instead he emptied himself
by assuming the form of a servant,
taking on the likeness of humanity.
And when he had come as a man,
he humbled himself by becoming obedient
to the point of death—even to death on a cross.
For this reason God highly exalted him
and gave him the name
that is above every name,
so that at the name of Jesus
every knee will bow—in heaven and on earth
and under the earth—and every tongue will confess
that Jesus Christ is Lord,
to the glory of God the Father.
Philippians 2:6–11

CANTICLE

Give thanks to the LORD, for he is good;
his faithful love endures forever.
Let Israel say,
"His faithful love endures forever."
LORD, save us!
LORD, please grant us success!

He who comes in the name
of the LORD is blessed.
From the house of the LORD we bless you.
The LORD is God and has given us light.
Bind the festival sacrifice with cords
to the horns of the altar.
You are my God, and I will give you thanks.
You are my God; I will exalt you.
Give thanks to the LORD, for he is good;
his faithful love endures forever.
Psalm 118:1–2,25–29

MORNING READINGS

Mark 11:1–10

When they approached Jerusalem, at Bethphage and Bethany
near the Mount of Olives, he sent two of his disciples and told
them, "Go into the village ahead of you. As soon as you enter it,
you will find a colt tied there, on which no one has ever sat. Untie
it and bring it. If anyone says to you, 'Why are you doing this?'
say, 'The Lord needs it and will send it back here right away.'"

So they went and found a colt outside in the street, tied by a
door. They untied it, and some of those standing there said to
them, "What are you doing, untying the colt?" They answered
them just as Jesus had said; so they let them go.

They brought the colt to Jesus and threw their clothes on it,
and he sat on it. Many people spread their clothes on the road,
and others spread leafy branches cut from the fields. Those who
went ahead and those who followed shouted:

> **Hosanna!**
> **Blessed is he who comes**
> **in the name of the Lord!**
> Blessed is the coming kingdom
> of our father David!
> **Hosanna** in the highest heaven!

Matthew 21:12–22

Jesus went into the temple and threw out all those buying and
selling. He overturned the tables of the money changers and the

chairs of those selling doves. He said to them, "It is written, **my house will be called a house of prayer,** but you are making it a den of thieves!"

The blind and the lame came to him in the temple, and he healed them. When the chief priests and the scribes saw the wonders that he did and the children shouting in the temple, "Hosanna to the Son of David!" they were indignant and said to him, "Do you hear what these children are saying?"

Jesus replied, "Yes, have you never read:

> **You have prepared praise**
> **from the mouths of infants and nursing babies**?"

Then he left them, went out of the city to Bethany, and spent the night there.

Early in the morning, as he was returning to the city, he was hungry. Seeing a lone fig tree by the road, he went up to it and found nothing on it except leaves. And he said to it, "May no fruit ever come from you again!" At once the fig tree withered.

When the disciples saw it, they were amazed and said, "How did the fig tree wither so quickly?"

Jesus answered them, "Truly I tell you, if you have faith and do not doubt, you will not only do what was done to the fig tree, but even if you tell this mountain, 'Be lifted up and thrown into the sea,' it will be done. And if you believe, you will receive whatever you ask for in prayer."

This is the Word of the Lord. Thanks be to God.

Gloria

Glory be to God the Father, God the Son, and God the Holy Spirit. As it was in the beginning, is now, and will be forever, world without end.

The Lord's Prayer

Our Father in heaven,
Hallowed be your name.
Your kingdom come,
Your will be done

on earth as it is in heaven.
Give us this day our daily bread.
And forgive us our debts,
as we also have forgiven our debtors.
And lead us not into temptation
But deliver us from the evil one.
For yours is the kingdom and the power and the glory forever.
Amen.

Intercessions and Personal Requests

Prayer of the Church

Almighty and everlasting God, in your tender love for us you
sent your Son our Savior Jesus Christ to take upon himself
our nature, and to suffer death upon the Cross, giving us the
example of his great humility: Mercifully grant that we may
walk in the way of his suffering, and come to share in his
resurrection; through Jesus Christ our Lord, who lives and
reigns with you and the Holy Spirit, one God, for ever and ever.
Amen.
The Book of Common Prayer

Blessing

The grace of the Lord Jesus Christ, and the love of God, and the
fellowship of the Holy Spirit be with us all.
2 Corinthians 13:14

DAY 21 MIDDAY PRAYER

Call to Prayer

The Lord is in his holy temple; let the whole earth be silent in
his presence.
Habakkuk 2:20

John 12:20–50

Now some Greeks were among those who went up to worship at the festival. So they came to Philip, who was from Bethsaida in Galilee, and requested of him, "Sir, we want to see Jesus." Philip went and told Andrew; then Andrew and Philip went and told Jesus.

Jesus replied to them, "The hour has come for the Son of Man to be glorified. Truly I tell you, unless a grain of wheat falls to the ground and dies, it remains by itself. But if it dies, it produces much fruit. The one who loves his life will lose it, and the one who hates his life in this world will keep it for eternal life. If anyone serves me, he must follow me. Where I am, there my servant also will be. If anyone serves me, the Father will honor him.

"Now my soul is troubled. What should I say—Father, save me from this hour? But that is why I came to this hour. Father, glorify your name."

Then a voice came from heaven: "I have glorified it, and I will glorify it again."

The crowd standing there heard it and said it was thunder. Others said, "An angel has spoken to him."

Jesus responded, "This voice came, not for me, but for you. Now is the judgment of this world. Now the ruler of this world will be cast out. As for me, if I am lifted up from the earth I will draw all people to myself." He said this to indicate what kind of death he was about to die.

Then the crowd replied to him, "We have heard from the law that the Messiah will remain forever. So how can you say, 'The Son of Man must be lifted up'? Who is this Son of Man?"

Jesus answered, "The light will be with you only a little longer. Walk while you have the light so that darkness doesn't overtake you. The one who walks in darkness doesn't know where he's going. While you have the light, believe in the light so that you may become children of light." Jesus said this, then went away and hid from them.

Even though he had performed so many signs in their presence, they did not believe in him. This was to fulfill the word of Isaiah the prophet, who said:

> **Lord, who has believed our message?**
> **And to whom has the arm of the Lord been revealed?**

This is why they were unable to believe, because Isaiah also said:

> **He has blinded their eyes**
> **and hardened their hearts,**
> **so that they would not see with their eyes**
> **or understand with their hearts,**
> **and turn,**
> **and I would heal them.**

Isaiah said these things because he saw his glory and spoke about him.

Nevertheless, many did believe in him even among the rulers, but because of the Pharisees they did not confess him, so that they would not be banned from the synagogue. For they loved human praise more than praise from God.

Jesus cried out, "The one who believes in me believes not in me, but in him who sent me. And the one who sees me sees him who sent me. I have come as light into the world, so that everyone who believes in me would not remain in darkness. If anyone hears my words and doesn't keep them, I do not judge him; for I did not come to judge the world but to save the world. The one who rejects me and doesn't receive my sayings has this as his judge: The word I have spoken will judge him on the last day. For I have not spoken on my own, but the Father himself who sent me has given me a command to say everything I have said. I know that his command is eternal life. So the things that I speak, I speak just as the Father has told me."

This is the Word of the Lord. Thanks be to God.

Gloria

Glory be to God the Father, God the Son, and God the Holy Spirit. As it was in the beginning, is now, and will be forever, world without end.

The Lord's Prayer

Our Father in heaven,
Hallowed be your name.
Your kingdom come,
Your will be done
on earth as it is in heaven.
Give us this day our daily bread.
And forgive us our debts,
as we also have forgiven our debtors.
And lead us not into temptation
But deliver us from the evil one.
For yours is the kingdom and the power and the glory forever.
Amen.

Blessing

May the Lord cause you to increase and overflow with love for
one another and for everyone. . . . May he make your hearts
blameless in holiness before our God and Father at the coming
of our Lord Jesus with all his saints. Amen.
1 Thessalonians 2:12–13

DAY 21 EVENING PRAYER

Call to Prayer

Compassion and forgiveness belong to the Lord our God,
though we have rebelled against him.
Daniel 9:9

Confession of Sin

O Word of our God, I betrayed you, the Truth, with my
falsehood. I betrayed you when I promised to hallow the hours
that vanish away. In overtaking me, night does not find me
undarkened by sin. I did indeed pray, and I thought to stand
blameless at evening. But someway and somewhere my feet
have stumbled and fallen; for a storm-cloud swooped on me,

envious lest I be saved. Kindle for me your light, O Christ, restore me by your Presence.
Gregory of Nazianzus

The sacrifice pleasing to God is a broken spirit. You will not despise a broken and humbled heart, God.
Psalm 51:17

CANTICLE

Open the gates of righteousness for me;
I will enter through them
and give thanks to the LORD.
This is the LORD's gate;
the righteous will enter through it.
I will give thanks to you
because you have answered me
and have become my salvation.
The stone that the builders rejected
has become the cornerstone.
This came from the LORD;
it is wondrous in our sight.
This is the day the LORD has made;
let's rejoice and be glad in it.
Psalm 118:19–24

EVENING READING

Matthew 21:23–46
When he entered the temple, the chief priests and the elders of the people came to him as he was teaching and said, "By what authority are you doing these things? Who gave you this authority?"

Jesus answered them, "I will also ask you one question, and if you answer it for me, then I will tell you by what authority I do these things. Did John's baptism come from heaven, or was it of human origin?"

They discussed it among themselves, "If we say, 'From heaven,' he will say to us, 'Then why didn't you believe him?'

But if we say, 'Of human origin,' we're afraid of the crowd, because everyone considers John to be a prophet." So they answered Jesus, "We don't know."

And he said to them, "Neither will I tell you by what authority I do these things.

"What do you think? A man had two sons. He went to the first and said, 'My son, go work in the vineyard today.'

"He answered, 'I don't want to,' but later he changed his mind and went. Then the man went to the other and said the same thing. 'I will, sir,' he answered, but he didn't go. Which of the two did his father's will?"

They said, "The first."

Jesus said to them, "Truly I tell you, tax collectors and prostitutes are entering the kingdom of God before you. For John came to you in the way of righteousness, and you didn't believe him. Tax collectors and prostitutes did believe him; but you, when you saw it, didn't even change your minds then and believe him.

"Listen to another parable: There was a landowner, who planted a vineyard, put a fence around it, dug a winepress in it, and built a watchtower. He leased it to tenant farmers and went away. When the time came to harvest fruit, he sent his servants to the farmers to collect his fruit. The farmers took his servants, beat one, killed another, and stoned a third. Again, he sent other servants, more than the first group, and they did the same to them. Finally, he sent his son to them. 'They will respect my son,' he said.

"But when the tenant farmers saw the son, they said to each other, 'This is the heir. Come, let's kill him and take his inheritance.' So they seized him, threw him out of the vineyard, and killed him. Therefore, when the owner of the vineyard comes, what will he do to those farmers?"

"He will completely destroy those terrible men," they told him, "and lease his vineyard to other farmers who will give him his fruit at the harvest."

Jesus said to them, "Have you never read in the Scriptures:

The stone that the builders rejected
has become the cornerstone.

**This is what the Lord has done
and it is wonderful in our eyes?**

Therefore I tell you, the kingdom of God will be taken away from you and given to a people producing its fruit. Whoever falls on this stone will be broken to pieces; but on whomever it falls, it will shatter him."

When the chief priests and the Pharisees heard his parables, they knew he was speaking about them. Although they were looking for a way to arrest him, they feared the crowds, because the people regarded him as a prophet.

This is the Word of the Lord. Thanks be to God.

GLORIA

Glory be to God the Father, God the Son, and God the Holy Spirit. As it was in the beginning, is now, and will be forever, world without end.

THE LORD'S PRAYER

Our Father in heaven,
Hallowed be your name.
Your kingdom come,
Your will be done
on earth as it is in heaven.
Give us this day our daily bread.
And forgive us our debts,
as we also have forgiven our debtors.
And lead us not into temptation
But deliver us from the evil one.
For yours is the kingdom and the power and the glory forever.
Amen.

PRAYER OF THE CHURCH

Almighty and everlasting God, you hate nothing you have made
and forgive the sins of all who are penitent: Create and make in
us new and contrite hearts, that we, worthily lamenting our sins
and acknowledging our wretchedness, may obtain of you, the
God of all mercy, perfect remission and forgiveness; through
Jesus Christ our Lord, who lives and reigns with you and the
Holy Spirit, one God, for ever and ever. Amen.
The Book of Common Prayer

BLESSING

The Lord Almighty grant us a peaceful night and a perfect end.
Amen.

DAY 22 MORNING PRAYER

CALL TO PRAYER

You who fear the LORD, praise him! All you descendants of
Jacob, honor him! All you descendants of Israel, revere him!
Psalm 22:23

CONFESSION OF FAITH

I believe in God, the Father almighty,
creator of heaven and earth;
I believe in Jesus Christ, his only Son, our Lord.
He was conceived by the power of the Holy Spirit
and born of the Virgin Mary.
He suffered under Pontius Pilate,
was crucified, died, and was buried.
He descended to the dead.
On the third day he rose again.
He ascended into heaven,
and is seated at the right hand of the Father.
He will come again to judge the living and the dead.
I believe in the Holy Spirit,
the holy catholic Church,
the communion of saints,
the forgiveness of sins
the resurrection of the body,
and the life everlasting. Amen.
The Apostles' Creed

CANTICLE

How happy is the one who does not
walk in the advice of the wicked
or stand in the pathway with sinners
or sit in the company of mockers!
Instead, his delight is in the LORD's instruction,
and he meditates on it day and night.

He is like a tree planted beside flowing streams
that bears its fruit in its season,
and its leaf does not wither.
Whatever he does prospers.
The wicked are not like this;
instead, they are like chaff that the wind blows away.
Therefore the wicked will not stand up in the judgment,
nor sinners in the assembly of the righteous.
For the LORD watches over the way of the righteous,
but the way of the wicked leads to ruin.
Psalm 1

MORNING READING
Matthew 22:15–46
Then the Pharisees went and plotted how to trap him by what
he said. So they sent their disciples to him, along with the
Herodians. "Teacher," they said, "we know that you are truthful
and teach truthfully the way of God. You don't care what anyone
thinks nor do you show partiality. Tell us, then, what you think.
Is it lawful to pay taxes to Caesar or not?"

Perceiving their malicious intent, Jesus said, "Why are you
testing me, hypocrites? Show me the coin used for the tax."
They brought him a denarius. "Whose image and inscription is
this?" he asked them.

"Caesar's," they said to him.

Then he said to them, "Give, then, to Caesar the things that
are Caesar's, and to God the things that are God's." When they
heard this, they were amazed. So they left him and went away.

That same day some Sadducees, who say there is no
resurrection, came up to him and questioned him: "Teacher,
Moses said, **if a man dies, having no children, his brother is
to marry his wife and raise up offspring for his brother.** Now
there were seven brothers among us. The first got married and
died. Having no offspring, he left his wife to his brother. The
same thing happened to the second also, and the third, and so
on to all seven. Last of all, the woman died. In the resurrection,
then, whose wife will she be of the seven? For they all had
married her."

Jesus answered them, "You are mistaken, because you don't know the Scriptures or the power of God. For in the resurrection they neither marry nor are given in marriage but are like angels in heaven. Now concerning the resurrection of the dead, haven't you read what was spoken to you by God: **I am the God of Abraham and the God of Isaac and the God of Jacob**? He is not the God of the dead, but of the living."

And when the crowds heard this, they were astonished at his teaching.

When the Pharisees heard that he had silenced the Sadducees, they came together. And one of them, an expert in the law, asked a question to test him: "Teacher, which command in the law is the greatest?"

He said to him, "**Love the Lord your God with all your heart, with all your soul, and with all your mind.** This is the greatest and most important command. The second is like it: **Love your neighbor as yourself.** All the Law and the Prophets depend on these two commands."

While the Pharisees were together, Jesus questioned them, "What do you think about the Messiah? Whose son is he?"

They replied, "David's."

He asked them, "How is it then that David, inspired by the Spirit, calls him 'Lord':

> **The Lord declared to my Lord,**
> **'Sit at my right hand**
> **until I put your enemies under your feet'**?

"If David calls him 'Lord,' how, then, can he be his son?" No one was able to answer him at all, and from that day no one dared to question him anymore.

This is the Word of the Lord. Thanks be to God.

GLORIA

Glory be to God the Father, God the Son, and God the Holy Spirit. As it was in the beginning, is now, and will be forever, world without end.

The Lord's Prayer

Our Father in heaven,
Hallowed be your name.
Your kingdom come,
Your will be done
on earth as it is in heaven.
Give us this day our daily bread.
And forgive us our debts,
as we also have forgiven our debtors.
And lead us not into temptation
But deliver us from the evil one.
For yours is the kingdom and the power and the glory forever.
Amen.

Intercessions and Personal Requests

Prayer of the Church

Lord, because you have made me, I owe you the whole of my
love; because you have redeemed me, I owe you the whole of
myself; because you have promised so much, I owe you my
whole being. I pray you, Lord, make me taste by love what
I taste by knowledge; let me know by love what I know by
understanding. I owe you more than my whole self, but I have
no more, and by myself I cannot render the whole of it to you.
Draw me to you, Lord, in the fullness of your love. I am wholly
yours by creation; make me all yours, too, in love. Amen.
Anselm

Blessing

The grace of the Lord Jesus Christ, and the love of God, and the
fellowship of the Holy Spirit be with us all.
2 Corinthians 13:14

DAY 22 MIDDAY PRAYER

Call to Prayer

Exalt the Lord our God; bow in worship at his footstool. He is holy.
Psalm 99:5

Midday Reading

Matthew 23:1–12
Then Jesus spoke to the crowds and to his disciples: "The scribes and the Pharisees are seated in the chair of Moses. Therefore do whatever they tell you, and observe it. But don't do what they do, because they don't practice what they teach. They tie up heavy loads that are hard to carry and put them on people's shoulders, but they themselves aren't willing to lift a finger to move them. They do everything to be seen by others: They enlarge their phylacteries and lengthen their tassels. They love the place of honor at banquets, the front seats in the synagogues, greetings in the marketplaces, and to be called 'Rabbi' by people.

"But you are not to be called 'Rabbi,' because you have one Teacher, and you are all brothers and sisters. Do not call anyone on earth your father, because you have one Father, who is in heaven. You are not to be called instructors either, because you have one Instructor, the Messiah. The greatest among you will be your servant. Whoever exalts himself will be humbled, and whoever humbles himself will be exalted."

This is the Word of the Lord. Thanks be to God.

Gloria

Glory be to God the Father, God the Son, and God the Holy Spirit. As it was in the beginning, is now, and will be forever, world without end.

The Lord's Prayer

Our Father in heaven,
Hallowed be your name.
Your kingdom come,
Your will be done
on earth as it is in heaven.
Give us this day our daily bread.
And forgive us our debts,
as we also have forgiven our debtors.
And lead us not into temptation
But deliver us from the evil one.
For yours is the kingdom and the power and the glory forever.
Amen.

Blessing

May the Lord bless you and protect you; may the Lord make
his face shine on you and be gracious to you; may
the Lord look with favor on you and give you peace.
Numbers 6:24–26

DAY 22 EVENING PRAYER

Call to Prayer

We will sing of the Lord's ways, for the Lord's glory is great.
Though the Lord is exalted, he takes note of the humble; but he
knows the haughty from a distance.
Adapted from Psalm 138:5–6

Confession of Sin

Most merciful God,
we confess that we have sinned against you
in thought, word, and deed,
by what we have done,
and by what we have left undone.
We have not loved you with our whole heart;

we have not loved our neighbors as ourselves.
We are truly sorry and we humbly repent.
For the sake of your Son Jesus Christ,
have mercy on us and forgive us;
that we may delight in your will,
and walk in your ways,
to the glory of your Name. Amen.
The Book of Common Prayer

If we confess our sins, he is faithful and righteous to forgive us
our sins and to cleanse us from all unrighteousness.
1 John 1:9

CANTICLE

My heart rejoices in the LORD;
my horn is lifted up by the LORD.
My mouth boasts over my enemies,
because I rejoice in your salvation.
There is no one holy like the LORD.
There is no one besides you!
And there is no rock like our God.
Do not boast so proudly,
or let arrogant words come out of your mouth,
for the LORD is a God of knowledge,
and actions are weighed by him.
The LORD brings poverty and gives wealth;
he humbles and he exalts.
He raises the poor from the dust
and lifts the needy from the trash heap.
He seats them with noblemen
and gives them a throne of honor.
For the foundations of the earth are the LORD's;
he has set the world on them.
1 Samuel 2:1–3,7–8

Matthew 23:13–36

"Woe to you, scribes and Pharisees, hypocrites! You shut the door of the kingdom of heaven in people's faces. For you don't go in, and you don't allow those entering to go in.

"Woe to you, scribes and Pharisees, hypocrites! You travel over land and sea to make one convert, and when he becomes one, you make him twice as much a child of hell as you are!

"Woe to you, blind guides, who say, 'Whoever takes an oath by the temple, it means nothing. But whoever takes an oath by the gold of the temple is bound by his oath.' Blind fools! For which is greater, the gold or the temple that sanctified the gold? Also, 'Whoever takes an oath by the altar, it means nothing; but whoever takes an oath by the gift that is on it is bound by his oath.' Blind people! For which is greater, the gift or the altar that sanctifies the gift? Therefore, the one who takes an oath by the altar takes an oath by it and by everything on it. The one who takes an oath by the temple takes an oath by it and by him who dwells in it. And the one who takes an oath by heaven takes an oath by God's throne and by him who sits on it.

"Woe to you, scribes and Pharisees, hypocrites! You pay a tenth of mint, dill, and cumin, and yet you have neglected the more important matters of the law—justice, mercy, and faithfulness. These things should have been done without neglecting the others. Blind guides! You strain out a gnat, but gulp down a camel!

"Woe to you, scribes and Pharisees, hypocrites! You clean the outside of the cup and dish, but inside they are full of greed and self-indulgence. Blind Pharisee! First clean the inside of the cup, so that the outside of it may also become clean.

"Woe to you, scribes and Pharisees, hypocrites! You are like whitewashed tombs, which appear beautiful on the outside, but inside are full of the bones of the dead and every kind of impurity. In the same way, on the outside you seem righteous to people, but inside you are full of hypocrisy and lawlessness.

"Woe to you, scribes and Pharisees, hypocrites! You build the tombs of the prophets and decorate the graves of the righteous, and you say, 'If we had lived in the days of our ancestors, we wouldn't have taken part with them in shedding the prophets' blood.' So you testify against yourselves that you are descendants of those who murdered the prophets. Fill up, then, the measure of your ancestors' sins!

"Snakes! Brood of vipers! How can you escape being condemned to hell? This is why I am sending you prophets, sages, and scribes. Some of them you will kill and crucify, and some of them you will flog in your synagogues and pursue from town to town. So all the righteous blood shed on the earth will be charged to you, from the blood of righteous Abel to the blood of Zechariah, son of Berechiah, whom you murdered between the sanctuary and the altar. Truly I tell you, all these things will come on this generation."

Mark 12:41–44
Sitting across from the temple treasury, he watched how the crowd dropped money into the treasury. Many rich people were putting in large sums. Then a poor widow came and dropped in two tiny coins worth very little. Summoning his disciples, he said to them, "Truly I tell you, this poor widow has put more into the treasury than all the others. For they all gave out of their surplus, but she out of her poverty has put in everything she had—all she had to live on."

This is the Word of the Lord. Thanks be to God.

Gloria
Glory be to God the Father, God the Son, and God the Holy Spirit. As it was in the beginning, is now, and will be forever, world without end.

The Lord's Prayer
Our Father in heaven,
Hallowed be your name.
Your kingdom come,
Your will be done
on earth as it is in heaven.
Give us this day our daily bread.

And forgive us our debts,
as we also have forgiven our debtors.
And lead us not into temptation
But deliver us from the evil one.
For yours is the kingdom and the power and the glory forever.
Amen.

INTERCESSIONS AND PERSONAL REQUESTS

PRAYER OF THE CHURCH

O Lord my God, instruct my ignorance and enlighten my
darkness. You are my King, take possession of all my powers
and abilities and let me be no longer under the dominion of sin.
Give me a sincere and heartfelt repentance for all my offenses
and strengthen by your grace my resolution to amend my ways.
Grant me also the spirit of prayer and supplication according to
your own most gracious promises.
Phillis Wheatley

BLESSING

The Almighty and merciful Lord, Father, Son, and Holy Spirit,
bless us and keep us, this night and evermore. Amen.

DAY 23 MORNING PRAYER

CALL TO PRAYER
Ascribe power to God. His majesty is over Israel; his power is among the clouds.
Psalm 68:34

CONFESSION OF FAITH
I believe that in God's own time and way, the bodily risen and ascended Christ will visibly return to consummate God's purpose for the whole cosmos through his victory over death and the devil. He will judge the world, consigning any who persist in unbelief to an everlasting fate apart from him, where his life and light are no more. Yet he will prepare his people as a bride for the marriage supper of the Lamb, giving rest to restless hearts and life to glorified bodies as we exult in joyful fellowship with our Lord and delight in the new heaven and the new earth. There we shall reign with him and see him face to face, forever rapt in wonder, love, and praise.
Adapted from the Reforming Catholic Confession

CANTICLE
Gather yourselves together;
gather together, undesirable nation,
before the decree takes effect
and the day passes like chaff,
before the burning of the LORD's anger overtakes you,
before the day of the LORD's anger overtakes you.
Seek the LORD, all you humble of the earth,
who carry out what he commands.
Seek righteousness, seek humility;
perhaps you will be concealed
on the day of the LORD's anger.
Zephaniah 2:1–3

Matthew 24:1–28

As Jesus left and was going out of the temple, his disciples came up and called his attention to its buildings. He replied to them, "Do you see all these things? Truly I tell you, not one stone will be left here on another that will not be thrown down."

While he was sitting on the Mount of Olives, the disciples approached him privately and said, "Tell us, when will these things happen? And what is the sign of your coming and of the end of the age?"

Jesus replied to them, "Watch out that no one deceives you. For many will come in my name, saying, 'I am the Messiah,' and they will deceive many. You are going to hear of wars and rumors of wars. See that you are not alarmed, because these things must take place, but the end is not yet. For nation will rise up against nation, and kingdom against kingdom. There will be famines and earthquakes in various places. All these events are the beginning of labor pains.

"Then they will hand you over to be persecuted, and they will kill you. You will be hated by all nations because of my name. Then many will fall away, betray one another, and hate one another. Many false prophets will rise up and deceive many. Because lawlessness will multiply, the love of many will grow cold. But the one who endures to the end will be saved. This good news of the kingdom will be proclaimed in all the world as a testimony to all nations, and then the end will come.

"So when you see **the abomination of desolation**, spoken of by the prophet Daniel, standing in the holy place" (let the reader understand), "then those in Judea must flee to the mountains. A man on the housetop must not come down to get things out of his house, and a man in the field must not go back to get his coat. Woe to pregnant women and nursing mothers in those days! Pray that your escape may not be in winter or on a Sabbath. For at that time there will be great distress, the kind that hasn't taken place from the beginning of the world until now and never will again. Unless those days were cut short, no one would be saved. But those days will be cut short because of the elect.

"If anyone tells you then, 'See, here is the Messiah!' or, 'Over here!' do not believe it. For false messiahs and false prophets will arise and perform great signs and wonders to lead astray, if possible, even the elect. Take note: I have told you in advance. So if they tell you, 'See, he's in the wilderness!' don't go out; or, 'See, he's in the storerooms!' do not believe it. For as the lightning comes from the east and flashes as far as the west, so will be the coming of the Son of Man. Wherever the carcass is, there the vultures will gather."

This is the Word of the Lord. Thanks be to God.

GLORIA

Glory be to God the Father, God the Son, and God the Holy Spirit. As it was in the beginning, is now, and will be forever, world without end.

THE LORD'S PRAYER

Our Father in heaven,
Hallowed be your name.
Your kingdom come,
Your will be done
on earth as it is in heaven.
Give us this day our daily bread.
And forgive us our debts,
as we also have forgiven our debtors.
And lead us not into temptation
But deliver us from the evil one.
For yours is the kingdom and the power and the glory forever.
Amen.

PRAYER OF THE CHURCH

Stir up your power, O Lord, and with great might come among
us; and, because we are sorely hindered by our sins, let your
bountiful grace and mercy speedily help and deliver us; through
Jesus Christ our Lord, to whom, with you and the Holy Spirit,
be honor and glory, now and for ever. Amen.
The Book of Common Prayer

BLESSING

Now to him who is able to do above and beyond all that we
ask or think according to the power that works in us—to him
be glory in the church and in Christ Jesus to all generations,
forever and ever. Amen.
Ephesians 3:20–21

DAY 23 MIDDAY PRAYER

CALL TO PRAYER

Sing to God! Sing praises to his name. Exalt him who rides on
the clouds—his name is the LORD—and celebrate before him.
Psalm 68:4

MIDDAY READING

Matthew 24:29–44
"Immediately after the distress of those days, the sun will be
darkened, and the moon will not shed its light; the stars will
fall from the sky, and the powers of the heavens will be shaken.
Then the sign of the Son of Man will appear in the sky, and then
all the peoples of the earth will mourn; and they will see the Son
of Man coming on the clouds of heaven with power and great
glory. He will send out his angels with a loud trumpet, and they

will gather his elect from the four winds, from one end of the sky to the other.

"Learn this lesson from the fig tree: As soon as its branch becomes tender and sprouts leaves, you know that summer is near. In the same way, when you see all these things, recognize that he is near—at the door. Truly I tell you, this generation will certainly not pass away until all these things take place. Heaven and earth will pass away, but my words will never pass away.

"Now concerning that day and hour no one knows—neither the angels of heaven nor the Son—except the Father alone. As the days of Noah were, so the coming of the Son of Man will be. For in those days before the flood they were eating and drinking, marrying and giving in marriage, until the day Noah boarded the ark. They didn't know until the flood came and swept them all away. This is the way the coming of the Son of Man will be. Then two men will be in the field; one will be taken and one left. Two women will be grinding grain with a hand mill; one will be taken and one left. Therefore be alert, since you don't know what day your Lord is coming. But know this: If the homeowner had known what time the thief was coming, he would have stayed alert and not let his house be broken into. This is why you are also to be ready, because the Son of Man is coming at an hour you do not expect."

This is the Word of the Lord. Thanks be to God.

Gloria

Glory be to God the Father, God the Son, and God the Holy Spirit. As it was in the beginning, is now, and will be forever, world without end.

The Lord's Prayer

Our Father in heaven,
Hallowed be your name.
Your kingdom come,
Your will be done
on earth as it is in heaven.

Give us this day our daily bread.
And forgive us our debts,
as we also have forgiven our debtors.
And lead us not into temptation
But deliver us from the evil one.
For yours is the kingdom and the power and the glory forever.
Amen.

BLESSING

The grace of the Lord Jesus Christ, and the love of God, and the
fellowship of the Holy Spirit be with us all.
2 Corinthians 13:14

DAY 23 EVENING PRAYER

CALL TO PRAYER

Be alert, since you don't know when the master of the house
is coming—whether in the evening or at midnight or at the
crowing of the rooster or early in the morning. Otherwise,
when he comes suddenly he might find you sleeping.
Mark 13:35–36

CONFESSION OF SIN

Lord Jesus Christ, Son of God, have mercy on me, a sinner.

The sacrifice pleasing to God is a broken spirit. You will not
despise a broken and humbled heart, God.
Psalm 51:17

CANTICLE

Now, Lord,
you can dismiss your servant in peace,
as you promised.
For my eyes have seen your salvation.

You have prepared it
in the presence of all peoples—
a light for revelation to the Gentiles
and glory to your people Israel.
Luke 2:29–32

Evening Reading

Matthew 25:1–30

"At that time the kingdom of heaven will be like ten virgins who took their lamps and went out to meet the groom. Five of them were foolish and five were wise. When the foolish took their lamps, they didn't take oil with them; but the wise ones took oil in their flasks with their lamps. When the groom was delayed, they all became drowsy and fell asleep.

"In the middle of the night there was a shout: 'Here's the groom! Come out to meet him.'

"Then all the virgins got up and trimmed their lamps. The foolish ones said to the wise ones, 'Give us some of your oil, because our lamps are going out.'

"The wise ones answered, 'No, there won't be enough for us and for you. Go instead to those who sell oil, and buy some for yourselves.'

"When they had gone to buy some, the groom arrived, and those who were ready went in with him to the wedding banquet, and the door was shut. Later the rest of the virgins also came and said, 'Master, master, open up for us!'

"He replied, 'Truly I tell you, I don't know you!'

"Therefore be alert, because you don't know either the day or the hour.

"For it is just like a man about to go on a journey. He called his own servants and entrusted his possessions to them. To one he gave five talents, to another two talents, and to another one talent, depending on each one's ability. Then he went on a journey. Immediately the man who had received five talents went, put them to work, and earned five more. In the same way the man with two earned two more. But the man who had received one talent went off, dug a hole in the ground, and hid his master's money.

"After a long time the master of those servants came and settled accounts with them. The man who had received five talents approached, presented five more talents, and said, 'Master, you gave me five talents. See, I've earned five more talents.'

"His master said to him, 'Well done, good and faithful servant! You were faithful over a few things; I will put you in charge of many things. Share your master's joy.'

"The man with two talents also approached. He said, 'Master, you gave me two talents. See, I've earned two more talents.'

"His master said to him, 'Well done, good and faithful servant! You were faithful over a few things; I will put you in charge of many things. Share your master's joy.'

"The man who had received one talent also approached and said, 'Master, I know you. You're a harsh man, reaping where you haven't sown and gathering where you haven't scattered seed. So I was afraid and went off and hid your talent in the ground. See, you have what is yours.'

"His master replied to him, 'You evil, lazy servant! If you knew that I reap where I haven't sown and gather where I haven't scattered, then you should have deposited my money with the bankers, and I would have received my money back with interest when I returned.

"'So take the talent from him and give it to the one who has ten talents. For to everyone who has, more will be given, and he will have more than enough. But from the one who does not have, even what he has will be taken away from him. And throw this good-for-nothing servant into the outer darkness, where there will be weeping and gnashing of teeth.'"

This is the Word of the Lord. Thanks be to God.

GLORIA

Glory be to God the Father, God the Son, and God the Holy Spirit. As it was in the beginning, is now, and will be forever, world without end.

THE LORD'S PRAYER

Our Father in heaven,
Hallowed be your name.
Your kingdom come,
Your will be done
on earth as it is in heaven.
Give us this day our daily bread.
And forgive us our debts,
as we also have forgiven our debtors.
And lead us not into temptation
But deliver us from the evil one.
For yours is the kingdom and the power and the glory forever.
Amen.

INTERCESSIONS AND PERSONAL REQUESTS

PRAYER OF THE CHURCH

O Lord of my life, take away from me the spirit of laziness,
faint-heartedness, lust for power and idle talk. Instead grant me,
your servant, the spirit of purity, humility, patience, and love.
Yes, O Lord and King! Grant me to see my own sins and faults
and not to judge my neighbor, for you are truly blessed forever.
Ephrem of Syria

BLESSING

The Lord Almighty grant us a peaceful night and a perfect end.
Amen.

DAY 24 MORNING PRAYER

CALL TO PRAYER

Sing a new song to the LORD; let the whole earth sing to
the LORD . . . for he is coming—for he is coming to judge the
earth. He will judge the world with righteousness and the
peoples with his faithfulness.
Psalm 96:1,13

CONFESSION OF FAITH

I believe that the one, holy, catholic, and apostolic church is
God's new society, the first fruit of the new creation, the whole
company of the redeemed through the ages, of which Christ is
Lord and head. The truth that Jesus is the Christ, the Son of the
living God, is the church's firm foundation. The local church is
both embassy and parable of the kingdom of heaven, an earthly
place where his will is done and he is now present, existing
visibly everywhere two or three gather in his name to proclaim
and spread the gospel in word and works of love, and by
obeying the Lord's command to baptize disciples and celebrate
the Lord's Supper.
Adapted from the Reforming Catholic Confession

CANTICLE

Happy is one who is considerate of the poor;
the LORD will save him in a day of adversity.
The LORD will keep him and preserve him;
he will be blessed in the land.
You will not give him over to the desire of his enemies.
The LORD will sustain him on his sickbed;
you will heal him on the bed where he lies.
Psalm 41:1–3

Matthew 25:31–46

"When the Son of Man comes in his glory, and all the angels with him, then he will sit on his glorious throne. All the nations will be gathered before him, and he will separate them one from another, just as a shepherd separates the sheep from the goats. He will put the sheep on his right and the goats on the left. Then the King will say to those on his right, 'Come, you who are blessed by my Father; inherit the kingdom prepared for you from the foundation of the world.

"'For I was hungry and you gave me something to eat; I was thirsty and you gave me something to drink; I was a stranger and you took me in; I was naked and you clothed me; I was sick and you took care of me; I was in prison and you visited me.'

"Then the righteous will answer him, 'Lord, when did we see you hungry and feed you, or thirsty and give you something to drink? When did we see you a stranger and take you in, or without clothes and clothe you? When did we see you sick, or in prison, and visit you?'

"And the King will answer them, 'Truly I tell you, whatever you did for one of the least of these brothers and sisters of mine, you did for me.'

"Then he will also say to those on the left, 'Depart from me, you who are cursed, into the eternal fire prepared for the devil and his angels! For I was hungry and you gave me nothing to eat; I was thirsty and you gave me nothing to drink; I was a stranger and you didn't take me in; I was naked and you didn't clothe me, sick and in prison and you didn't take care of me.'

"Then they too will answer, 'Lord, when did we see you hungry, or thirsty, or a stranger, or without clothes, or sick, or in prison, and not help you?'

"Then he will answer them, 'Truly I tell you, whatever you did not do for one of the least of these, you did not do for me.'

"And they will go away into eternal punishment, but the righteous into eternal life."

Matthew 26:1–5

When Jesus had finished saying all these things, he told his disciples, "You know that the Passover takes place after two days, and the Son of Man will be handed over to be crucified."

Then the chief priests and the elders of the people assembled in the courtyard of the high priest, who was named Caiaphas, and they conspired to arrest Jesus in a treacherous way and kill him. "Not during the festival," they said, "so there won't be rioting among the people."

This is the Word of the Lord. Thanks be to God.

GLORIA

Glory be to God the Father, God the Son, and God the Holy Spirit. As it was in the beginning, is now, and will be forever, world without end.

THE LORD'S PRAYER

Our Father in heaven,
Hallowed be your name.
Your kingdom come,
Your will be done
on earth as it is in heaven.
Give us this day our daily bread.
And forgive us our debts,
as we also have forgiven our debtors.
And lead us not into temptation
But deliver us from the evil one.
For yours is the kingdom and the power and the glory forever.
Amen.

Prayer of the Church

Lord of all power and might, the author and giver of all good things: Graft in our hearts the love of your Name; increase in us true religion; nourish us with all goodness; and bring forth in us the fruit of good works; through Jesus Christ our Lord, who lives and reigns with you and the Holy Spirit, one God, for ever and ever. Amen.

The Book of Common Prayer

Blessing

May God be gracious to us and bless us; may he make his face shine upon us so that your way may be known on earth, your salvation among all nations.

Psalm 67:1–2

DAY 24 MIDDAY PRAYER

Call to Prayer

Hallelujah! Sing to the LORD a new song, his praise in the assembly of the faithful. For the LORD takes pleasure in his people; he adorns the humble with salvation.

Psalm 149:1,4

Midday Readings

Luke 22:7–13

Then the Day of Unleavened Bread came when the Passover lamb had to be sacrificed. Jesus sent Peter and John, saying, "Go and make preparations for us to eat the Passover."

"Where do you want us to prepare it?" they asked him.

"Listen," he said to them, "when you've entered the city, a man carrying a water jug will meet you. Follow him into the house he enters. Tell the owner of the house, 'The Teacher asks you,

"Where is the guest room where I can eat the Passover with my disciples?"' Then he will show you a large, furnished room upstairs. Make the preparations there."

So they went and found it just as he had told them, and they prepared the Passover.

John 13:1–11
Before the Passover Festival, Jesus knew that his hour had come to depart from this world to the Father. Having loved his own who were in the world, he loved them to the end.

Now when it was time for supper, the devil had already put it into the heart of Judas, Simon Iscariot's son, to betray him. Jesus knew that the Father had given everything into his hands, that he had come from God, and that he was going back to God. So he got up from supper, laid aside his outer clothing, took a towel, and tied it around himself. Next, he poured water into a basin and began to wash his disciples' feet and to dry them with the towel tied around him.

He came to Simon Peter, who asked him, "Lord, are you going to wash my feet?"

Jesus answered him, "What I'm doing you don't realize now, but afterward you will understand."

"You will never wash my feet," Peter said.

Jesus replied, "If I don't wash you, you have no part with me."

Simon Peter said to him, "Lord, not only my feet, but also my hands and my head."

"One who has bathed," Jesus told him, "doesn't need to wash anything except his feet, but he is completely clean. You are clean, but not all of you." For he knew who would betray him. This is why he said, "Not all of you are clean."

This is the Word of the Lord. Thanks be to God.

Gloria
Glory be to God the Father, God the Son, and God the Holy Spirit. As it was in the beginning, is now, and will be forever, world without end.

The Lord's Prayer

Our Father in heaven,
Hallowed be your name.
Your kingdom come,
Your will be done
on earth as it is in heaven.
Give us this day our daily bread.
And forgive us our debts,
as we also have forgiven our debtors.
And lead us not into temptation
But deliver us from the evil one.
For yours is the kingdom and the power and the glory forever.
Amen.

Blessing

May [the LORD] give you what your heart desires and fulfill
your whole purpose. May the LORD fulfill all your requests.
Psalm 20:4–5

DAY 24 EVENING PRAYER

Call to Prayer

Worship the LORD in the splendor of his holiness; let the whole
earth tremble before him.
Psalm 96:9

Confession of Sin

Lamb of God, you take away the sin of the world;
have mercy on us.
Lamb of God, you take away the sin of the world;
have mercy on us.
Lamb of God, you take away the sin of the world;
grant us your peace.

As far as the east is from the west, so far has he removed our transgressions from us.
Psalm 103:12

O gladsome light,
pure brightness of the everlasting Father in heaven,
O Jesus Christ, holy and blessed!
Now as we come to the setting of the sun,
and our eyes behold the vesper light,
we sing your praises, O God: Father, Son, and Holy Spirit.
You are worthy at all times to be praised by happy voices,
O Son of God, O Giver of Life,
and to be glorified through all the worlds.
Phos Hilaron

EVENING READINGS

John 13:12–20
When Jesus had washed their feet and put on his outer clothing, he reclined again and said to them, "Do you know what I have done for you? You call me Teacher and Lord—and you are speaking rightly, since that is what I am. So if I, your Lord and Teacher, have washed your feet, you also ought to wash one another's feet. For I have given you an example, that you also should do just as I have done for you.

"Truly I tell you, a servant is not greater than his master, and a messenger is not greater than the one who sent him. If you know these things, you are blessed if you do them.

"I'm not speaking about all of you; I know those I have chosen. But the Scripture must be fulfilled: **The one who eats my bread has raised his heel against me.** I am telling you now before it happens, so that when it does happen you will believe that I am he. Truly I tell you, whoever receives anyone I send receives me, and the one who receives me receives him who sent me."

When Jesus had said this, he was troubled in his spirit and testified, "Truly I tell you, one of you will betray me."

The disciples started looking at one another—uncertain which one he was speaking about. One of his disciples, the one Jesus loved, was reclining close beside Jesus. Simon Peter motioned to him to find out who it was he was talking about. So he leaned back against Jesus and asked him, "Lord, who is it?"

Jesus replied, "He's the one I give the piece of bread to after I have dipped it." When he had dipped the bread, he gave it to Judas, Simon Iscariot's son. After Judas ate the piece of bread, Satan entered him. So Jesus told him, "What you're doing, do quickly."

None of those reclining at the table knew why he said this to him. Since Judas kept the money-bag, some thought that Jesus was telling him, "Buy what we need for the festival," or that he should give something to the poor. After receiving the piece of bread, he immediately left. And it was night.

Matthew 26:26–29
As they were eating, Jesus took bread, blessed and broke it, gave it to the disciples, and said, "Take and eat it; this is my body." Then he took a cup, and after giving thanks, he gave it to them and said, "Drink from it, all of you. For this is my blood of the covenant, which is poured out for many for the forgiveness of sins. But I tell you, I will not drink from this fruit of the vine from now on until that day when I drink it new with you in my Father's kingdom."

This is the Word of the Lord. Thanks be to God.

GLORIA
Glory be to God the Father, God the Son, and God the Holy Spirit. As it was in the beginning, is now, and will be forever, world without end.

THE LORD'S PRAYER
Our Father in heaven,
Hallowed be your name.
Your kingdom come,

Your will be done
on earth as it is in heaven.
Give us this day our daily bread.
And forgive us our debts,
as we also have forgiven our debtors.
And lead us not into temptation
But deliver us from the evil one.
For yours is the kingdom and the power and the glory forever.
Amen.

INTERCESSIONS AND PERSONAL REQUESTS

PRAYER OF THE CHURCH

We give you thanks, Father most holy, through Jesus Christ our
Lord, who girded himself with a towel and, taking the form
of a servant, washed the feet of his disciples. He gave us a new
commandment that we should love one another as he has loved
us. Knowing that his hour had come, in his great love he gave
this supper to his disciples to be a memorial of his passion,
that we might proclaim his death until he comes again, and
feast with him in his kingdom. Therefore earth unites with
heaven to sing a new song of praise; we too join with angels and
archangels as they proclaim your glory without end.
The Book of Common Prayer

BLESSING

The Almighty and merciful Lord, Father, Son, and Holy Spirit,
bless us and keep us, this night and evermore. Amen.

DAY 25 MORNING PRAYER

CALL TO PRAYER

I lift my eyes to you, the one enthroned in heaven.
Psalm 123:1

CONFESSION OF FAITH

I believe there is one God, infinitely great and good, the creator and sustainer of all things visible and invisible, the one true source of light and life, who has life in himself and lives eternally in glorious light and sovereign love in three persons—Father, Son, and Holy Spirit—co-equal in nature, majesty, and glory. Everything God does in creating, sustaining, judging, and redeeming the world reflects who God is, the one whose perfections, including love, holiness, knowledge, wisdom, power, and righteousness, have been revealed in the history of salvation. God has freely purposed from before the foundation of the world to elect and form a people for himself to be his treasured possession, to the praise of his glory.
Adapted from the Reforming Catholic Confession

CANTICLE

Show us your faithful love, LORD,
and give us your salvation.
I will listen to what God will say;
surely the LORD will declare peace
to his people, his faithful ones,
and not let them go back to foolish ways.
His salvation is very near those who fear him,
so that glory may dwell in our land.
Psalm 85:7–9

John 13:31–38

Jesus said, "Now the Son of Man is glorified, and God is glorified in him. If God is glorified in him, God will also glorify him in himself and will glorify him at once. Little children, I am with you a little while longer. You will look for me, and just as I told the Jews, so now I tell you, 'Where I am going, you cannot come.'

"I give you a new command: Love one another. Just as I have loved you, you are also to love one another. By this everyone will know that you are my disciples, if you love one another."

"Lord," Simon Peter said to him, "where are you going?"

Jesus answered, "Where I am going you cannot follow me now, but you will follow later."

"Lord," Peter asked, "why can't I follow you now? I will lay down my life for you."

Jesus replied, "Will you lay down your life for me? Truly I tell you, a rooster will not crow until you have denied me three times."

John 14:1–14

"Don't let your heart be troubled. Believe in God; believe also in me. In my Father's house are many rooms. If it were not so, would I have told you that I am going to prepare a place for you? If I go away and prepare a place for you, I will come again and take you to myself, so that where I am you may be also. You know the way to where I am going."

"Lord," Thomas said, "we don't know where you're going. How can we know the way?"

Jesus told him, "I am the way, the truth, and the life. No one comes to the Father except through me. If you know me, you will also know my Father. From now on you do know him and have seen him."

"Lord," said Philip, "show us the Father, and that's enough for us."

Jesus said to him, "Have I been among you all this time and you do not know me, Philip? The one who has seen me has seen the Father. How can you say, 'Show us the Father'? Don't you believe that I am in the Father and the Father is in me? The words I speak to you I do not speak on my own. The Father who lives in me does his works. Believe me that I am in the Father and the Father is in me. Otherwise, believe because of the works themselves.

"Truly I tell you, the one who believes in me will also do the works that I do. And he will do even greater works than these, because I am going to the Father. Whatever you ask in my name, I will do it so that the Father may be glorified in the Son. If you ask me anything in my name, I will do it."

This is the Word of the Lord. Thanks be to God.

GLORIA

Glory be to God the Father, God the Son, and God the Holy Spirit. As it was in the beginning, is now, and will be forever, world without end.

THE LORD'S PRAYER

Our Father in heaven,
Hallowed be your name.
Your kingdom come,
Your will be done
on earth as it is in heaven.
Give us this day our daily bread.
And forgive us our debts,
as we also have forgiven our debtors.
And lead us not into temptation
But deliver us from the evil one.
For yours is the kingdom and the power and the glory forever.
Amen.

INTERCESSIONS AND PERSONAL REQUESTS

PRAYER OF THE CHURCH

Lord, make me an instrument of your peace. Where there is hatred, let me sow love; where there is injury, pardon; where

there is doubt, faith; where there is despair, hope; where there is darkness, light; where there is sadness, joy. O, Divine Master, grant that I may not so much seek to be consoled as to console; to be understood as to understand; to be loved as to love; for it is in giving that we receive; it is in pardoning that we are pardoned; it is in dying that we are born again to eternal life.
Francis of Assisi

BLESSING

May the Lord cause you to increase and overflow with love for one another and for everyone. . . . May he make your hearts blameless in holiness before our God and Father at the coming of our Lord Jesus with all his saints. Amen.
1 Thessalonians 2:12–13

DAY 25 MIDDAY PRAYER

CALL TO PRAYER

Teach me to do your will, for you are my God. May your gracious Spirit lead me on level ground.
Psalm 143:10

MIDDAY READING

John 14:15–31
"If you love me, you will keep my commands. And I will ask the Father, and he will give you another Counselor to be with you forever. He is the Spirit of truth. The world is unable to receive him because it doesn't see him or know him. But you do know him, because he remains with you and will be in you.

"I will not leave you as orphans; I am coming to you. In a little while the world will no longer see me, but you will see me. Because I live, you will live too. On that day you will know that I am in my Father, you are in me, and I am in you. The one who has my commands and keeps them is the one who loves me.

And the one who loves me will be loved by my Father. I also will love him and will reveal myself to him."

Judas (not Iscariot) said to him, "Lord, how is it you're going to reveal yourself to us and not to the world?"

Jesus answered, "If anyone loves me, he will keep my word. My Father will love him, and we will come to him and make our home with him. The one who doesn't love me will not keep my words. The word that you hear is not mine but is from the Father who sent me.

"I have spoken these things to you while I remain with you. But the Counselor, the Holy Spirit, whom the Father will send in my name, will teach you all things and remind you of everything I have told you.

"Peace I leave with you. My peace I give to you. I do not give to you as the world gives. Don't let your heart be troubled or fearful. You have heard me tell you, 'I am going away and I am coming to you.' If you loved me, you would rejoice that I am going to the Father, because the Father is greater than I. I have told you now before it happens so that when it does happen you may believe. I will not talk with you much longer, because the ruler of the world is coming. He has no power over me. On the contrary, so that the world may know that I love the Father, I do as the Father commanded me."

This is the Word of the Lord. Thanks be to God.

Gloria

Glory be to God the Father, God the Son, and God the Holy Spirit. As it was in the beginning, is now, and will be forever, world without end.

The Lord's Prayer

Our Father in heaven,
Hallowed be your name.
Your kingdom come,
Your will be done
on earth as it is in heaven.

Give us this day our daily bread.
And forgive us our debts,
as we also have forgiven our debtors.
And lead us not into temptation
But deliver us from the evil one.
For yours is the kingdom and the power and the glory forever.
Amen.

Blessing
The grace of the Lord Jesus Christ, and the love of God, and the fellowship of the Holy Spirit be with us all.
2 Corinthians 13:14

DAY 25 EVENING PRAYER

Call to Prayer
Holy, holy, holy is the Lord of Armies; his glory fills the whole earth.
Isaiah 6:3

Confession of Sin
Lord Jesus, give me a deeper repentance, a horror of sin, a dread of its approach. Help me to flee it and jealously to resolve that my heart shall be yours alone. Give me a deeper trust, that I may lose myself to find myself in you, the ground of my rest, the spring of my being. Give me a deeper knowledge of you as Savior, Master, Lord, and King. Give me deeper power in private prayer, more sweetness in your Word, more steadfast grip on its truth. Give me deeper holiness in speech, thought, action, and let me not seek moral virtue apart from you.
The Valley of Vision

If we confess our sins, he is faithful and righteous to forgive us our sins and to cleanse us from all unrighteousness.
1 John 1:9

Canticle

Glory to you, Lord God of our fathers;
you are worthy of praise; glory to you.
Glory to you for the radiance of your holy Name;
we will praise you and highly exalt you for ever.
Glory to you in the splendor of your temple;
on the throne of your majesty, glory to you.
Glory to you, seated between the Cherubim;
we will praise you and highly exalt you for ever.
Glory to you, beholding the depths;
in the high vault of heaven, glory to you.
Glory to you, Father, Son, and Holy Spirit;
we will praise you and highly exalt you for ever.
Song of the Three Young Men

Evening Readings

Luke 22:39
He went out and made his way as usual to the Mount of Olives,
and the disciples followed him.

John 15:1–27
"I am the true vine, and my Father is the gardener. Every branch
in me that does not produce fruit he removes, and he prunes
every branch that produces fruit so that it will produce more
fruit. You are already clean because of the word I have spoken
to you. Remain in me, and I in you. Just as a branch is unable
to produce fruit by itself unless it remains on the vine, neither
can you unless you remain in me. I am the vine; you are the
branches. The one who remains in me and I in him produces
much fruit, because you can do nothing without me. If anyone
does not remain in me, he is thrown aside like a branch and he
withers. They gather them, throw them into the fire, and they
are burned. If you remain in me and my words remain in you,
ask whatever you want and it will be done for you. My Father is
glorified by this: that you produce much fruit and prove to be
my disciples.

"As the Father has loved me, I have also loved you. Remain
in my love. If you keep my commands you will remain in my

love, just as I have kept my Father's commands and remain in his love.

"I have told you these things so that my joy may be in you and your joy may be complete.

"This is my command: Love one another as I have loved you. No one has greater love than this: to lay down his life for his friends. You are my friends if you do what I command you. I do not call you servants anymore, because a servant doesn't know what his master is doing. I have called you friends, because I have made known to you everything I have heard from my Father. You did not choose me, but I chose you. I appointed you to go and produce fruit and that your fruit should remain, so that whatever you ask the Father in my name, he will give you.

"This is what I command you: Love one another.

"If the world hates you, understand that it hated me before it hated you. If you were of the world, the world would love you as its own. However, because you are not of the world, but I have chosen you out of it, the world hates you. Remember the word I spoke to you: 'A servant is not greater than his master.' If they persecuted me, they will also persecute you. If they kept my word, they will also keep yours. But they will do all these things to you on account of my name, because they don't know the one who sent me. If I had not come and spoken to them, they would not be guilty of sin. Now they have no excuse for their sin. The one who hates me also hates my Father. If I had not done the works among them that no one else has done, they would not be guilty of sin. Now they have seen and hated both me and my Father. But this happened so that the statement written in their law might be fulfilled: **They hated me for no reason.**

"When the Counselor comes, the one I will send to you from the Father—the Spirit of truth who proceeds from the Father—he will testify about me. You also will testify, because you have been with me from the beginning."

This is the Word of the Lord. Thanks be to God.

Gloria

Glory be to God the Father, God the Son, and God the Holy Spirit. As it was in the beginning, is now, and will be forever, world without end.

The Lord's Prayer

Our Father in heaven,
Hallowed be your name.
Your kingdom come,
Your will be done
on earth as it is in heaven.
Give us this day our daily bread.
And forgive us our debts,
as we also have forgiven our debtors.
And lead us not into temptation
But deliver us from the evil one.
For yours is the kingdom and the power and the glory forever.
Amen.

Intercessions and Personal Requests

Prayer of the Church

O Lord, reassure me with your enlivening Spirit; without you I can do nothing. Mortify in me all ambition, vanity, vainglory, worldliness, pride, selfishness, and resistance from God, and fill me with love, peace, and all the fruit of the Spirit. O Lord, I know not what I am, but to you I flee for refuge. I surrender myself to you, trusting your precious promises and against hope believing in hope.
William Wilberforce

Blessing

The Lord Almighty grant us a peaceful night and a perfect end. Amen.

DAY 26 MORNING PRAYER

CALL TO PRAYER

The Spirit of the Lord renews the face of the earth: O come, let us adore him.

CONFESSION OF FAITH

I believe the Holy Spirit is the third person of the Trinity, the unseen yet active personal presence of God in the world, who unites believers to Christ, regenerating and making us new creatures with hearts oriented to the light and life of the kingdom of God and to peace and justice on earth. The Spirit indwells those whom he makes alive with Christ, through faith incorporates us into the body of Christ, and conforms us to the image of Christ so that we may glorify him as we grow in knowledge, wisdom, and love into mature sainthood, the measure of the stature of the fullness of Christ. The Spirit is the light of truth and fire of love who continues to sanctify the people of God, prompting us to repentance and faith, diversifying our gifts, directing our witness, and empowering our discipleship.
Adapted from the Reforming Catholic Confession

CANTICLE

"This is my servant; I strengthen him,
this is my chosen one; I delight in him.
I have put my Spirit on him;
he will bring justice to the nations.
He will not cry out or shout
or make his voice heard in the streets.
He will not break a bruised reed,
and he will not put out a smoldering wick;
he will faithfully bring justice.
He will not grow weak or be discouraged
until he has established justice on earth.

The coasts and islands will wait for his instruction."
Isaiah 42:1–4

Morning Reading
John 16:1–15

"I have told you these things to keep you from stumbling. They will ban you from the synagogues. In fact, a time is coming when anyone who kills you will think he is offering service to God. They will do these things because they haven't known the Father or me. But I have told you these things so that when their time comes you will remember I told them to you. I didn't tell you these things from the beginning, because I was with you. But now I am going away to him who sent me, and not one of you asks me, 'Where are you going?' Yet, because I have spoken these things to you, sorrow has filled your heart. Nevertheless, I am telling you the truth. It is for your benefit that I go away, because if I don't go away the Counselor will not come to you. If I go, I will send him to you. When he comes, he will convict the world about sin, righteousness, and judgment: About sin, because they do not believe in me; about righteousness, because I am going to the Father and you will no longer see me; and about judgment, because the ruler of this world has been judged.

"I still have many things to tell you, but you can't bear them now. When the Spirit of truth comes, he will guide you into all the truth. For he will not speak on his own, but he will speak whatever he hears. He will also declare to you what is to come. He will glorify me, because he will take from what is mine and declare it to you. Everything the Father has is mine. This is why I told you that he takes from what is mine and will declare it to you."

This is the Word of the Lord. Thanks be to God.

Gloria

Glory be to God the Father, God the Son, and God the Holy Spirit. As it was in the beginning, is now, and will be forever, world without end.

The Lord's Prayer

Our Father in heaven,
Hallowed be your name.
Your kingdom come,
Your will be done
on earth as it is in heaven.
Give us this day our daily bread.
And forgive us our debts,
as we also have forgiven our debtors.
And lead us not into temptation
But deliver us from the evil one.
For yours is the kingdom and the power and the glory forever.
Amen.

Intercessions and Personal Requests

Prayer of the Church

As a reconciled Father, take me to be your child; and give me your renewing Spirit, to be in me a principle of holy life, and light, and love, and your seal and witness that I am yours. Let him enliven my dead and hardened heart. Let him enlighten my dark and unbelieving mind, by clearer knowledge and firm belief. Let him turn my will to the ready obedience of your holy will. Let him reveal to my soul the wonders of your love in Christ, and fill it with love to you and my Redeemer, and to all your holy Word and works. Amen.
Richard Baxter

Now to him who is able to do above and beyond all that we ask or think according to the power that works in us—to him be glory in the church and in Christ Jesus to all generations, forever and ever. Amen.
Ephesians 3:20–21

DAY 26 MIDDAY PRAYER

Call to Prayer

An hour is coming, and is now here, when the true worshipers will worship the Father in Spirit and in truth. Yes, the Father wants such people to worship him.
John 4:23

Midday Reading

John 16:16–33
"In a little while, you will no longer see me; again in a little while, you will see me."

Then some of his disciples said to one another, "What is this he's telling us: 'In a little while, you will not see me; again in a little while, you will see me,' and, 'Because I am going to the Father'?" They said, "What is this he is saying, 'In a little while'? We don't know what he's talking about."

Jesus knew they wanted to ask him, and so he said to them, "Are you asking one another about what I said, 'In a little while, you will not see me; again in a little while, you will see me'? Truly I tell you, you will weep and mourn, but the world will rejoice. You will become sorrowful, but your sorrow will turn to joy. When a woman is in labor, she has pain because her time has come. But when she has given birth to a child, she no longer remembers the suffering because of the joy that a person has been born into the world. So you also have sorrow now. But I will see you again. Your hearts will rejoice, and no one will take away your joy from you.

"In that day you will not ask me anything. Truly I tell you, anything you ask the Father in my name, he will give you. Until now you have asked for nothing in my name. Ask and you will receive, so that your joy may be complete.

"I have spoken these things to you in figures of speech. A time is coming when I will no longer speak to you in figures, but I will tell you plainly about the Father. On that day you will ask in my name, and I am not telling you that I will ask the Father on your behalf. For the Father himself loves you, because you have loved me and have believed that I came from God. I came from the Father and have come into the world. Again, I am leaving the world and going to the Father."

His disciples said, "Look, now you're speaking plainly and not using any figurative language. Now we know that you know everything and don't need anyone to question you. By this we believe that you came from God."

Jesus responded to them, "Do you now believe? Indeed, an hour is coming, and has come, when each of you will be scattered to his own home, and you will leave me alone. Yet I am not alone, because the Father is with me. I have told you these things so that in me you may have peace. You will have suffering in this world. Be courageous! I have conquered the world."

This is the Word of the Lord. Thanks be to God.

Gloria

Glory be to God the Father, God the Son, and God the Holy Spirit. As it was in the beginning, is now, and will be forever, world without end.

The Lord's Prayer

Our Father in heaven,
Hallowed be your name.
Your kingdom come,
Your will be done
on earth as it is in heaven.
Give us this day our daily bread.

And forgive us our debts,
as we also have forgiven our debtors.
And lead us not into temptation
But deliver us from the evil one.
For yours is the kingdom and the power and the glory forever.
Amen.

BLESSING

May your faithful love rest on us, LORD, for we put our hope
in you.
Psalm 33:22

DAY 26 EVENING PRAYER

CALL TO PRAYER

Father, Son, and Holy Spirit, one God: O come, let us adore
him.

CONFESSION OF SIN

I, a poor sinful person, confess to you, my Lord God and Maker,
that sadly I have sinned much, with my senses, thoughts, words,
and deeds, as you, eternal God, know very well. I regret them
and beg your grace. Amen.
Heinrich Bullinger

How joyful is the one whose transgression is forgiven, whose
sin is covered!
Psalm 32:1

CANTICLE

Our Lord and God,
you are worthy to receive
glory and honor and power,
because you have created all things,

and by your will
they exist and were created.
You are worthy to take the scroll
and to open its seals,
because you were slaughtered,
and you purchased people
for God by your blood
from every tribe and language
and people and nation.
You made them a kingdom
and priests to our God,
and they will reign on the earth.
Blessing and honor and glory and power
be to the one seated on the throne,
and to the Lamb, forever and ever!
Amen.
Revelation 4:11; 5:9–10,13,14

Evening Reading
John 17:1–26
Jesus spoke these things, looked up to heaven, and said, "Father, the hour has come. Glorify your Son so that the Son may glorify you, since you gave him authority over all people, so that he may give eternal life to everyone you have given him. This is eternal life: that they may know you, the only true God, and the one you have sent—Jesus Christ. I have glorified you on the earth by completing the work you gave me to do. Now, Father, glorify me in your presence with that glory I had with you before the world existed.

"I have revealed your name to the people you gave me from the world. They were yours, you gave them to me, and they have kept your word. Now they know that everything you have given me is from you, because I have given them the words you gave me. They have received them and have known for certain that I came from you. They have believed that you sent me.

"I pray for them. I am not praying for the world but for those you have given me, because they are yours. Everything I have is yours, and everything you have is mine, and I am glorified in them. I am no longer in the world, but they are in the world, and I am coming to you. Holy Father, protect them by your name that you have given me, so that they may be one as we are one. While I was with them, I was protecting them by your name that you have given me. I guarded them and not one of them is lost, except the son of destruction, so that the Scripture may be fulfilled. Now I am coming to you, and I speak these things in the world so that they may have my joy completed in them. I have given them your word. The world hated them because they are not of the world, just as I am not of the world. I am not praying that you take them out of the world but that you protect them from the evil one. They are not of the world, just as I am not of the world. Sanctify them by the truth; your word is truth. As you sent me into the world, I also have sent them into the world. I sanctify myself for them, so that they also may be sanctified by the truth.

"I pray not only for these, but also for those who believe in me through their word. May they all be one, as you, Father, are in me and I am in you. May they also be in us, so that the world may believe you sent me. I have given them the glory you have given me, so that they may be one as we are one. I am in them and you are in me, so that they may be made completely one, that the world may know you have sent me and have loved them as you have loved me.

"Father, I want those you have given me to be with me where I am, so that they will see my glory, which you have given me because you loved me before the world's foundation. Righteous Father, the world has not known you. However, I have known you, and they have known that you sent me. I made your name known to them and will continue to make it known, so that the love you have loved me with may be in them and I may be in them."

This is the Word of the Lord. Thanks be to God.

Gloria

Glory be to God the Father, God the Son, and God the Holy Spirit. As it was in the beginning, is now, and will be forever, world without end.

The Lord's Prayer

Our Father in heaven,
Hallowed be your name.
Your kingdom come,
Your will be done
on earth as it is in heaven.
Give us this day our daily bread.
And forgive us our debts,
as we also have forgiven our debtors.
And lead us not into temptation
But deliver us from the evil one.
For yours is the kingdom and the power and the glory forever.
Amen.

Intercessions and Personal Requests

Prayer of the Church

Father Almighty, Creator of heaven and earth: Set up your
kingdom in our midst. Lord Jesus Christ, Son of the Living
God: Have mercy on us sinners. Holy Spirit, Breath of the
Living God: Renew us and all the world.
N. T. Wright

Blessing

The Almighty and merciful Lord, Father, Son, and Holy Spirit,
bless us and keep us, this night and evermore. Amen.

DAY 27 MORNING PRAYER

CALL TO PRAYER

I cry to you, LORD; I say, "You are my shelter, my portion in the land of the living."
Psalm 142:5

CONFESSION OF FAITH

My only comfort in life and death is that I am not my own, but belong—body and soul, in life and death—to my faithful Savior, Jesus Christ. He has fully paid for all my sins with his precious blood, and has set me free from the tyranny of the devil. He also watches over me in such a way that not a hair can fall from my head without the will of my Father in heaven; in fact, all things must work together for my salvation. Because I belong to him, Christ, by his Holy Spirit, assures me of eternal life, and makes me wholeheartedly willing and ready from now on to live for him.
Adapted from the Heidelberg Catechism

CANTICLE

God, listen to my prayer
and do not hide from my plea for help.
Pay attention to me and answer me.
I am restless and in turmoil with my complaint,
because of the enemy's words,
because of the pressure of the wicked.
For they bring down disaster on me
and harass me in anger.
My heart shudders within me;
terrors of death sweep over me.
Fear and trembling grip me;
horror has overwhelmed me.
I said, "If only I had wings like a dove!
I would fly away and find rest.

How far away I would flee;
I would stay in the wilderness. *Selah*
I would hurry to my shelter
from the raging wind and the storm."
Psalm 55:1–8

Morning Readings

Mark 14:32–42

Then they came to a place named Gethsemane, and he told his disciples, "Sit here while I pray." He took Peter, James, and John with him, and he began to be deeply distressed and troubled. He said to them, "I am deeply grieved to the point of death. Remain here and stay awake." He went a little farther, fell to the ground, and prayed that if it were possible, the hour might pass from him. And he said, "Abba, Father! All things are possible for you. Take this cup away from me. Nevertheless, not what I will, but what you will." Then he came and found them sleeping. He said to Peter, "Simon, are you sleeping? Couldn't you stay awake one hour? Stay awake and pray so that you won't enter into temptation. The spirit is willing, but the flesh is weak." Once again he went away and prayed, saying the same thing. And again he came and found them sleeping, because they could not keep their eyes open. They did not know what to say to him. Then he came a third time and said to them, "Are you still sleeping and resting? Enough! The time has come. See, the Son of Man is betrayed into the hands of sinners. Get up; let's go. See, my betrayer is near."

Matthew 26:47–56

While he was still speaking, Judas, one of the Twelve, suddenly arrived. A large mob with swords and clubs was with him from the chief priests and elders of the people. His betrayer had given them a sign: "The one I kiss, he's the one; arrest him." So immediately he went up to Jesus and said, "Greetings, Rabbi!" and kissed him.

"Friend," Jesus asked him, "why have you come?"

Then they came up, took hold of Jesus, and arrested him. At that moment one of those with Jesus reached out his hand and drew his sword. He struck the high priest's servant and cut off his ear.

Then Jesus told him, "Put your sword back in its place because all who take up the sword will perish by the sword. Or do you think that I cannot call on my Father, and he will provide me here and now with more than twelve legions of angels? How, then, would the Scriptures be fulfilled that say it must happen this way?"

At that time Jesus said to the crowds, "Have you come out with swords and clubs, as if I were a criminal, to capture me? Every day I used to sit, teaching in the temple, and you didn't arrest me. But all this has happened so that the writings of the prophets would be fulfilled." Then all the disciples deserted him and ran away.

This is the Word of the Lord. Thanks be to God.

Gloria

Glory be to God the Father, God the Son, and God the Holy Spirit. As it was in the beginning, is now, and will be forever, world without end.

The Lord's Prayer

Our Father in heaven,
Hallowed be your name.
Your kingdom come,
Your will be done
on earth as it is in heaven.
Give us this day our daily bread.
And forgive us our debts,
as we also have forgiven our debtors.
And lead us not into temptation
But deliver us from the evil one.
For yours is the kingdom and the power and the glory forever.
Amen.

PRAYER OF THE CHURCH

Almighty God, you know that we have no power in ourselves
to help ourselves: Keep us both outwardly in our bodies and
inwardly in our souls, that we may be defended from all
adversities which may happen to the body, and from all evil
thoughts which may assault and hurt the soul; through Jesus
Christ our Lord, who lives and reigns with you and the Holy
Spirit, one God, for ever and ever.
The Book of Common Prayer

BLESSING

Now may the God of hope fill you with all joy and peace as you
believe, so that you may overflow with hope by the power of the
Holy Spirit.
Romans 15:13

DAY 27 MIDDAY PRAYER

CALL TO PRAYER

God, hear my cry; pay attention to my prayer.
Psalm 61:1

MIDDAY READINGS

John 18:13–14
First they led him to Annas, since he was the father-in-law of
Caiaphas, who was high priest that year. Caiaphas was the one
who had advised the Jews that it would be better for one man to
die for the people.

John 18:19–24
The high priest questioned Jesus about his disciples and about
his teaching.

"I have spoken openly to the world," Jesus answered him. "I have always taught in the synagogue and in the temple, where all the Jews gather, and I haven't spoken anything in secret. Why do you question me? Question those who heard what I told them. Look, they know what I said."

When he had said these things, one of the officials standing by slapped Jesus, saying, "Is this the way you answer the high priest?"

"If I have spoken wrongly," Jesus answered him, "give evidence about the wrong; but if rightly, why do you hit me?" Then Annas sent him bound to Caiaphas the high priest.

Matthew 26:59–68
The chief priests and the whole Sanhedrin were looking for false testimony against Jesus so that they could put him to death, but they could not find any, even though many false witnesses came forward. Finally, two who came forward stated, "This man said, 'I can destroy the temple of God and rebuild it in three days.'"

The high priest stood up and said to him, "Don't you have an answer to what these men are testifying against you?" But Jesus kept silent. The high priest said to him, "I charge you under oath by the living God: Tell us if you are the Messiah, the Son of God."

"You have said it," Jesus told him. "But I tell you, in the future you will see **the Son of Man seated at the right hand** of Power and **coming on the clouds of heaven**."

Then the high priest tore his robes and said, "He has blasphemed! Why do we still need witnesses? See, now you've heard the blasphemy. What is your decision?"

They answered, "He deserves death!" Then they spat in his face and beat him; others slapped him and said, "Prophesy to us, Messiah! Who was it that hit you?"

This is the Word of the Lord. Thanks be to God.

Glory be to God the Father, God the Son, and God the Holy Spirit. As it was in the beginning, is now, and will be forever, world without end.

THE LORD'S PRAYER

Our Father in heaven,
Hallowed be your name.
Your kingdom come,
Your will be done
on earth as it is in heaven.
Give us this day our daily bread.
And forgive us our debts,
as we also have forgiven our debtors.
And lead us not into temptation
But deliver us from the evil one.
For yours is the kingdom and the power and the glory forever.
Amen.

BLESSING

May [the LORD] give you what your heart desires and fulfill your whole purpose. May the LORD fulfill all your requests.
Psalm 20:4–5

DAY 27 EVENING PRAYER

CALL TO PRAYER

The LORD will fulfill his purpose for me. LORD, your faithful love endures forever; do not abandon the work of your hands.
Psalm 138:8

CONFESSION OF SIN

Holy Spirit, grant us each a true conviction leading to a true repentance. Indeed it was our desire to serve you well

in this day, O God, but we have again fallen short of your righteousness in our thoughts, our intentions, our actions, and our utterances. We have responded at times without grace. We have chosen sometimes that which is unprofitable and which leads neither to our own flourishing nor to the proclamation of your glory. Forgive us, O King, for treasons both known and unknown. Forgive us for the harms we have done this day, and for the goods we might have done but failed to do; forgive us also for the constant condition of our hearts, for the self-serving impulses, inclinations, and desires which stand us every moment in need of a savior.
Every Moment Holy

The sacrifice pleasing to God is a broken spirit. You will not despise a broken and humbled heart, God.
Psalm 51:17

Canticle

See, my servant will be successful;
he will be raised and lifted up and greatly exalted.
Just as many were appalled at you—
his appearance was so disfigured
that he did not look like a man,
and his form did not resemble a human being—
so he will sprinkle many nations.
Kings will shut their mouths because of him,
for they will see what had not been told them,
and they will understand what they had not heard.
Isaiah 52:13–14

Evening Readings

Matthew 26:69–75
Now Peter was sitting outside in the courtyard. A servant girl approached him and said, "You were with Jesus the Galilean too."

But he denied it in front of everyone: "I don't know what you're talking about."

When he had gone out to the gateway, another woman saw him and told those who were there, "This man was with Jesus the Nazarene!"

And again he denied it with an oath: "I don't know the man!"

After a little while those standing there approached and said to Peter, "You really are one of them, since even your accent gives you away."

Then he started to curse and to swear with an oath, "I don't know the man!" Immediately a rooster crowed, and Peter remembered the words Jesus had spoken, "Before the rooster crows, you will deny me three times." And he went outside and wept bitterly.

Luke 22:66–71
When daylight came, the elders of the people, both the chief priests and the scribes, convened and brought him before their Sanhedrin. They said, "If you are the Messiah, tell us."

But he said to them, "If I do tell you, you will not believe. And if I ask you, you will not answer. But from now on, the Son of Man will be seated at the right hand of the power of God."

They all asked, "Are you, then, the Son of God?"

And he said to them, "You say that I am."

"Why do we need any more testimony," they said, "since we've heard it ourselves from his mouth?"

Matthew 27:2–10
After tying him up, they led him away and handed him over to Pilate, the governor.

Then Judas, his betrayer, seeing that Jesus had been condemned, was full of remorse and returned the thirty pieces of silver to the chief priests and elders. "I have sinned by betraying innocent blood," he said.

"What's that to us?" they said. "See to it yourself!" So he threw the silver into the temple and departed. Then he went and hanged himself.

The chief priests took the silver and said, "It's not permitted to put it into the temple treasury, since it is blood money." They conferred together and bought the potter's field with it as a burial place for foreigners. Therefore that field has been called "Field of

Blood" to this day. Then what was spoken through the prophet Jeremiah was fulfilled: **They took the thirty pieces of silver, the price of him whose price was set by the Israelites, and they gave them for the potter's field, as the Lord directed me.**

This is the Word of the Lord. Thanks be to God.

GLORIA

Glory be to God the Father, God the Son, and God the Holy Spirit. As it was in the beginning, is now, and will be forever, world without end.

THE LORD'S PRAYER

Our Father in heaven,
Hallowed be your name.
Your kingdom come,
Your will be done
on earth as it is in heaven.
Give us this day our daily bread.
And forgive us our debts,
as we also have forgiven our debtors.
And lead us not into temptation
But deliver us from the evil one.
For yours is the kingdom and the power and the glory forever.
Amen.

INTERCESSIONS AND PERSONAL REQUESTS

PRAYER OF THE CHURCH

I am pardoned through the blood of Jesus—give me a new sense of it, continue to pardon me by it, may I come every day to the fountain, and every day be washed anew, that I may worship you always in spirit and truth.
The Valley of Vision

The Lord Almighty grant us a peaceful night and a perfect end. Amen.

DAY 28 MORNING PRAYER

CALL TO PRAYER

Turn your face from all my sins and blot out all my guilt.
Psalm 51:9

CONFESSION OF FAITH

I believe that God, who is rich in mercy towards the
undeserving, has made gracious provision for human
wrongdoing, corruption, and guilt, provisionally and
typologically through Israel's Temple and sin offerings, then
definitively and gloriously in the gift of Jesus's once-for-all
sufficient and perfect sacrificial death on the cross in the temple
of his human flesh. By his death in our stead, he revealed God's
love and upheld God's justice, removing our guilt, vanquishing
the powers that held us captive, and reconciling us to God. It
is wholly by grace, not our own works or merits, that we have
been forgiven; it is wholly by Jesus's shed blood, not by our own
sweat and tears, that we have been cleansed.
Adapted from the Reforming Catholic Confession

CANTICLE

Who has believed what we have heard?
And to whom has the arm of the LORD been revealed?
He grew up before him like a young plant
and like a root out of dry ground.
He didn't have an impressive form
or majesty that we should look at him,
no appearance that we should desire him.
He was despised and rejected by men,
a man of suffering who knew what sickness was.
He was like someone people turned away from;
he was despised, and we didn't value him.
Yet he himself bore our sicknesses,
and he carried our pains;

but we in turn regarded him stricken,
struck down by God, and afflicted.
But he was pierced because of our rebellion,
crushed because of our iniquities;
punishment for our peace was on him,
and we are healed by his wounds.
We all went astray like sheep;
we all have turned to our own way;
and the LORD has punished him
for the iniquity of us all.
Isaiah 53:1–6

MORNING READING

John 18:28–19:16

Then they led Jesus from Caiaphas to the governor's headquarters. It was early morning. They did not enter the headquarters themselves; otherwise they would be defiled and unable to eat the Passover.

So Pilate came out to them and said, "What charge do you bring against this man?"

They answered him, "If this man weren't a criminal, we wouldn't have handed him over to you."

Pilate told them, "You take him and judge him according to your law."

"It's not legal for us to put anyone to death," the Jews declared. They said this so that Jesus's words might be fulfilled indicating what kind of death he was going to die.

Then Pilate went back into the headquarters, summoned Jesus, and said to him, "Are you the king of the Jews?"

Jesus answered, "Are you asking this on your own, or have others told you about me?"

"I'm not a Jew, am I?" Pilate replied. "Your own nation and the chief priests handed you over to me. What have you done?"

"My kingdom is not of this world," said Jesus. "If my kingdom were of this world, my servants would fight, so that I wouldn't be handed over to the Jews. But as it is, my kingdom is not from here."

"You are a king then?" Pilate asked.

"You say that I'm a king," Jesus replied. "I was born for this, and I have come into the world for this: to testify to the truth. Everyone who is of the truth listens to my voice."

"What is truth?" said Pilate.

After he had said this, he went out to the Jews again and told them, "I find no grounds for charging him. You have a custom that I release one prisoner to you at the Passover. So, do you want me to release to you the king of the Jews?"

They shouted back, "Not this man, but Barabbas!" Now Barabbas was a revolutionary.

Then Pilate took Jesus and had him flogged. The soldiers also twisted together a crown of thorns, put it on his head, and clothed him in a purple robe. And they kept coming up to him and saying, "Hail, king of the Jews!" and were slapping his face.

Pilate went outside again and said to them, "Look, I'm bringing him out to you to let you know I find no grounds for charging him." Then Jesus came out wearing the crown of thorns and the purple robe. Pilate said to them, "Here is the man!"

When the chief priests and the temple servants saw him, they shouted, "Crucify! Crucify!"

Pilate responded, "Take him and crucify him yourselves, since I find no grounds for charging him."

"We have a law," the Jews replied to him, "and according to that law he ought to die, because he made himself the Son of God."

When Pilate heard this statement, he was more afraid than ever. He went back into the headquarters and asked Jesus, "Where are you from?" But Jesus did not give him an answer. So Pilate said to him, "Do you refuse to speak to me? Don't you know that I have the authority to release you and the authority to crucify you?"

"You would have no authority over me at all," Jesus answered him, "if it hadn't been given you from above. This is why the one who handed me over to you has the greater sin."

From that moment Pilate kept trying to release him. But the Jews shouted, "If you release this man, you are not Caesar's friend. Anyone who makes himself a king opposes Caesar!"

When Pilate heard these words, he brought Jesus outside. He sat down on the judge's seat in a place called the Stone Pavement (but in Aramaic, *Gabbatha*). It was the preparation day for the Passover, and it was about noon. Then he told the Jews, "Here is your king!"

They shouted, "Take him away! Take him away! Crucify him!"

Pilate said to them, "Should I crucify your king?"

"We have no king but Caesar!" the chief priests answered.

Then he handed him over to be crucified.

This is the Word of the Lord. Thanks be to God.

GLORIA

Glory be to God the Father, God the Son, and God the Holy Spirit. As it was in the beginning, is now, and will be forever, world without end.

THE LORD'S PRAYER

Our Father in heaven,
Hallowed be your name.
Your kingdom come,
Your will be done
on earth as it is in heaven.
Give us this day our daily bread.
And forgive us our debts,
as we also have forgiven our debtors.
And lead us not into temptation
But deliver us from the evil one.
For yours is the kingdom and the power and the glory forever.
Amen.

PRAYER OF THE CHURCH

Lord Jesus Christ, you stretched out your arms of love on the hard wood of the cross that everyone might come within the reach of your saving embrace: So clothe us in your Spirit that we, reaching forth our hands in love, may bring those who do not know you to the knowledge and love of you; for the honor of your name. Amen.

The Book of Common Prayer

BLESSING

The grace of the Lord Jesus Christ, and the love of God, and the fellowship of the Holy Spirit be with us all.

2 Corinthians 13:14

DAY 28 MIDDAY PRAYER

CALL TO PRAYER

The mercy of the Lord is everlasting: O come, let us adore him.

MIDDAY READINGS

Luke 23:26–43

As they led him away, they seized Simon, a Cyrenian, who was coming in from the country, and laid the cross on him to carry behind Jesus. A large crowd of people followed him, including women who were mourning and lamenting him. But turning to them, Jesus said, "Daughters of Jerusalem, do not weep for me, but weep for yourselves and your children. Look, the days are coming when they will say, 'Blessed are the women without children, the wombs that never bore, and the breasts that never nursed!' **Then they will begin to say to the mountains, 'Fall on us!' and to the hills, 'Cover us!'** For if they do these things when the wood is green, what will happen when it is dry?"

Two others—criminals—were also led away to be executed with him. When they arrived at the place called The Skull, they crucified him there, along with the criminals, one on the right and one on the left. Then Jesus said, "Father, forgive them, because they do not know what they are doing." And they divided his clothes and cast lots.

The people stood watching, and even the leaders were scoffing: "He saved others; let him save himself if this is God's Messiah, the Chosen One!" The soldiers also mocked him. They came offering him sour wine and said, "If you are the king of the Jews, save yourself!"

An inscription was above him: THIS IS THE KING OF THE JEWS.

Then one of the criminals hanging there began to yell insults at him: "Aren't you the Messiah? Save yourself and us!"

But the other answered, rebuking him: "Don't you even fear God, since you are undergoing the same punishment? We are punished justly, because we're getting back what we deserve for the things we did, but this man has done nothing wrong." Then he said, "Jesus, remember me when you come into your kingdom."

And he said to him, "Truly I tell you, today you will be with me in paradise."

Matthew 27:45–49
From noon until three in the afternoon, darkness came over the whole land. About three in the afternoon Jesus cried out with a loud voice, "*Elí, Elí, lemá sabachtháni?*" that is, "**My God, my God, why have you abandoned me?**"

When some of those standing there heard this, they said, "He's calling for Elijah."

Immediately one of them ran and got a sponge, filled it with sour wine, put it on a stick, and offered him a drink. But the rest said, "Let's see if Elijah comes to save him."

John 19:25–30
Standing by the cross of Jesus were his mother, his mother's sister, Mary the wife of Clopas, and Mary Magdalene. When Jesus saw his mother and the disciple he loved standing there,

he said to his mother, "Woman, here is your son." Then he said to the disciple, "Here is your mother." And from that hour the disciple took her into his home.

After this, when Jesus knew that everything was now finished that the Scripture might be fulfilled, he said, "I'm thirsty." A jar full of sour wine was sitting there; so they fixed a sponge full of sour wine on a hyssop branch and held it up to his mouth.

When Jesus had received the sour wine, he said, "It is finished."

Luke 23:45–46
The curtain of the sanctuary was split down the middle. And Jesus called out with a loud voice, "Father, **into your hands I entrust my spirit.**" Saying this, he breathed his last.

Mark 15:39–41
When the centurion, who was standing opposite him, saw the way he breathed his last, he said, "Truly this man was the Son of God!"

There were also women watching from a distance. Among them were Mary Magdalene, Mary the mother of James the younger and of Joses, and Salome. In Galilee these women followed him and took care of him. Many other women had come up with him to Jerusalem.

This is the Word of the Lord. Thanks be to God.

Gloria

Glory be to God the Father, God the Son, and God the Holy Spirit. As it was in the beginning, is now, and will be forever, world without end.

The Lord's Prayer

Our Father in heaven,
Hallowed be your name.
Your kingdom come,
Your will be done

on earth as it is in heaven.
Give us this day our daily bread.
And forgive us our debts,
as we also have forgiven our debtors.
And lead us not into temptation
But deliver us from the evil one.
For yours is the kingdom and the power and the glory forever.
Amen.

BLESSING

The peace of God, which passes all understanding, keep your
hearts and minds in the knowledge and love of God, and of his
Son Jesus Christ our Lord; and the blessing of God Almighty,
the Father, the Son, and the Holy Spirit, be among you, and
remain with you always. Amen.

DAY 28 EVENING PRAYER

CALL TO PRAYER

We all went astray like sheep; we all have turned to our own
way; and the LORD has punished him for the iniquity of us all.
Isaiah 53:6

CONFESSION OF SIN

Lord Jesus Christ, who stretched out your hands on the cross,
and redeemed us by your blood: forgive me, a sinner, for none
of my thoughts are hidden from you. Pardon I ask, pardon I
hope for, pardon I trust to have. You who are full of pity and
mercy: spare me, and forgive.
Ambrose

If we confess our sins, he is faithful and righteous to forgive us
our sins and to cleanse us from all unrighteousness.
1 John 1:9

He was oppressed and afflicted,
yet he did not open his mouth.
Like a lamb led to the slaughter
and like a sheep silent before her shearers,
he did not open his mouth.
He was taken away because of oppression and judgment,
and who considered his fate?
For he was cut off from the land of the living;
he was struck because of my people's rebellion.
He was assigned a grave with the wicked,
but he was with a rich man at his death,
because he had done no violence
and had not spoken deceitfully.
Yet the LORD was pleased to crush him severely.
When you make him a guilt offering,
he will see his seed, he will prolong his days,
and by his hand, the LORD's pleasure will be accomplished.
After his anguish,
he will see light and be satisfied.
By his knowledge,
my righteous servant will justify many,
and he will carry their iniquities.
Therefore I will give him the many as a portion,
and he will receive the mighty as spoil,
because he willingly submitted to death,
and was counted among the rebels;
yet he bore the sin of many
and interceded for the rebels.
Isaiah 53:7–12

EVENING READINGS

John 19:31–42

Since it was the preparation day, the Jews did not want the
bodies to remain on the cross on the Sabbath (for that Sabbath
was a special day). They requested that Pilate have the men's
legs broken and that their bodies be taken away. So the soldiers
came and broke the legs of the first man and of the other one

who had been crucified with him. When they came to Jesus, they did not break his legs since they saw that he was already dead. But one of the soldiers pierced his side with a spear, and at once blood and water came out. He who saw this has testified so that you also may believe. His testimony is true, and he knows he is telling the truth. For these things happened so that the Scripture would be fulfilled: **Not one of his bones will be broken.** Also, another Scripture says: **They will look at the one they pierced.**

After this, Joseph of Arimathea, who was a disciple of Jesus—but secretly because of his fear of the Jews—asked Pilate that he might remove Jesus's body. Pilate gave him permission; so he came and took his body away. Nicodemus (who had previously come to him at night) also came, bringing a mixture of about seventy-five pounds of myrrh and aloes. They took Jesus's body and wrapped it in linen cloths with the fragrant spices, according to the burial custom of the Jews. There was a garden in the place where he was crucified. A new tomb was in the garden; no one had yet been placed in it. They placed Jesus there because of the Jewish day of preparation and since the tomb was nearby.

Matthew 27:62–66
The next day, which followed the preparation day, the chief priests and the Pharisees gathered before Pilate and said, "Sir, we remember that while this deceiver was still alive he said, 'After three days I will rise again.' So give orders that the tomb be made secure until the third day. Otherwise, his disciples may come, steal him, and tell the people, 'He has been raised from the dead,' and the last deception will be worse than the first."

"Take guards," Pilate told them. "Go and make it as secure as you know how." They went and secured the tomb by setting a seal on the stone and placing the guards.

This is the Word of the Lord. Thanks be to God.

GLORIA

Glory be to God the Father, God the Son, and God the Holy Spirit. As it was in the beginning, is now, and will be forever, world without end.

THE LORD'S PRAYER

Our Father in heaven,
Hallowed be your name.
Your kingdom come,
Your will be done
on earth as it is in heaven.
Give us this day our daily bread.
And forgive us our debts,
as we also have forgiven our debtors.
And lead us not into temptation
But deliver us from the evil one.
For yours is the kingdom and the power and the glory forever.
Amen.

INTERCESSIONS AND PERSONAL REQUESTS

PRAYER OF THE CHURCH

Almighty God, whose dear Son went not up to joy but first he suffered pain, and entered not into glory before he was crucified: Mercifully grant that we, walking in the way of the cross, may find it none other than the way of life and peace; through Jesus Christ your Son our Lord, who lives and reigns with you and the Holy Spirit, one God, for ever and ever. Amen.
The Book of Common Prayer

BLESSING

The Almighty and merciful Lord, Father, Son, and Holy Spirit, bless us and keep us, this night and evermore. Amen.

DAY 29 MORNING PRAYER

Alleluia. The Lord is risen indeed: O come, let us adore him.
Alleluia.

I believe that Christ died for our sins according to the
Scriptures, that he was buried, that he was raised on the
third day according to the Scriptures, and that he appeared
to Cephas, then to the Twelve. Then he appeared to over five
hundred brothers and sisters at one time.
1 Corinthians 15:3–6

I will sing to the Lord,
for he is highly exalted;
he has thrown the horse
and its rider into the sea.
The Lord is my strength and my song;
he has become my salvation.
This is my God, and I will praise him,
my father's God, and I will exalt him.
The Lord is a warrior;
the Lord is his name.
He threw Pharaoh's chariots
and his army into the sea;
the elite of his officers
were drowned in the Red Sea.
The floods covered them;
they sank to the depths like a stone.
Lord, your right hand is glorious in power.
Lord, your right hand shattered the enemy.
Lord, who is like you among the gods?
Who is like you, glorious in holiness,

revered with praises, performing wonders?
You stretched out your right hand,
and the earth swallowed them.
With your faithful love,
you will lead the people
you have redeemed;
you will guide them to your holy dwelling
with your strength.
You will bring them in and plant them
on the mountain of your possession;
LORD, you have prepared the place
for your dwelling;
Lord, your hands have established the sanctuary.
The LORD will reign forever and ever!
Exodus 15:1–6,11–13,17–18

MORNING READINGS

Luke 24:1–11

On the first day of the week, very early in the morning, they
came to the tomb, bringing the spices they had prepared. They
found the stone rolled away from the tomb. They went in
but did not find the body of the Lord Jesus. While they were
perplexed about this, suddenly two men stood by them in
dazzling clothes. So the women were terrified and bowed down
to the ground.

"Why are you looking for the living among the dead?" asked
the men. "He is not here, but he has risen! Remember how he
spoke to you when he was still in Galilee, saying, 'It is necessary
that the Son of Man be betrayed into the hands of sinful men,
be crucified, and rise on the third day'?" And they remembered
his words.

Returning from the tomb, they reported all these things to
the Eleven and to all the rest. Mary Magdalene, Joanna, Mary
the mother of James, and the other women with them were

telling the apostles these things. But these words seemed like nonsense to them, and they did not believe the women.

John 20:3–18
At that, Peter and the other disciple went out, heading for the tomb. The two were running together, but the other disciple outran Peter and got to the tomb first. Stooping down, he saw the linen cloths lying there, but he did not go in. Then, following him, Simon Peter also came. He entered the tomb and saw the linen cloths lying there. The wrapping that had been on his head was not lying with the linen cloths but was folded up in a separate place by itself. The other disciple, who had reached the tomb first, then also went in, saw, and believed. For they did not yet understand the Scripture that he must rise from the dead. Then the disciples returned to the place where they were staying.

But Mary stood outside the tomb, crying. As she was crying, she stooped to look into the tomb. She saw two angels in white sitting where Jesus's body had been lying, one at the head and the other at the feet. They said to her, "Woman, why are you crying?"

"Because they've taken away my Lord," she told them, "and I don't know where they've put him."

Having said this, she turned around and saw Jesus standing there, but she did not know it was Jesus. "Woman," Jesus said to her, "why are you crying? Who is it that you're seeking?"

Supposing he was the gardener, she replied, "Sir, if you've carried him away, tell me where you've put him, and I will take him away."

Jesus said to her, "Mary."

Turning around, she said to him in Aramaic, "*Rabboni!*"— which means "Teacher."

"Don't cling to me," Jesus told her, "since I have not yet ascended to the Father. But go to my brothers and tell them that I am ascending to my Father and your Father, to my God and your God."

Mary Magdalene went and announced to the disciples, "I have seen the Lord!" And she told them what he had said to her.

Matthew 28:11–15
As they were on their way, some of the guards came into the city and reported to the chief priests everything that had happened. After the priests had assembled with the elders and agreed on a plan, they gave the soldiers a large sum of money and told them, "Say this, 'His disciples came during the night and stole him while we were sleeping.' If this reaches the governor's ears, we will deal with him and keep you out of trouble." They took the money and did as they were instructed, and this story has been spread among Jewish people to this day.

This is the Word of the Lord. Thanks be to God.

Gloria

Glory be to God the Father, God the Son, and God the Holy Spirit. As it was in the beginning, is now, and will be forever, world without end.

The Lord's Prayer

Our Father in heaven,
Hallowed be your name.
Your kingdom come,
Your will be done
on earth as it is in heaven.
Give us this day our daily bread.
And forgive us our debts,
as we also have forgiven our debtors.
And lead us not into temptation
But deliver us from the evil one.
For yours is the kingdom and the power and the glory forever.
Amen.

Prayer of the Church

O God, who by the glorious resurrection of your Son Jesus Christ destroyed death and brought life and immortality to light: Grant that we, who have been raised with him, may abide in his presence and rejoice in the hope of eternal glory; through Jesus Christ our Lord, to whom, with you and the Holy Spirit, be dominion and praise for ever and ever.

The Book of Common Prayer

Blessing

Now to him who is able to do above and beyond all that we ask or think according to the power that works in us—to him be glory in the church and in Christ Jesus to all generations, forever and ever. Amen.

Ephesians 3:20–21

DAY 29 MIDDAY PRAYER

Call to Prayer

The LORD lives—blessed be my rock! The God of my salvation is exalted.

Psalm 18:46

Midday Reading

Luke 24:13–35

Now that same day two of them were on their way to a village called Emmaus, which was about seven miles from Jerusalem. Together they were discussing everything that had taken place. And while they were discussing and arguing, Jesus himself came near and began to walk along with them. But they were prevented from recognizing him. Then he asked them, "What is this dispute that you're having with each other as you are walking?" And they stopped walking and looked discouraged.

The one named Cleopas answered him, "Are you the only visitor in Jerusalem who doesn't know the things that happened there in these days?"

"What things?" he asked them.

So they said to him, "The things concerning Jesus of Nazareth, who was a prophet powerful in action and speech before God and all the people, and how our chief priests and leaders handed him over to be sentenced to death, and they crucified him. But we were hoping that he was the one who was about to redeem Israel. Besides all this, it's the third day since these things happened. Moreover, some women from our group astounded us. They arrived early at the tomb, and when they didn't find his body, they came and reported that they had seen a vision of angels who said he was alive. Some of those who were with us went to the tomb and found it just as the women had said, but they didn't see him."

He said to them, "How foolish you are, and how slow to believe all that the prophets have spoken! Wasn't it necessary for the Messiah to suffer these things and enter into his glory?" Then beginning with Moses and all the Prophets, he interpreted for them the things concerning himself in all the Scriptures.

They came near the village where they were going, and he gave the impression that he was going farther. But they urged him, "Stay with us, because it's almost evening, and now the day is almost over." So he went in to stay with them.

It was as he reclined at the table with them that he took the bread, blessed and broke it, and gave it to them. Then their eyes were opened, and they recognized him, but he disappeared from their sight. They said to each other, "Weren't our hearts burning within us while he was talking with us on the road and explaining the Scriptures to us?" That very hour they got up and returned to Jerusalem. They found the Eleven and those with them gathered together, who said, "The Lord has truly been raised and has appeared to Simon!" Then they began to describe what had happened on the road and how he was made known to them in the breaking of the bread.

This is the Word of the Lord. Thanks be to God.

Glory be to God the Father, God the Son, and God the Holy
Spirit. As it was in the beginning, is now, and will be forever,
world without end.

THE LORD'S PRAYER
Our Father in heaven,
Hallowed be your name.
Your kingdom come,
Your will be done
on earth as it is in heaven.
Give us this day our daily bread.
And forgive us our debts,
as we also have forgiven our debtors.
And lead us not into temptation
But deliver us from the evil one.
For yours is the kingdom and the power and the glory forever.
Amen.

BLESSING
The grace of the Lord Jesus Christ, and the love of God, and the
fellowship of the Holy Spirit be with us all.
2 Corinthians 13:14

DAY 29 EVENING PRAYER

CALL TO PRAYER
Thanks be to God, who gives us the victory through our Lord
Jesus Christ!
1 Corinthians 15:57

Confession of Sin

Lord, have mercy on us.
Christ, have mercy on us.
Lord, have mercy on us.

The sacrifice pleasing to God is a broken spirit. You will not
despise a broken and humbled heart, God.
Psalm 51:17

Canticle

Alleluia. Christ our Passover has been sacrificed,
therefore let us observe the feast,
Not with old leaven, or with the leaven of malice and evil,
but with the unleavened bread of sincerity and truth. Alleluia.
Christ, having been raised from the dead, will not die again;
death no longer rules over him.
For the death that he died, he died to sin once for all time,
but the life he lives, he lives to God.
So, you too consider yourselves dead to sin
and alive to God in Christ Jesus. Alleluia.
Christ has been raised from the dead,
the firstfruits of those who have fallen asleep.
For since death came through a man,
the resurrection of the dead also comes through a man.
For as in Adam all die,
so also in Christ all will be made alive. Alleluia.
1 Corinthians 5:7–8; Romans 6:9–11; 1 Corinthians 15:20–22

Evening Readings

John 20:19
When it was evening on that first day of the week, the disciples
were gathered together with the doors locked because they
feared the Jews. Jesus came, stood among them, and said to
them, "Peace be with you."

Luke 24:37–43

But they were startled and terrified and thought they were seeing a ghost. "Why are you troubled?" he asked them. "And why do doubts arise in your hearts? Look at my hands and my feet, that it is I myself! Touch me and see, because a ghost does not have flesh and bones as you can see I have." Having said this, he showed them his hands and feet. But while they still were amazed and in disbelief because of their joy, he asked them, "Do you have anything here to eat?" So they gave him a piece of a broiled fish, and he took it and ate in their presence.

John 20:21–29

Jesus said to them again, "Peace be with you. As the Father has sent me, I also send you." After saying this, he breathed on them and said, "Receive the Holy Spirit. If you forgive the sins of any, they are forgiven them; if you retain the sins of any, they are retained."

But Thomas (called "Twin"), one of the Twelve, was not with them when Jesus came. So the other disciples were telling him, "We've seen the Lord!"

But he said to them, "If I don't see the mark of the nails in his hands, put my finger into the mark of the nails, and put my hand into his side, I will never believe."

A week later his disciples were indoors again, and Thomas was with them. Even though the doors were locked, Jesus came and stood among them and said, "Peace be with you."

Then he said to Thomas, "Put your finger here and look at my hands. Reach out your hand and put it into my side. Don't be faithless, but believe."

Thomas responded to him, "My Lord and my God!"

Jesus said, "Because you have seen me, you have believed. Blessed are those who have not seen and yet believe."

This is the Word of the Lord. Thanks be to God.

GLORIA

Glory be to God the Father, God the Son, and God the Holy
Spirit. As it was in the beginning, is now, and will be forever,
world without end.

THE LORD'S PRAYER

Our Father in heaven,
Hallowed be your name.
Your kingdom come,
Your will be done
on earth as it is in heaven.
Give us this day our daily bread.
And forgive us our debts,
as we also have forgiven our debtors.
And lead us not into temptation
But deliver us from the evil one.
For yours is the kingdom and the power and the glory forever.
Amen.

INTERCESSIONS AND PERSONAL REQUESTS

PRAYER OF THE CHURCH

O God of my exodus, great was the joy of Israel's sons when
Egypt died upon the shore, far greater the joy when the
Redeemer's foe lay crushed in the dust! Jesus strides forth as
the victor, conqueror of death, hell, and all opposing might;
he bursts the bands of death, tramples the powers of darkness
down, and lives forever. He, my gracious surety, apprehended for
payment of my debt, comes forth from the prison house of the
grave free, and triumphant over sin, Satan, and death. Show me
the proof that his vicarious offering is accepted, that the claims
of justice are satisfied, that the devil's scepter is shivered, that his
wrongful throne is leveled. Give me the assurance that in Christ
I died, in him I rose, in his life I live, in his victory I triumph, in
his ascension I shall be glorified.
The Valley of Vision

Blessing

The Lord Almighty grant us a peaceful night and a perfect end.
Amen.

DAY 30 MORNING PRAYER

So if you have been raised with Christ, seek the things above,
where Christ is, seated at the right hand of God.
Colossians 3:1

CONFESSION OF FAITH

I believe the Son of God was manifested in the flesh,
vindicated in the Spirit,
seen by angels,
preached among the nations,
believed on in the world,
taken up in glory.
1 Timothy 3:16

CANTICLE

You are God: we praise you;
you are the Lord; we acclaim you;
you are the eternal Father:
All creation worships you.
To you all angels, all the powers of heaven,
Cherubim and Seraphim, sing in endless praise:
Holy, holy, holy Lord, God of power and might,
heaven and earth are full of your glory.
The glorious company of apostles praise you.
The noble fellowship of prophets praise you.
The white-robed army of martyrs praise you.
Throughout the world the holy Church acclaims you;
Father, of majesty unbounded,
your true and only Son, worthy of all worship,
and the Holy Spirit, advocate and guide.
You, Christ, are the king of glory,
the eternal Son of the Father.
When you became man to set us free

you did not shun the Virgin's womb.
You overcame the sting of death
and opened the kingdom of heaven to all believers.
You are seated at God's right hand in glory.
We believe that you will come and be our judge.
Come then, Lord, and help your people,
bought with the price of your own blood,
and bring us with your saints
to glory everlasting.
Te Deum

Morning Reading

John 21:1–14

After this, Jesus revealed himself again to his disciples by the Sea of Tiberias. He revealed himself in this way:

Simon Peter, Thomas (called "Twin"), Nathanael from Cana of Galilee, Zebedee's sons, and two others of his disciples were together.

"I'm going fishing," Simon Peter said to them.

"We're coming with you," they told him. They went out and got into the boat, but that night they caught nothing.

When daybreak came, Jesus stood on the shore, but the disciples did not know it was Jesus. "Friends," Jesus called to them, "you don't have any fish, do you?"

"No," they answered.

"Cast the net on the right side of the boat," he told them, "and you'll find some." So they did, and they were unable to haul it in because of the large number of fish. The disciple, the one Jesus loved, said to Peter, "It is the Lord!"

When Simon Peter heard that it was the Lord, he tied his outer clothing around him (for he had taken it off) and plunged into the sea. Since they were not far from land (about a hundred yards away), the other disciples came in the boat, dragging the net full of fish.

When they got out on land, they saw a charcoal fire there, with fish lying on it, and bread. "Bring some of the fish you've just caught," Jesus told them. So Simon Peter climbed up and hauled the net ashore, full of large fish—153 of them. Even though there were so many, the net was not torn.

"Come and have breakfast," Jesus told them. None of the disciples dared ask him, "Who are you?" because they knew it was the Lord. Jesus came, took the bread, and gave it to them. He did the same with the fish. This was now the third time Jesus appeared to the disciples after he was raised from the dead.

This is the Word of the Lord. Thanks be to God.

GLORIA

Glory be to God the Father, God the Son, and God the Holy Spirit. As it was in the beginning, is now, and will be forever, world without end.

THE LORD'S PRAYER

Our Father in heaven,
Hallowed be your name.
Your kingdom come,
Your will be done
on earth as it is in heaven.
Give us this day our daily bread.
And forgive us our debts,
as we also have forgiven our debtors.
And lead us not into temptation
But deliver us from the evil one.
For yours is the kingdom and the power and the glory forever.
Amen.

INTERCESSIONS AND PERSONAL REQUESTS

PRAYER OF THE CHURCH

O God, who for our redemption gave your only-begotten Son to the death of the cross, and by his glorious resurrection delivered us from the power of our enemy: Grant us so to die daily to sin, that we may evermore live with him in the joy of his resurrection; through Jesus Christ your Son our Lord, who lives and reigns with you and the Holy Spirit, one God, now and for ever. Amen.

The Book of Common Prayer

BLESSING

Now to him who is able to protect you from stumbling and to make you stand in the presence of his glory, without blemish and with great joy, to the only God our Savior, through Jesus Christ our Lord, be glory, majesty, power, and authority before all time, now and forever. Amen.

Jude 24–25

DAY 30 MIDDAY PRAYER

CALL TO PRAYER

If you confess with your mouth, "Jesus is Lord," and believe in your heart that God raised him from the dead, you will be saved.

Romans 10:9

MIDDAY READINGS

John 21:15–23

When they had eaten breakfast, Jesus asked Simon Peter, "Simon, son of John, do you love me more than these?"

"Yes, Lord," he said to him, "you know that I love you."

"Feed my lambs," he told him. A second time he asked him, "Simon, son of John, do you love me?"

"Yes, Lord," he said to him, "you know that I love you."

"Shepherd my sheep," he told him.

He asked him the third time, "Simon, son of John, do you love me?"

Peter was grieved that he asked him the third time, "Do you love me?" He said, "Lord, you know everything; you know that I love you."

"Feed my sheep," Jesus said. "Truly I tell you, when you were younger, you would tie your belt and walk wherever you wanted. But when you grow old, you will stretch out your hands and someone else will tie you and carry you where you don't want to go." He said this to indicate by what kind of death Peter would glorify God. After saying this, he told him, "Follow me."

So Peter turned around and saw the disciple Jesus loved following them, the one who had leaned back against Jesus at the supper and asked, "Lord, who is the one that's going to betray you?" When Peter saw him, he said to Jesus, "Lord, what about him?"

"If I want him to remain until I come," Jesus answered, "what is that to you? As for you, follow me."

So this rumor spread to the brothers and sisters that this disciple would not die. Yet Jesus did not tell him that he would not die, but, "If I want him to remain until I come, what is that to you?"

Matthew 28:16–20
The eleven disciples traveled to Galilee, to the mountain where Jesus had directed them. When they saw him, they worshiped, but some doubted. Jesus came near and said to them, "All authority has been given to me in heaven and on earth. Go, therefore, and make disciples of all nations, baptizing them in the name of the Father and of the Son and of the Holy Spirit, teaching them to observe everything I have commanded you. And remember, I am with you always, to the end of the age."

This is the Word of the Lord. Thanks be to God.

GLORIA
Glory be to God the Father, God the Son, and God the Holy Spirit. As it was in the beginning, is now, and will be forever, world without end.

The Lord's Prayer

Our Father in heaven,
Hallowed be your name.
Your kingdom come,
Your will be done
on earth as it is in heaven.
Give us this day our daily bread.
And forgive us our debts,
as we also have forgiven our debtors.
And lead us not into temptation
But deliver us from the evil one.
For yours is the kingdom and the power and the glory forever.
Amen.

Blessing

Now may the God of hope fill you with all joy and peace as you
believe, so that you may overflow with hope by the power of the
Holy Spirit.
Romans 15:13

DAY 30 EVENING PRAYER

Call to Prayer

Therefore, since we have a great high priest who has passed
through the heavens—Jesus the Son of God—let us hold fast to
our confession. Therefore, let us approach the throne of grace
with boldness, so that we may receive mercy and grace to help
us in time of need.
Hebrews 4:14,16

Confession of Sin

Most holy and merciful Father: I have not loved you with my
whole heart, and mind, and strength. I have not loved my
neighbors as myself. I have not forgiven others, as I have been
forgiven. I have been deaf to your call to serve, as Christ served

us. I have not been true to the mind of Christ. I have grieved your Holy Spirit. Restore me, good Lord, and let your anger depart from me. By the cross of your Son, our Lord, bring me with all your saints to the joy of his resurrection.
The Book of Common Prayer

If we confess our sins, he is faithful and righteous to forgive us our sins and to cleanse us from all unrighteousness.
1 John 1:9

Canticle

He is the image of the invisible God,
the firstborn over all creation.
For everything was created by him,
in heaven and on earth,
the visible and the invisible,
whether thrones or dominions
or rulers or authorities—
all things have been created through him and for him.
He is before all things,
and by him all things hold together.
He is also the head of the body, the church;
he is the beginning,
the firstborn from the dead,
so that he might come to have
first place in everything.
For God was pleased to have
all his fullness dwell in him,
and through him to reconcile
everything to himself,
whether things on earth or things in heaven,
by making peace
through his blood, shed on the cross.
Colossians 1:15–20

Luke 24:44–49
He told them, "These are my words that I spoke to you while I was still with you—that everything written about me in the Law of Moses, the Prophets, and the Psalms must be fulfilled." Then he opened their minds to understand the Scriptures. He also said to them, "This is what is written: The Messiah will suffer and rise from the dead the third day, and repentance for forgiveness of sins will be proclaimed in his name to all the nations, beginning at Jerusalem. You are witnesses of these things. And look, I am sending you what my Father promised. As for you, stay in the city until you are empowered from on high."

Acts 1:3–11
After he had suffered, he also presented himself alive to them by many convincing proofs, appearing to them over a period of forty days and speaking about the kingdom of God.

While he was with them, he commanded them not to leave Jerusalem, but to wait for the Father's promise. "Which," he said, "you have heard me speak about; for John baptized with water, but you will be baptized with the Holy Spirit in a few days."

So when they had come together, they asked him, "Lord, are you restoring the kingdom to Israel at this time?"

He said to them, "It is not for you to know times or periods that the Father has set by his own authority. But you will receive power when the Holy Spirit has come on you, and you will be my witnesses in Jerusalem, in all Judea and Samaria, and to the ends of the earth."

After he had said this, he was taken up as they were watching, and a cloud took him out of their sight. While he was going, they were gazing into heaven, and suddenly two men in white clothes stood by them. They said, "Men of Galilee, why do you stand looking up into heaven? This same Jesus, who has been taken from you into heaven, will come in the same way that you have seen him going into heaven."

This is the Word of the Lord. Thanks be to God.

GLORIA

Glory be to God the Father, God the Son, and God the Holy Spirit. As it was in the beginning, is now, and will be forever, world without end.

THE LORD'S PRAYER

Our Father in heaven,
Hallowed be your name.
Your kingdom come,
Your will be done
on earth as it is in heaven.
Give us this day our daily bread.
And forgive us our debts,
as we also have forgiven our debtors.
And lead us not into temptation
But deliver us from the evil one.
For yours is the kingdom and the power and the glory forever.
Amen.

INTERCESSIONS AND PERSONAL REQUESTS

PRAYER OF THE CHURCH

Praise and thanksgiving be unto you, O God, who brought again from the dead our Lord Jesus Christ and set him at your right hand in the kingdom of glory. Praise and thanksgiving be unto you, O Lord Jesus Christ, you Lamb of God who has redeemed us by your blood, you heavenly Priest who ever lives to make intercession for us, you eternal King who comes again to make all things new. Praise and thanksgiving be unto you, O Holy Spirit, who has shed abroad the love of God, who makes us alive together with Christ, and makes us to sit with him in heavenly places, and to taste the good Word of God and the powers of the age to come. Blessing and glory, and wisdom and thanksgiving, and honor and power and might, be unto you our God forever and ever. Amen

Thomas F. Torrance

BLESSING

The Almighty and merciful Lord, Father, Son, and Holy Spirit,
bless us and keep us, this night and evermore. Amen.

SOURCES

Quote from Jaroslav Pelikan from *Jesus Through the Centuries: His Place in the History of Culture* (New Haven: Yale University Press, 1999), 1.

Selections from *The Book of Common Prayer* are from *The Book of Common Prayer*, 2019 Anglican Church in North America and from *The Book of Common Prayer*, 1979 Episcopal Church of North America

Selections from *The Valley of Vision* are adapted from Arthur Bennett, *The Valley of Vision*, Banner of Truth Trust, 2002.

The Reforming Catholic Confession is available here: https://reformingcatholicconfession.com/

Prayer of Augustine (Day 2, 16) adapted from *Augustine's Confessions* (A. A. Knopf, 2001), 8.

Prayer of Anselm (Day 3, 17) adapted from *ESV Prayer Bible*, Deuteronomy 26:1–15.

Prayer of Benedict (Day 3) adapted from *A Pocket Book of Prayers for Busy People* (Christian Art Gifts)

Prayer of Patrick of Ireland (Day 4) adapted from *100 Prayers Every Christian Should Know* (Bloomington, Minnesota: Bethany House Publishers, 2021), 226–229.

Prayer of John Wesley (Day 4) adapted from *John and Charles Wesley: Selected Prayers, Hymns, Journal Notes, and Sermons* (Paulist Press, 1981), 59.

Prayer of Absalom Jones (Day 5) adapted from *Conversations with God: Two Centuries of Prayer by African Americans* edited by John Melvin Washington (New York: Amistad: Harper Perennial, 1995), 12–13.

Prayer of Zacharias Ursinus (Day 5) adapted from Jonathan Gibson, *Be Thou My Vision: A Liturgy for Daily Worship* (Wheaton, IL: Crossway, 2021), 138.

Prayer of George Matheson (Day 6, 20) adapted from Jonathan Gibson, *Be Thou My Vision: A Liturgy for Daily Worship* (Wheaton, IL: Crossway, 2021), 88–89.

Prayer of Polycarp (Day 6) adapted from *Our Common Prayer* by Winfield Bevins (Simeon Press, 2013), 91.

Prayer of Jerome (Day 7) adapted from *Our Common Prayer* by Winfield Bevins (Simeon Press, 2013), 99.

Prayer of Gregory of Nazianzus (Day 7, 21) adapted from *On the Way to the Cross: 40 Days with the Church Fathers* by Thomas Oden (InterVarsity Press, 2011), 55.

Prayer of Thomas à Kempis (Day 7) adapted from Jonathan Gibson, *Be Thou My Vision: A Liturgy for Daily Worship* (Wheaton, IL: Crossway, 2021), 158.

Prayer of Thomas Dorsey (Day 8) adapted from *Conversations with God: Two Centuries of Prayer by African Americans* edited by John Melvin Washington (New York: Amistad: Harper Perennial, 1995), 154.

Prayer of William Wilberforce (Day 9) adapted from *ESV Prayer Bible,* Ezekiel 16:1–22.

Prayer of Balthasar Hubmaier (Day 9) adapted from *A Form for Christ's Supper* (1527), quoted in Luke, edited by Beth Kreitzer, vol. 3 in *Reformation Commentary on Scripture: New Testament* (Downers Grove, IL: InterVarsity Press, 2015), 490.

Prayer from Middelburg Liturgy (Day 10) adapted from Jonathan Gibson, *Be Thou My Vision: A Liturgy for Daily Worship (*Wheaton, IL: Crossway, 2021), 41–42.

Prayer of Ambrose (Day 10, Day 28) adapted from *The Macmillan Book of Earliest Christian Prayers (*Collier Books, 1990), 107.

Prayer of Basil the Great (Day 10) adapted from *On the Way to the Cross: 40 Days with the Church Fathers* by Thomas Oden (InterVarsity Press, 2011), 78.

Prayer of Anselm (Day 11) adapted from *100 Prayers Every Christian Should Know* (Bloomington, Minnesota: Bethany House Publishers, 2021), 81.

Prayer of Richard Allen (Day 12) adapted from *Conversations with God: Two Centuries of Prayer by African Americans* edited by John Melvin Washington (New York: Amistad: Harper Perennial, 1995), 11.

Prayer of Melito of Sardis (Day 13) adapted from Kurt Bjorklund, *Prayers for Today: A Yearlong Journey for Contemplative Prayer* (Chicago, IL: Moody Publishers, 2011), 111.

Prayer of Hilary of Poitiers (Day 13) adapted from *Ancient Christian Devotional: Lectionary Cycle A* edited by Cindy Crosby (InterVarsity Press, 2007), 140.

Prayers of Every Moment Holy (Day 14, 17, 27) adapted from Douglas McKelvey, *Every Moment Holy: Volume 1 Pocket Edition* (Nashville, TN: Rabbit Room Press, 2019), 11, 139.

Prayer of Maria W. Stewart (Day 14) adapted from *Conversations with God: Two Centuries of Prayer by African American*s edited by John Melvin Washington (New York: Amistad: Harper Perennial, 1995), 26.

Prayer of Columbanus (Day 15) adapted from Thomas Oden and Joel Elowsky (editors) *On the Way to the Cross: 40 Days with the Church Fathers* (Downers Grove, IL: InterVarsity Press, 2011), 34.

Prayer of John Chrysostom (Day 15) adapted from *ESV Prayer Bible*, Job 26:1–14.

Prayer of Lancelot Andrewes (Day 16) adapted from *The HarperCollins Book of Prayers* compiled by Robert Van de Weyer (Castle Books, 1993), 29–30.

Prayer of Clement of Rome (Day 18) adapted from *The HarperCollins Book of Prayers* compiled by Robert Van de Weyer (Castle Books, 1993), 108–109.

Prayer of Basil of Caesarea (Day 18) adapted from *The HarperCollins Book of Prayers* compiled by Robert Van de Weyer (Castle Books, 1993), 58.

Prayer of Martin Luther (Day 18) adapted from *The Complete Sermons of Martin Luther: Volume 5* (Delmarva Publications)

Prayer of Arthur Dent (Day 19) adapted from *Piercing Heaven: Prayers of the Puritans*, Robert Elmer, editor (Bellingham, WA: Lexham Press, 2019), 257.

Prayer of Wilhelm Loehe (Day 19) adapted from Jonathan Gibson, *Be Thou My Vision: A Liturgy for Daily Worship* (Wheaton, IL: Crossway, 2021), 115.

Prayer of Jane Austen (Day 19) adapted from *30-Day Journey with Jane Austen* (Fortress Press, 2020), 60.

Prayer of Thomas à Kempis (Day 20) adapted from *100 Prayers Every Christian Should Know* (Bloomington, Minnesota: Bethany House Publishers, 2021), 21–22.

Prayer of Anselm (Day 22) adapted from *The Westminster Collection of Christian Prayers*, edited by Dorothy M. Stewart (Louisville: Westminster John Knox, 1999), 38.

Prayer of Phillis Wheatley (Day 22) adapted from *Phillis Wheatley, Complete Writings* (Penguin, 2001), 96.

Prayer of Ephrem of Syria (Day 23) adapted from *Our Common Prayer* by Winfield Bevins (Simeon Press, 2013), 99.

Prayer of Francis of Assisi (Day 25) adapted from *The HarperCollins Book of Prayers* compiled by Robert Van de Weyer (Castle Books, 1993), 150–151.

Prayer of William Wilberforce (Day 25) adapted from *100 Prayers Every Christian Should Know* (Bloomington, Minnesota: Bethany House Publishers, 2021), 33.

Prayer of Richard Baxter (Day 26) adapted from Jonathan Gibson, *Be Thou My Vision: A Liturgy for Daily Worship* (Wheaton, IL: Crossway, 2021), 61.

Prayer of Heinrich Bullinger (Day 26) adapted from Jonathan Gibson, *Be Thou My Vision: A Liturgy for Daily Worship* (Wheaton, IL: Crossway, 2021), 76.

Prayer of N. T. Wright (Day 26) adapted from *Simply Christian: Why Christianity Makes Sense (Zondervan*, 2010), 169.

Prayer of Thomas F. Torrance (Day 30) adapted from *Christian Doctrine of God: One Being Three Persons* by Thomas F. Torrance (A&C Black, 2001), 256.